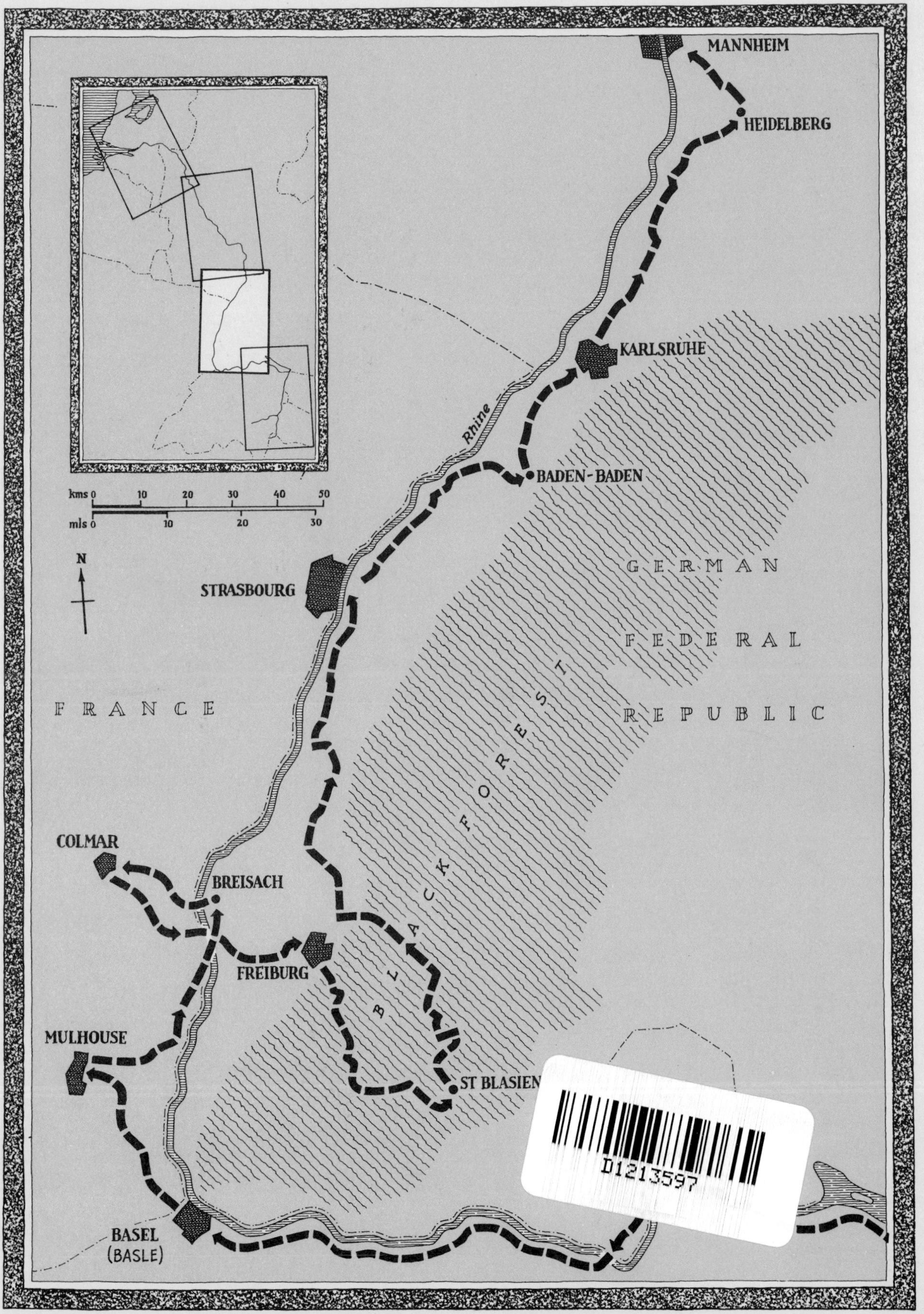
MANNHEIM
HEIDELBERG
KARLSRUHE
Rhine
BADEN-BADEN
kms 0 10 20 30 40 50
mls 0 10 20 30
N
STRASBOURG
GERMAN
FEDERAL
REPUBLIC
FRANCE
BLACK FOREST
COLMAR
BREISACH
FREIBURG
MULHOUSE
ST BLASIEN
BASEL
(BASLE)

TO THE END OF THE RHINE

Happy Birthday!

Love,

Nancy

xxxx

by the same author

THE PENDULUM YEARS
TAKING SIDES
CONDUCTED TOUR
SPEAKING UP
ENTHUSIASMS
THE WAY WE LIVE NOW
HANNIBAL'S FOOTSTEPS
IN THESE TIMES

TO THE END OF THE RHINE

Bernard Levin

JONATHAN CAPE
THIRTY-TWO BEDFORD SQUARE
LONDON

First published 1987

Jonathan Cape Ltd, 32 Bedford Square, London WC1B 3EL

British Library Cataloguing in Publication Data

Levin, Bernard
To the End of the Rhine
1. Rhine River Region—Description and travel
I. Title
914.3′404878 D923

ISBN 0 224 02498 1

Typeset by Computape (Pickering) Ltd, North Yorkshire
Printed in Great Britain by
R. J. Acford Ltd, Chichester, Sussex

for T-P

Contents

Illustrations

All the photographs, including those on the jacket, were taken by Graham Edgar

Acknowledgments

A JOURNEY OF this kind (and this length) cannot be done without the help of many people; I was struck by the willingness of so many, in so many countries, to provide that help. They are too numerous to list in full, but they included His Excellency Baron Rüdiger von Wechmar, German Ambassador to Britain, who smoothed the path into Germany; Herr Erwin Lauterwasser and his fellow-huntsmen, who took me shooting in the Black Forest, but (quite rightly) would not let me shoot; Hans Peter Kaufmann, Director of Tourism for Schaffhausen, who entered most enthusiastically into the spirit of the journey; Divisionnaire Andreas Gadient, who lent me his helicopter and indeed his Division; Christian and Leonie Patt, who gave me a magical musical day; Dr jur. Werner Keicher, one of the leading lawyers and financial consultants of Liechtenstein, who knows many secrets and tells none; Myriam and Roseline Bouret and their children, who carried me many miles on their barge, the *Fleurie*; Herr Hermann Hecher, Lord of Burgstein Castle, who put me up in a room with a view that would make eagles dizzy; Dr Walter Hönig, Chief Perfumier at 4711, whose nose is his fortune; Herr Richard Schmitz, General Manager of the Brenner Park Hotel in Baden-Baden, who provided limitless hospitality and explained the philosophy of hotel-keeping; and Fritz Schlumpf, who managed to make me interested in motor-cars, which I would have thought impossible.

These helped on the journey; others helped at home. Once again, Oula Jones of the Society of Indexers brought her unique combination of skill, diligence, charm and wit to bear on the preparation of the index; once again, Brian Inglis passed his basilisk eye over the proofs, and spotted many an error; once again, Stephen and Penny Ross and their flawless *brigade* at Homewood Park, where I wrote this book,* looked after me, guarded me from distraction, cosseted me, fed me, wined me, and above all befriended me; once again, my assistant, Sally Chichester, ran things in my absence so efficiently that I wondered why I bothered to come home at all.

And once again, the team who made the television series which accompanied my previous travel book, *Hannibal's Footsteps*, made the one which accompanied this.

There was almost no change in the personnel, though some had changed roles. Bernard Clark, previously the producer and director, was producer only; the director was David Edgar, who last time was assistant cameraman; Steve Egleton was again the sound-recordist, effortlessly coping with the multilingual Babel of the European Parliament; Nathalie Ferrier – researcher, scout, opener of doors locked and barred – deployed her perfect German as last time she had provided perfect French.

Only one face was missing from the previous group; Mike Hutchinson, who had been assistant producer, was otherwise engaged. He was replaced by Kate Brown, who speedily made herself at home and indispensable, and even, among her countless contributions, provided us with an epic, now known for ever as The Day Kate Lost the Car-Keys. In addition, there was Mark Milson, appointed in a mysterious category of which I had never heard: a Jobfit Trainee. He was, I suppose, a sort of apprentice, but he could have taught many a sorcerer new tricks. As far as I could see, he never slept, never ate, never stopped working, and never complained. He will go far.

We were a happy band, even on The Day Kate Lost the Car-Keys. It is possible to do satisfying work in uncongenial company; it is much better to do it among amiable companions; best of all is to work with friends. The bonds forged during the Hannibal journey were this time renewed, reinforced and widened, and in extending to all my colleagues my warmest thanks, I do so not only for the work they did and the care they took of me, but also for the friendship we shared, and will continue to share.

* The fourth I have written there? The fifth? Not the last, anyway.

I

The Noblest River

THE FIRST THING I ever learned about the Rhine, at school, was that it flowed through something mysteriously called a Rift Valley, presumably a geographical term used to distinguish it from other kinds of valley. What the difference is, how it came about, and whether the inexpert eye can tell a Rift Valley from its rivals, I no longer remember, if indeed I grasped the explanation at the time; probably not, for I have a much clearer memory of finding geography unendurably tedious, involving as it did the incessant tracing of maps depicting the principal jute-exporting nations. (To this day I do not know what jute is.)

An unpromising start, perhaps, to a book which records a journey I made, in 1986, along the entire course of the Rhine, from its first tricklings in the Swiss mountains to the mighty delta it becomes in the Netherlands before emptying its waters into the North Sea. But this, the noblest of Europe's rivers, has drawn me to its banks all my life, from my first sight of it as a hitch-hiking student, and there are stretches of it that I know as well as any place on earth.

I call it Europe's noblest river, and surely it is. Not the longest; that title belongs to the Volga, and even if we exclude anything east of Poland as not really Europe, we shall find that the Danube still beats the Rhine in length. Nor is it the most beautiful, though the Judgment of Paris was simple and free of risk compared with an attempt to adjudicate in a beauty contest among rivers; I would give the apple to the Loire, prepared for objections by the supporters of fifty others, from the Tay to the Guadalquivir. More important, and with a more subtle distinction, the Rhine is not a *lovable* river, as are, say, the

Thames, the Mosel and the Po. But its failure to inspire the deepest affection has nothing to do with questions of beauty or size, still less of history, though it must have seen more blood spilt than any other river (well, perhaps not the Somme), or of what Germany has done to it since the Second World War, which is to turn it into the most polluted stream in Europe. (Though that melancholy record is at last in danger, for a belated repentance has led to measures that may yet save it, and salmon have been sighted in places where for years a fisherman could catch nothing but effluent – or, if he fell in, typhoid.*)

The truth is that the Rhine, though it can be sportive, particularly in its upper reaches, is too *grand* to be loved; its nobility inspires awe and admiration, but it stands on its dignity, and a very masculine dignity it is, too. It is Father Rhine to the Germans (who, after all, have more of it than any of the other five nations it visits); well, the British have Old Father Thames, but the adjective is significant, softening the soubriquet and turning the stern patriarch into a benevolent white-haired octogenarian with a pocketful of sweets for the local children.

If it is impossible to envisage the Rhine *en pantoufles*, if the beauty is beside it rather than on its surface, if the pure, clean colour of its origins soon turns to an impenetrable mixture of mud-brown and rainbow-decay, if its severely utilitarian function as one of the greatest freight-ways in the world (at one point on my journey I counted sixty-seven giant barges going past in an hour – and that was in one direction only) makes the student of it sometimes wonder whether it is a river at all, if very few of its 120-odd bridges are beautiful (and a river may be known by its bridges), then wherein lies the fascination that it has exerted for many centuries, and continues to exert today?

I shall try to answer that question – indeed, this book *is* my answer – but first I must make clear the extent and strength of that fascination. For I am by no means alone in finding the Rhine irresistible; there is a vast Rhenish literature, starting with Julius Caesar, who expressed surprise that some of the tribes along the river's course were reputed to live entirely on eggs and fish, but did not find it equally odd that the Black Forest (so named – *Silva Nigra* – by the Romans) contained

---

* Not long before this book went to press, the hopeful note became abruptly discordant, when the Rhine was reported to have turned bright green. Upon investigation, it proved to be the fault of the Swiss, of all people, who had been discharging chemical waste into it, to the fury of the French, the Germans and the Dutch.

animals unknown elsewhere, such as bulls the size of elephants and monster oxen with a single horn in the centre of their foreheads. (That suggests the rhinoceros, which is impossible; at least, I presume it is, but the beast's very name makes a Rhine devotee's heart beat faster in a wild hope that everyone, from zoologists to lexicographers, has got it wrong.) Caesar's remarks about the Black Forest, incidentally, were not confined to such marginalia; the way he estimates its size sweeps the reader twenty centuries back in an instant, to a world without maps, roads or trigonometry: he said it was 'sixty days long and nine days wide'.

Petrarch visited Cologne, and watched the annual purification ceremony take place in the river; he expressed his astonishment that in a land of barbarians the people of the city were highly civilised, their manners gracious, the men dignified, the women well-dressed. On the other hand, Coleridge went berserk with hatred of the same city (God knows what they must have done to him there):

In Köln, a town of monks and bones,
And pavements fang'd with murderous stones
And rags, and hags, and hideous wenches;
I counted two-and-seventy stenches,
All well defined and several stinks!
Ye nymphs that reign o'er sewers and sinks
The river Rhine, it is well known,
Doth wash your city of Cologne;
But tell me, Nymphs, what power divine
Shall henceforth wash the river Rhine?

A curious memory floats to the surface; at the end of the Second World War, when the concentration camps were liberated and the first authenticated details and pictures given to a stunned world, *The Times* quoted the four last lines in a leader, as apposite a comment as can ever have been made out of a verse designed for a different purpose. For his part, Coleridge wasn't quite finished; he left Cologne with a postscript:

As I am a Rhymer
And now at least a merry one,
Mr Mum's Rudesheimer
And the church of St Geryon

Are the two things alone
That deserve to be known
In the body-and-soul-stinking town of Cologne.

Victor Hugo, on the other hand, was so inspired by the Rhine that he gave it all the qualities of all the other rivers put together:

> . . . swift as the Rhône, broad as the Loire, embanked like the Meuse, serpentine as the Seine, limpid and green as the Somme, as historic as the Tiber, royal like the Danube, mysterious as the Nile, sprinkled with gold like a river of America, crammed with fables and phantoms like a river of Asia . . . The Rhine is the river of which everyone speaks and which no one studies, which everyone visits and no one knows, which is seen in passing and forgotten in hurrying . . . its ruins engage the loftiest imagination, its destiny the most thoughtful intelligence; this admirable river catches the eye of the poet as well as of the publicist, the past and the future of Europe.

The *Nibelungenlied* takes place on its waters and its banks, and Wagner set to music not only the legend but the river itself; the *Rheingold* Prelude is one of the most lifelike musical depictions of a tangible scene ever written, and a blind man who had never heard of the composer, or for that matter the Rhine, could be in no doubt that he was listening to the flowing of a mighty river. (Schumann wrote a Rhenish Symphony, but the poor devil had a more literal immersion in the Rhine; at the height of his madness he threw himself into it in an attempt at suicide.)

The painters have not been idle, either. Turner was fascinated by the Rhine, and so was that strange man Fuseli, whose work gives me nightmares (though not such violent ones as Piranesi's does); so was Edward Lear. But the nineteenth century is littered with hundreds of artists, many of them amateurs, and very few inspired ones, who drew, painted, water-coloured and etched it from its source to the sea; there can hardly be a print-gallery in Europe with fewer than forty boxes of unsaleable Rhine views.

Southey enshrined in verse, or at least in doggerel, the legend of the wicked Bishop Hatto, who responded to the complaints of the poor that they were starving by shutting them up in a granary and setting it on fire, then fled, in fear of retribution, to his Rhine-castle:

'I'll go to my tower on the Rhine,' said he,
'It's the safest place in Germany;
The walls are high and the shores are steep,
And the stream is strong and the water deep.'

But, as all the world knows, the stream was not strong enough, nor the water deep enough, for the mice came swimming across to his impregnable fortress and devoured him. Serve him right, we say, but we are shockingly wrong, for the whole story is a wicked libel; the original of the cruel prelate was a kindly and generous man and a wise ruler, and if the mice did eat him it was an appalling miscarriage of justice. (There is a *Mauseturm*, however, its base washed by the waters of the river, but the unjust legend has proved stronger than the innocent facts; a rare victory to the Manichee.) Southey, of course, was only one among a vast catalogue of poets who have hymned the Rhine: even Longfellow had a shot at it:

At Bacharach on the Rhine,
At Hochheim on the Main,
And at Würzburg on the Stein,
Grow the three best kinds of wine!

The Rhine seems to have brought out the facetiousness in many a poet; C. S. Calverley contributed his own version:

For king-like rolls the Rhine
And the scenery's divine,
And the victuals and the wine
Rather good.

Heine's poem is the most celebrated of all poetic tributes to the Rhine, though the verses are far from his best. Perhaps that is why Schubert never set it, so that we have to put up with the dreadful sugary thing that is its only music; if a visitor sits on the shore by the Lorelei all day he will hear the music wafting across the water a couple of dozen times, for every pleasure-boat captain feels obliged to entertain his passengers with it as the boat approaches the fatal rock.

But Heine, Coleridge, Southey, Longfellow and Calverley all put together at their worst are preferable to Johannes Becker, who wrote

The Watch on the Rhine, and deserves to have the horrible thing quoted in the original:

Es braut ein Ruf wie Donnerhall,
Wie Schwertgeklirr und Wogenprall;
Zum Rhein, zum Rhein, zum deutschen Rhein,
Wer will des Strömes Hüter sein?
Lieb Vaterland, magst ruhig sein,
Fest steht und treu die Wacht am Rhein.*

Becker's tomorrow-the-world fervour was not the first expression of the *furor teutonicus* which has so often troubled the peace of Europe, and it was certainly not the last, as tens of millions of corpses in my own lifetime would testify if they could. Travelling along the whole stretch of the river where it forms the frontier between Germany and France, I could not stop marvelling at the fact that the two great nations which face each other across it will never fight in opposite camps again.

The Romans – not only Julius but also Augustus, Tiberius and Drusus – saw the Rhine as a frontier across which lay implacable enemies of their *imperium*; they fortified it from Constance to Cologne, and built a fleet to patrol it, since when all Europe, on both sides, has taken much the same view, even though it was not until the unification of Germany and the Franco-Prussian War that the mutual enmity narrowed down to Germany versus France. But I know of nothing to compare with the apotheosis of Germany, one of the most astonishing in all history. The Federal Republic's journey to Canossa took only *nine* years after the overthrow of Nazism; thereafter, Germany's democracy was among the most complete in the world, and those who – reasonably enough – doubted whether the roots would ever go deep enough have seen another three decades of evidence that they do. Who could have predicted that?

Clovis, Charlemagne and Barbarossa (to say nothing of Siegfried) may sleep sound; Luther, if that burning spirit could ever find rest in

* There sounds a call like a thunderclap
Like the clash of swords and crash of waves;
To the Rhine, to the Rhine, to the German Rhine,
Who will the river's guardian be?
Dear Fatherland, you may be calm,
Fast and true stands the Watch on the Rhine.

this world or the next, may be content; neither the French Revolution nor its enemies need plot and plan; Metternich himself (he was born in Koblenz, a most unlikely Rhinelander) may stop worrying; Alsace, which has changed hands throughout history as often as a worn coin, will never be spent again; that great chain of Romanesque cathedrals – Mainz, Speyer, Worms – and the Gothic ones – Cologne, Freiburg, Strasbourg – stand like watch-towers that need never more sound the alarm; and Erasmus of Rotterdam, adopted son of Basle, may correct his proofs in Froben's printing-house, secure in the knowledge that he will never have such another fright as when Dürer, hearing a rumour that Luther had been killed in battle, wrote to him with a call to pick up the fallen standard: 'O, Erasmus of Rotterdam! Where art thou? Listen, thou Knight of Christ, ride out with the Lord Christ, defend the truth and earn for thyself the martyr's crown.' (Erasmus, of all people! 'Let others strive for martyrdom,' he said modestly, 'I am not worthy of such an honour.' But I shall come to Erasmus, whom I love more than any other figure in history, when I arrive in Basle.)

Lincoln, at the end of the Civil War, speaking of the Mississippi, said, 'The father of waters rolls unvexed to the sea,' and the words are apt for the Rhine today. After the Second World War, it took a year for it to be cleared sufficiently for serious navigation to begin again, and now it has heavier traffic than any other river in Europe; we must not forget the Rhine in its role as an emblem of prosperity. (For that matter, we must not forget that Lake Constance, which the Germans and the Austrians call the Bodensee, into which the Rhine flows at one end, and out of which it flows at the other, has heavier traffic than any other European lake, even Lac Léman – which *we* call Lake Geneva – or Lake Balaton.)

This extraordinary waterway, which marked the divide between Romans and Teutons, civilisation and barbarism, even Christianity and paganism, before it ran between Germany and France, has been spawning legends for more than a thousand years, and it cannot be a coincidence that the majority of them are dark, mysterious and doom-laden, telling of death, loss and sorrow. The legend of St Ursula and her 11,000 virgins (so memorably portrayed by Carpaccio) is typical; so is that of the Seven Maidens who were turned to stone (the seven peaks are still there to prove it) for their cruel coldness to their wooers; so is that of Parsifal and Lohengrin; so is that of Hugo of Langenstein and Fair Rosine, which is *so* typical that it deserves to be told again.

These two were to be married, but just before the wedding Peter the Hermit called Europe to the crusade, and Hugo, deeming it his Christian duty, went to the holy war. He was captured and sold into slavery; the years went by, but the forlorn Rosine never lost hope. At length, Hugo swore a vow, promising that if he ever saw his native land again he would devote his life to religion, and abandon all thought of earthly joys. At once, a means of escape providentially appeared, and Hugo finally returned home, to find the ever-faithful Rosine still waiting for him to claim his bride. But his vow was stronger; he gave up his Penelope and enrolled in the Order of the Knights Templar, which demanded lifelong celibacy from its adherents. Rosine, still uncomplaining, retired to a convent.

Adenauer and Beethoven, Duden (of the dictionary) and Gutenberg, Heine and Gustav Gründgens (who taught Hitler his platform manner), Rembrandt (Rembrandt van Rijn, remember) and Holbein, Robert Schumann and Desiderius Erasmus, Albert Schweitzer and Count Zeppelin: these were all natives of the Rhine, however much difficulty some of them would have in recognising it today. (Heine, in Düsseldorf, said that the city of his birth was 'very beautiful', and so it may have been when he said it, in 1826. But he also said of the Rhine that 'in its green hills grows folly, which is gathered in the autumn, put away in cellars, then poured into barrels to be exported to other lands,' so perhaps he was joking about Düsseldorf.)

Another great Rhinelander was Karl Baedeker; it was only fitting that the very first guidebook he published was for the Rhine itself. I have always felt that Baedeker would have been a man to know; his wonderful combination of relentless hard work, attention to detail, elevated tone and air of primness would have been irresistible, for who could resist such a passage as this, in the section on general advice to the traveller from the old Rhine guide?

> When the traveller remains for a week or more at a hotel, it is advisable to pay, or at least call for, his account every two or three days in order that erroneous insertions may be detected. Verbal reckonings are objectionable except in some of the more remote and primitive districts where bills are never written. A waiter's mental arithmetic is faulty, and the faults are seldom in favour of the traveller. A favourite practice is to present the bill at the last moment, when mistakes or wilful imposition cannot easily be detected or rectified.

Those who purpose starting early in the morning will do well to ask for their bills on the previous evening.

And somebody in the modern Baedeker firm is clearly carrying on the tradition, for the current *Rhine*, discussing the modest improvement in the cleanliness of the water, says, 'At some points, too, bathing in the river is again possible, though not perhaps to be wholeheartedly indulged in.'

History, war, legend, religion, music, wine (twenty-five centuries of the last): the Rhine's spell is unique, or at any rate it is for me. In my previous travel book, *Hannibal's Footsteps*, I had a live hero to follow, in the person of the great Carthaginian, and he was beside me throughout my 320-mile march. On my journey down the Rhine, which this book records, I did not walk except for short stretches and when exploring towns on the route; the length of the journey was thrice that of the Hannibal expedition, which ruled out foot-slogging on the grounds of time, and I regretted the constraint, if only because when I started down into Italy from the Col d'Agnel on the earlier journey I was fitter than I had ever before been in all my life. But the other difference between the two explorations – the lack, this time, of a historic figure whose tracks I was following – turned out not to matter at all. For I had a hero beside me all the way, whether I was on foot, in a train or bus or car, a passenger in a huge steamer, a guest on a barge, a very modern traveller through the air or a very rash one in a rubber dinghy; and my hero was, of course, the river himself. Throughout the whole journey, he was rarely out of my sight, and when I had been away for a few hours, I greeted him as a friend newly met when I was back on his banks. I saw him from towpaths, from hills, from ferries, from the air, from castles, from terraces, from gravel-banks, from bridges, from balconies, from trains, from roads, from boulders in his midst, from the top of the biggest waterfall in Europe and from the ferris-wheel (180 feet up in the air with no visible means of support) at the Düsseldorf fun-fair, and I would have seen him, at the same place, from a vertiginous horror-ride called The Magic Carpet (which made me understand what an ice-cube feels in a cocktail-shaker), had I not been too terrified to open my eyes.

The Rhine, then, is the hero of this book, as he has been one of the heroes of my life, and in the end, it is the Rhine's extraordinary mixture that makes up its glory, a mixture of countries and peoples and languages, landscapes and cityscapes and skyscapes, historical events and mythological ones, individuals on my route like the mad helicopter-pilot who was not bent on suicide and the former ski-instructor who found genius lying in his hands, the Swiss army officer who enabled me to see the most spectacular view I have ever set eyes on and the manager of the finest hotel in Europe, the alchemist of Cologne and the man who raises the money for the Rijksmuseum in Amsterdam, the resolutely unhelpful girl behind the information counter at Strasbourg railway station and the man who stuffs the geese with corn, six-year-old Sophie who invited me to play with her remote-controlled lorry, and the President of Austria.

Carl Zuckmayer's play *The Devil's General** (there was a memorable production of it in London some thirty years ago, with Trevor Howard and Wilfrid Lawson) is loosely based on the life of a *Luftwaffe* General, Hans Udet, who hated and despised the Nazis, and struggled in vain to find some way of resolving the conflict between his duty to fight for Germany and his knowledge that Germany was possessed by monstrous evil. Zuckmayer's general is called Harras, and at one point a young officer on his staff reveals to General Harras that his engagement has been broken off; the reason is that he can discover nothing about the origins of one of his great-grandmothers, except that she had come from abroad, rather than from the Rhineland where all his other forebears were born and bred. It is possible, therefore, that she might have had Jewish blood; whence the officer's fear and the broken engagement. Harras tries to shame the young man out of this nonsense with sarcasm:

> So that's it! Poor chap running about with a great-grandmother from nowhere. And what do you know about this great-grandmother's extra-marital escapades, eh? I don't suppose *she* demanded proof of pure Aryan blood! Or are you possibly a descendant of that particular Knight of the Cross who married into a family of wine-merchants from Jerusalem?

But the boy says only, 'I don't suppose racial research goes back that far, General,' whereupon Harras explodes:

---

* *Des Teufels General* (© 1946 by Bermann-Fischer Verlag AB, Stockholm. Translated and quoted here by permission of S. Fischer Verlag GmbH, Frankfurt am Main; there is a students' text published in Britain, by Nelson, but to my knowledge no edition in English).

Well, it damn well ought to! In for a penny, in for a pound. Just imagine – the things that might have happened in an old family. From the Rhine, moreover! From the Rhine! The great human melting-pot! The wine-press of Europe! And now try to imagine your line of ancestors since the birth of Christ. There was a Roman general, a dark, swarthy fellow, skin like a ripe olive, who took a blonde maiden and taught her some Latin. And then came a Jewish spice-merchant, a serious fellow, who became a Christian before marrying into the family, and founded the Catholic tradition of the house. And then there was a Greek physician, or a Celtic legionnaire, a mercenary from the Grisons, a Swedish horseman, a soldier of Napoleon's, a Cossack deserter, a craftsman from the Black Forest, a journeyman miller from Alsace, a fat sailor from Holland, a Hungarian, a procurer, a Viennese officer, a French actor, a Bohemian musician – they all lived on the Rhine, fought there, got drunk there, sang songs there, sired their children there, and – and – Goethe, who came out of the same stewpot, and Beethoven, and Gutenberg, and Matthias Grünewald, and – oh, go and look it up in the encyclopaedia. They were the salt of the earth, my young friend! The world's best! And why? Because that's where people's blood was mixed. Mixed – like the water from springs and brooks and rivers, to flow together into one great, living stream. The Rhine – that means Western culture! Nature's own aristocracy! *That* is race! Be proud of it, Hartmann – and hang your great-grandmother's birth-certificate in the lavatory. *Prosit.*

That is as rich and telling a description of my hero as I could ever hope to come upon, let alone create. And with Zuckmayer's words for a great, rolling motto, I set out on my journey down the Rhine, 'From' (the words are Longfellow's, this time in more serious mood) 'its cradle in the snowy Alps to its grave in the sands of Holland.' I started near the end of May, and finished early in August; and what befell me on my travels I shall now relate.

2

Swiss Arms and Mr Patt's Hands

THE RHINE – for all that the Germans call it theirs, the French dispute their ownership, the Austrians grumble because they only just get a look in at one corner of the Bodensee, the Dutch change its name and the people of Liechtenstein are so busy trying to convince the world that there is such a place that they have no time to think about it – rises, without doubt, in Switzerland. I say 'without doubt' because that is the only thing about the Rhine's origins that cannot be disputed. There are two streams – the Hinterrhein and the Vorderrhein – which flow parallel, eyeing each other suspiciously, before merging in Tamins (after which the Rhine is one, until it breaks up in Holland); but which of the thousands of tiny rivulets feeding the two mini-Rhines can be described as *the* source of the great river will not be determined until geology yields its last secret, if then. So up I went, into the Swiss mountains, to start from the point at which everybody can agree that the river has begun, at the start of both ur-Rhines, Vorder and Hinter, and embark like them upon my journey to the sea. The Hinterrhein starts from the Soppot glacier, a blinding sheet of immaculate cold; the Vorderrhein near a miniature lake called the Tomasee; a little further and both would have been in Italy.

But they are in Switzerland. Switzerland, it cannot be denied, has had a bad press. Dorothy Parker's notorious description – 'Beautiful, but dumb' – has stuck, and Orson Welles's even better known interpolation in *The Third Man* has stuck even more firmly:

> In Italy for thirty years under the Borgias, they had warfare, terror, murder, bloodshed – but they produced Michelangelo, Leonardo da

Vinci, and the Renaissance. In Switzerland, they have had brotherly love, five hundred years of democracy and peace, and what did that produce? The cuckoo clock.

Deadly, but unfair; also inaccurate, for the cuckoo clock was invented in the Black Forest, which has had precious little brotherly love, democracy or peace in the last 500 years. But it is inaccurate in a more important sense, for Switzerland, so far from being a land of chocolate soldiers, is armed to the teeth, and the teeth are ready to bite; there is no country in the world, with the possible exception of Israel (and Israel's army is in any case modelled upon the Swiss), more prepared for war, and more resolute for resistance. If Britain's military forces constituted the same percentage of Britain's population as the Swiss forces of theirs, we would have 5.5 million men under arms; in Switzerland, they say, 'We don't *have* an army, we *are* an army,' and it is nothing but the truth. Every Swiss male is subject to conscription, and when he has done his basic training he remains a soldier for thirty years; every year he is recalled to the colours for anything up to two months, depending on his rank (the higher the longer). He keeps his gun at home, together with his uniform and a supply of ammunition; he has to pass, regularly and repeatedly, a test of proficiency in shooting; he and all his 650,000 fellow-soldiers can be fully mobilised within forty-eight hours; and in the exercises and manoeuvres which are the purpose of the annual recall, only live ammunition is used. (This last fact has led to a curiously Swiss problem; the country is so small that virtually every uninhabited snowfield, mountainside and granite peak has been repeatedly shelled, with the result that avalanches, where the shelling has loosened the rock, have steadily become more frequent.)

I spent a day, up near the Rhine's beginnings, with the Swiss Army – a tank regiment, to be precise – and watched the shelling; an absorbing day it was. But before I describe it, I must say something more about the extraordinary state of military readiness in which the Swiss live, and of the even more extraordinary origins of it.*

Switzerland is not only a country with a citizen army comprising 10 per cent of its entire population; it is, in its physical configuration, a minefield, a booby-trap, an ammunition-dump and an air-raid shelter.

---

* For many of the facts which follow I am indebted to *La Place de la Concorde Suisse* (Farrar, Straus, Giroux, 1983), by John McPhee, a book no less enthralling than the story it tells.

Take the air-raid shelter first. All new buildings put up in Switzerland for many years now – homes, offices, shops – have by law been obliged to incorporate an air-raid shelter built to specifications which provide complete protection from an explosion generating ten tons of pressure on every square metre; in less technical language that means survival for anyone half a mile from a nuclear bomb the size of the one dropped on Hiroshima, and essential installations such as hospitals and military command posts have protection built to three times the resistant capacity of the domestic shelter. Large public underground car-parks are built to be turned into bunkers at the press of a button operating the sliding doors; there is one in Zürich, at all times ready for an emergency, which will shelter 7000 people. Beneath the city of Lucerne, a tunnel carries the motorway to leave the city traffic in peace; at each end of the tunnel there is a sliding concrete door five feet thick, and when these doors have slid to, 20,000 people inside them will be supplied with food, water, beds, information and a fully equipped hospital.

I visited one of these hospitals, in the little skiing town of Chur; it was situated beneath the ground, and above the ground was an ordinary hospital. That is only logical; when the siren sounds everybody gets into the lifts and descends. The lifts are very big indeed.

Inside, I could only retreat into an overworked metaphor; it *was* like something out of science fiction. There were rows and rows and rows of bunks, each with its bedding, plastic containers for the patient's possessions and frame for details of treatment fixed to the end of the bed; there was, of course, a blank card already in each frame. I wandered about; there were neatly piled boxes full of hypodermics, stacks of plastic beakers, cases of dressings, mountains of instruments, lakes of distilled water. I turned a corner; before me there was an avenue of trucks, every truck entirely encased in stout plastic. I peered through the plastic; each of the trucks was piled high – high, but with meticulous symmetry – with tins, looking rather like paint-tins. I peered more closely, and read the labels. They said 'Survival Food', in all three of Switzerland's national languages, and each tin carried clear instructions, equally multilingual, for the preparation of the pabulum inside; each tin would make fifty meals. But there were three sizes of tin: why? I peered more closely still, and all was clear; the smallest was for Breakfast, the middle-sized for Lunch, the largest for Dinner. My temptation to laugh at the Swiss, which had been diminishing fast, vanished entirely, and did not return even when it struck me that since only the Swiss are ready for a nuclear war, if the final catastrophe should come about they would be the only nation to survive; the world, therefore, would be, over the years, repopulated entirely with Switzers. Well, well; it might have been the Swedes.

That does not exhaust Switzerland's planning for war; there is also the countryside to be considered. The Swiss have honeycombed their mountains, burrowing into them like mad woodpeckers, to make chambers that will hold soldiers and their equipment; there are some that will hold an entire division of the Swiss Army. Every bridge and every railway junction is mined and ready for blowing; clearings dot the forests with air-strips; trees have been felled to provide fields of fire; above roads which are narrow ledges on mountainsides, rocks have been cut and fitted to crash down and block them; in underground, man-made lakes, there are reserves of petroleum sufficient to fuel the entire Swiss Army *for a year*.

Switzerland is neutral; Swiss neutrality, indeed, is so implacable and complete that in other countries it would be counted as ruthless aggression. (She will not even join the United Nations.) But this is not the neutrality of Costa Rica, which has no army, or of Sweden, which cannot find a Russian submarine in Stockholm harbour,* or of Austria, where the cannons are loaded with *Guglhupf* and *Sachertorte* and where the retreat to *their* mountain redoubt, which is called *Schlamperei*, would take only five minutes. Swiss neutrality is based on the determination, which runs right through the national consciousness, that although they will attack no other nation, join no other nation in any military alliance, fight alongside no other nation, they will resist any attack on themselves by any other nation, and resist it *à outrance*. The reason for this determination, and for the unique state of readiness that it leads to, is even more astonishing than the thing itself. But to understand how it came about, it is necessary to go back to the Second World War, and to introduce the name of Henri Guisan.

There are no generals in the Swiss Army; the rank is unknown. The title is kept for the very gravest states of emergency, and the gravity of an emergency that can demand the appointment of a general may be gauged from the fact that Switzerland, in 472 years of neutrality, has had only four.

The last of these was Henri Guisan, made General of Switzerland at

---

* Or the assassins of the Prime Minister anywhere.

the beginning of the Second World War. The Swiss General's powers and position are like those of the dictator appointed by the Roman Republic in times of extreme danger; dictator is a word that sounds dark and ominous in modern ears, and so it should, but its original meaning was free of any associations with tyranny, and the Swiss leader is subject to the orders of the civilian, elected government, though the country's entire military structure and personnel are under his absolute, personal command.

Guisan took up his duties in the worst conditions possible. Switzerland was desperately unready to resist any aggressor, and there was a powerful faction, which included the President of the Council – that is, the Prime Minister – which wanted Switzerland to throw in her lot with Germany; when the rest of Europe was overrun, leaving Switzerland as the only nation not subjugated by the Axis between the Pyrenees and the Kattegat, the call for surrender became louder still.

Guisan would have none of it. He announced, and went on announcing, that Switzerland would fight any army which crossed her borders, and he set himself, by a combination of heroic effort and delicate guile, to put his country in a position to make good his pledge. The plan was to abandon the Swiss lowlands, undefendable against an attack by greatly superior numbers, and to retreat into the impenetrable Alps, to the preparation of which the Swiss effort was single-mindedly directed. He made concessions to Hitler when he could not avoid doing so; he bluffed Hitler whenever he could; as Switzerland grew stronger he tilted her stance further and further towards the Allies; and as soon as the war was over, he handed back his powers to the democratic, civilian government that had entrusted them to him, and retired into private life. He had not only saved Switzerland, but had ensured that never again would she face a crisis unprepared; Switzerland learned the lesson he taught her, and learned it to such effect that today the plan for the Swiss Army to retire, under attack, to the country's Alpine fortress has been superseded by a determination to stand and fight even in the streets of Basle, and if forced to retreat to make it virtually impossible for the enemy to follow; whence the explosives fitted into the bridges, the railway junctions and the overhanging rocks.

The only comparison with Guisan's achievement is the leadership Churchill gave Britain in 1940; the Swiss, too, understood that they were being offered nothing but blood, toil, tears and sweat, and they rose to their destiny in much the same manner as did Britain. In his

1 The view from Divisionnaire Gadient's helicopter 2 Back to the mountains 3 A civilian in the Swiss Army 4 The tanks will be here in a minute 5 Passing the initiative test

1

2

3

4

5

6

7

book *Spying for Peace*,* Jon Kimche includes a substantial account of what Guisan did for his country and how he did it, and he ends with this vivid and moving picture of what his country did for him at the moment of his death, after he had lived on for fifteen years as a private man:

> He . . . was buried in Lausanne on April 12, 1960. The world outside, if it had ever heard of General Guisan, had long forgotten him. But in the Swiss homes, without orders or instructions, without designation, over two hundred thousand former soldiers donned their full dress uniforms, put on their black bands of mourning, and travelled to Lausanne at their own expense to pay a last tribute such as was given to no other war commander anywhere. For these two hundred thousand Swiss knew what they – and the world – owed to Henri Guisan, their General.

It was with this knowledge that I set out for my day with the Swiss Army. The Swiss Army, for all its determination to face any hostile foreigner with the whole of its formidable fire-power, is extraordinarily hospitable to a visitor who comes with only friendly intent. Not only did they entertain me, feed me, and explain to me everything I wanted to know, they virtually put themselves under my orders, moving the tanks and opening fire in the manner I felt would give the most exciting show. After some time, I began to suffer from hallucinations, feeling more and more like Alexander the Great; it was all I could do to restrain myself from asking them to invade Italy and start a war. No doubt they would have declined politely, explaining that it would involve the abandonment of Switzerland's neutrality, but Divisionnaire Andreas Gadient did the next best thing: he offered me his own helicopter and pilot, and the surrounding terrain to explore.

We were in a valley, the valley of the Hinterrhein, the walls rising sheer on both sides and the far end of it closed by a range of mountains, their peaks savagely incised into the sky. The helicopter soared down the valley, straight at the wall, which loomed, with its spikes atop, before me. The inevitable optical illusion followed; it looked as though the helicopter was going to smash straight into the wall, but it sailed over the reef, and before me was a sight to make the imagination hold

---

* Weidenfeld & Nicolson, 1961.

6 Over the dam   7 A novel way to commit suicide

its breath. There were the Swiss-Italian Alps, standing up like ranks of soldiers, filling the view to the horizon ahead and to both sides. I have, of course, flown over the Alps many times, and in clear weather the sight of the carpet of peaks below the aircraft has been almost unbearably thrilling, but what made my hour in the Swiss divisionnaire's helicopter unique was that instead of the view being fifteen or twenty thousand feet below me, it was only a few *hundred* feet, and as the machine swooped in and out and over this wild, snow-clad and glorious landscape, I felt that I was looking at the surface of some other planet altogether; when we hovered over the Soppot glacier from which one arm of the Rhine springs, I felt I could lean out and scratch my initials on it.

But the thrill of this magic expedition through the sky was not yet finished, even when we turned to go back. As the helicopter climbed the vertical wall from the far side, and paused for a moment over the sharp stakes of bare rock that guarded it, a herd of mountain goats, startled by the noise and the rushing shadow, broke cover and scampered right along the top of the wall. Immediately, the phrase 'sure-footed as a mountain goat' sprang to life, because the terrain across which they were running seemed to make it impossible for them to put one foot down, let alone four. My excitement must have communicated itself to the pilot, for he turned the helicopter round, flew back towards the wall, and banked steeply so that I could get another and closer view of the animals, which made even more powerful the illusion that I was in another and unfamiliar part of the universe, where strange creatures, unknown on earth, gambol weightlessly among the silent mountains capped with eternal snow.

Divisionnaire Gadient was not quite what I thought a Swiss Army officer would be like (he was one of the tiny number of full-time professional soldiers, the principle of the citizen army and the speed with which it can be mobilised making it unnecessary to have a substantial standing army as well); he was an excellent deadpan comic, not only making a string of jokes, but finishing by asking me whether I was surprised to find a Swiss Army officer making any jokes at all. I could only answer that I *was* surprised, though afterwards I thought it might have been more tactful to say that I wasn't.

But it was time to join the Other Ranks. As we ate lunch out of metal mess-tins, I discovered who, or rather what, they were: one was a farmer, one a student, one a schoolteacher; one worked for an insurance company, one ran the area tourist office, one – older than the rest – was a director of a firm which makes window shutters. I asked the obvious question: didn't they feel irked at being called up every year for half their lives and spending at least three weeks back in the army? Nobody stuck his hand crossways in his jacket and made a speech about patriotism and defending his country; they simply explained that since it applied to everybody, it was so normal and natural that nobody really minded, or even noticed. Besides, the annual service is never part of their holidays: their employers are obliged to give them the time off, and to continue paying them for it. (There is one exception to this last rule; any Swiss soldier who fails his shooting test twice is obliged to go to a depot for extra target practice, and his time there does not count for payment from his employer.)

Then I asked another obvious question, basing it instinctively on Britain, or rather translating the Swiss method into British conditions. Never mind conscription and the annual recall; there are 650,000 modern rifles in Swiss homes, together with a supply of ammunition for every one of them; why has this not led to widespread violent crime? One of my platoon explained. First, he said crisply, an outbreak of violence in Switzerland is about as likely as an outbreak of democracy in Russia. Second, he went on, if anyone did commit what he called the ultimate Swiss crime – bank robbery – the criminal would not only, when caught, face a long term of imprisonment for the crime, he would have another sentence on top of it for misusing an Army rifle, which is in itself a very serious offence, even if the misuse is no more sinister than the shooting of a temptingly succulent rabbit. (A soldier recalled for his annual refresher who is unable to produce his ammunition-packet with the seals unbroken has some explaining to do, and the explanation had better be very convincing indeed.)

Translating that back into British terms was a somewhat unsettling experience. Even if we forget the IRA and other terrorists, what would even the most optimistic Briton imagine as the consequence of 650,000 men who could shoot straight keeping 650,000 rifles in 650,000 corner cupboards up and down the land? (No; 5,500,000, extrapolating as before from a country with less than an eighth of our population.) The question is not difficult to answer; but why is the answer what it is, rather than what it would be in Switzerland? Is it that the Swiss tradition, in which neutrality is not simply a refusal to take sides, but a positive thing, a determination to defend Switzerland against all comers, binds the nation into not only a unity, but a unity which elevates the very temper and soul of a people? But that leads to a strange and disturbing thought; perhaps Britain rose to the occasion in 1940, and allowed Churchill to inspire her, only because she was alone in the fight; as the Swiss know that their independent position means that they have no one to save them but themselves, so Britain knew the same in those days gone by.

For the Swiss, neutrality and self-defence are one. Their metaphor is the porcupine: when attacked, roll up into a ball, quills pointing outwards, and defy anyone to pick the ball up, let alone run away with it. That, it is true, does not explain where the Swiss porcupine gets his mettle from; nor does it explain why those 650,000 guns remain in their 650,000 cupboards, being taken out only for oiling or for their owner's annual recall to active service; nor, above all, does it explain why a citizen army like Switzerland's could not now exist in Britain, though it once might have.

I shook hands with Divisionnaire Gadient; he strode across the grass to his helicopter, then turned to raise a hand in a salute of farewell as he got in, and left me to the Rhine.

The Rhine here is almost entirely untamed, nor is it to be finally curbed and trammelled, made fit for through navigation, for another couple of hundred miles; true, the waters of Lake Constance are placid enough, and they are crowded with traffic, from ferries to freight and from holiday-cruisers to houseboats (though a storm on this lake is not to be trifled with, and rowing-boats are discouraged); true, also, that although south of the lake only the mad would entrust themselves to its waters, the stretch from the northern end to Schaffhausen is one of the most beautiful and charming reaches of the whole river; true, again, that one or two intrepid voyagers, madder than most, have gone over the Schaffhausen Falls in anything from a canoe to a barrel, though a high proportion of these have not lived to boast about it. All the same, as I sat on the banks of the turbulent young Rhine, while the troops packed away their equipment and prepared to bivouac, it was difficult to recognise it as the mighty, placid water I knew from lower down.

The Rhine, fed by Alpine snows, is numbingly cold here even at the height of summer and well into a day of blazing sun; it is also fast and fierce as it tumbles among the stones, for the snow will go on melting for months yet (we are scarcely in June). But its speed and its temperature are not what the traveller first notices; what strikes the eye and the imagination is its colour. Once more, the foolish, vain yearning for a painter's skill stabs at me; the whole place is a giant palette, from the white of the peaks to the grey-brown of the bare rocks beneath them, then down to the brilliant colours of the grass and trees lower still, then on to the valley floor, its grass already yellowing, then to the harebells that line the river's banks, then into the water among the now pale grey rocks, and finally to the water itself, a rich, thick, yet translucent pale green.

A little lower down is Zillis, a tiny scrap of a village; I would have gone straight through it without a pause if it had not been for half a dozen signposts bearing the conventional pictogram of a church. If Zillis is so insistent that its church is worth a visit, I reasoned, having dismissed the possibility that the signs were doing no more than call the faithful to *Gottesdienst* (this is a Protestant area), I had better believe it, at least as far as a peep inside.

The peep turned out to be one of the highlights of the entire journey; a week of day-long visits to St Martin in Zillis would hardly have been enough to encompass the treasure within. The building is part Romanesque, part Gothic; its walls are unadorned by anything other than whitewash, its altar is only a round slab, the floor is bare wood, a Gothic arch leads to the choir, handsome but unremarkable. So what is all the fuss about, and why all those pointing signposts?

Look up; above the visitor's head is a twelfth-century miracle. The flat ceiling is painted with 153 yard-square biblical scenes, forming a rectangle nine squares wide and seventeen long. The outer squares form a border, portraying a continuous, undulating sea inhabited by mythical creatures – serpents, mermaids, nereids, sea-horses; within this frame, the other squares record the life of Christ. Not quite all of it, though; the last row of *cartouches* depicts the life of St Martin, the Zillis church's patron saint, and Christ's Passion stops at the crown of thorns, omitting – surprisingly – the Crucifixion and Resurrection. It seems that the original painter broke off, perhaps through death, just before he finished his work, and another hand completed it with the St Martin scenes. The ceiling is in a state of perfect preservation, and scattered about the church are magnifying-mirrors; the visitor has only to take one and tilt it until he works out how to sweep up and down this astounding Book of Hours.

The twelfth century; the painter of Zillis (his very name is unknown to history, and I dare say he would not have found that either surprising or annoying) lived 100 years before Giotto, and there was nothing much in the way of perspective in his work. Yet the life and richness in this tapestry of wood were as direct and intelligible as anything painted 500 years later, and its faith-grounded simplicity led me instantly to thoughts of the medieval Mysteries, and in particular to our National Theatre's recent re-working of them. Christ's life and death and life again were more than a millennium away from the Mysteries and St Martin's, yet plainly the people of Wakefield and of Zillis alike felt them to have taken place only yesterday; just when did that attitude begin to die, when (and how and why) did the Christian faith begin to demand effort, become externalised rather than something that flowed through the blood and was breathed in from the surrounding air? Was it, I wonder, when Christians, no longer persecuted, began to persecute? The painter of Zillis, and the working men of medieval Wakefield, would have found all such questions incomprehensible. I left the artist to his certainty, and returned to the afternoon sunshine.

Just down the road the sunshine found itself baffled; a cleft in the rock turned into a gorge like a mineshaft, and not even the noon-day sun could have penetrated to the bottom, unless it was willing to tramp down the 321 steps, and then peer down into the depths, which go down more than 300 yards. There must be a legend (though I couldn't find one) to the effect that the shaft came about through a mistimed blow from a giant's axe, or a thunderbolt hurled from Heaven at someone who had displeased the gods. The gorge is part of what is called – and presumably has been since Roman times – the Via Mala, and a very Bad Road it was; I could well imagine how, before the modern passage (itself narrow and winding enough) was cut, the route would have been virtually impassable, though as I later discovered, a Roman general called Stilicho had managed to traverse it twice in the fourth century. The water that rushes along in this buried channel presumably enters the Rhine further along, and the depth and darkness in which it dwells must mean that it remains cold enough to make even the still-Alpine Rhine shiver at the blow.

That seemed a reasonable point to leave the Hinterrhein and explore its brother the Vorderrhein, and up it I went the next day. The Swiss have long since corralled their Rhine with dams, and the hydro-electricity these produce (no doubt they store it, like the petrol, in underground lakes, ready for any emergency) must make a considerable contribution to Switzerland's energy-supplies. The very first dam on the Vorderrhein curved round in a huge, graceful arc, leaning back against the blue-green lake it had produced like a line of policemen resisting a mob. Parallel with the top of the dam was a bridge, crossing the wider end of the lake; the cliffs descended steeply on both sides of it, while the road clung to them as best it might; so narrow was the path at the eastern end that the Swiss authorities had put up a signboard giving the precise times, in each hour, when traffic might proceed, the point being that for miles ahead no car could pass another.

Into this scene, with the modern dam and man-made lake strung between granite cliffs that must have seen most of earth's ages pass, there intruded the hornet-buzzing of a helicopter, and soon the hornet itself could be seen, flying up the valley towards the dam. On the other side of the dam the water runs underground, coming up for air half a mile or so further on, which meant that below the bridge there was a broad plateau on which a small winged aircraft could have landed safely, and a helicopter would have no problem at all; above the dam, and on both sides of the lake, there was no place on which even a gull could alight.

The pilot, however, was behaving oddly; having flown over his landing-place, he went on past the dam and the bridge, soaring out over the lake. Then he made a sweeping loop that took him from one cliff to the other; it looked as though he was seeking somewhere to land above the dam, which was strange, because it must have been as obvious to him as it was to me – *more* obvious, since from his bird's-eye view he could see the whole terrain at a glance – that there was not a patch of ground on which he could put down. Odder and odder; he went right round again, and just as I was assuming that he would now re-cross the roadway and land down on the plateau, he straightened up and flew directly at the rock wall. I was certain that I was about to witness a suicide (and a suicide, moreover, of a perhaps unique kind), for there was no possible way, if he held his course for another twenty yards, that he could survive. Or rather: *I* could see no possible way; but he could. He had noticed that directly before him there was a slight hollow in the cliff face, like an embrasure or the beginning of a cave, and he set down his hornet with such precision that, while the runners were only three-quarters of their length on the ground, the other quarter hanging over the drop, the rotor blades were using the depression in the wall to finish their revolving; he could not have had more than two feet to spare before or behind, if that. I assumed that he must be a film stunt-man (the dam-keeper came out of his cabin quite clearly under the impression that his visitor was a madman, which was certainly the only other explanation possible), but it transpired that although he was on an assignment to a film company, taking some aerial views for them, such death-defying aerobatics were in the ordinary day's round for him.

When I had recovered, I wandered out to the middle of the dam. The sun was high, with not a cloud to be seen; the day was very warm, but I was still some thousands of feet up, so it wasn't *too* warm; it was, in fact, the kind of weather (there was a light breeze, just untidying the surface of the lake) I love best.

I began to reflect on the very strange effect that weather has. In Britain, we grumble about it constantly, of course; we find a May too wet, an August too cold, a June too humid. But we know that we are lucky; we know that in Britain we almost never have extreme conditions of cold or heat or rain or drought. In other words, for all the changeability of Britain's weather, it very rarely takes us seriously by surprise. And yet we are psychologically subject to it in a very disturbing manner. When the weather is bad (and when it is, it is still bad only in British terms – it is, after all, never as cold as Siberia or as hot as Dubai) the depressive effect is extraordinarily powerful, though we know that in the ordinary course of events it will turn good again within a day or two. For not only do we behave like the cave-man who, when winter came, could not believe (because he had no understanding of the regularity of the season's return) that it would ever end; we allow ourselves to feel a profound dejection, frequently mixed with – of all useless emotions in the circumstances – real anger. And if bad weather persists for as long as a week, a feeling of something close to despair is likely to descend. It is said that winds like the *Mistral* or the *Föhn* sometimes drive people to madness and suicide if they persist, and I can understand it, because although in Britain we have no such winds, when even a mild gale has blown for even a few hours it produces a senseless rage against life itself.

Yet the opposite is also true. A few days of warmth in the sun, even if they have followed average weather, not bad, raise the spirits as high as the cold and rain lower them. I wonder if there are any statistics correlating the suicide-rate with the weather? No doubt few people, even in *Mistral* country, take their lives *only* because of the weather; but from my own experiences alone, swinging between emotions far too strong for any real cause that the weather ought to generate, I can well believe that it is a genuine contribution.

The next stop would still have been magic in a monsoon, a blizzard or a burning fiery furnace; it was a visit to Mr Patt. I had found his village, Malix, but I was making no progress in finding him, and in the sleepy afternoon there was nobody about to enquire of. Then three people came laughing up the hill; they didn't look part of Mr Patt's world, but I asked them anyway: 'Kennen Sie Herr Patt?' They didn't say a word, but swung round and pointed, in triple unison, to a house set a little off the path lower down. I knocked on the door; it was opened by Mrs Patt. I was expected; she greeted me warmly, and her very next words were, 'Haben Sie Durst?' I said I did indeed have thirst, considerable thirst, and she led me to a jug of her home-made elderflower cordial and left me with it. I sank a couple of tumblers; it was unimaginably delicious, and would have quenched Dives' thirst in Hell. Then she returned with her husband, and I took stock.

Christian and Leonie Patt are an elderly couple; they radiate contentment, wisdom and an unobtrusive charm; their house is furnished simply, but with great care and perfect taste, and their tiny patch of garden is immaculate. We went outside, with the jug; they left me there, and I sat on a bench in the mild, bone-cheering warmth. A breeze sprang up, and with it a ghostly sound, like the twanging of heavenly viols and tinkling of heavenly bells, a sound I could neither locate nor define; I thought of the ghostly music which accompanies the death of Enobarbus; indeed, I thought of ghosts, though I could not imagine what a ghost would be doing in this tranquil garden on such a day. Then I realised that the sound was coming from round the corner of the house; I followed it, and all was clear. Set beneath the eaves was an Aeolian harp, the instrument – indeed of the gods – that is silent when the air is still, but springs into life as the wind passes through its strings. It was time, I thought, to see what I had come for, and upon the thought, Leonie came out to summon me to it.

Christian Patt used to be a professional ski instructor, but a bad accident put paid to his career. It had happened twenty-five years ago, when he was in his forties, no age to retire, even if he could have afforded to. What next? What next was the flowering of a talent amounting to genius; when I was ushered into the drawing-room I ceased to wonder that the three strollers had known where Mr Patt lived, and marvelled only that there might be anybody in the country who did not. For the room was lined and criss-crossed with an entire gallery, a museumful, a world, of ravishingly beautiful musical instruments; every size and kind of woodwind, strings, percussion; organs and harpsichords; ancient things I could not put a name to (except a few I recognised from the days of David Munrow's Early Music Consort); hurdy-gurdies, pipes, horns made of horn, lutes, lyres, harps – except for the brass, the room could have equipped half the orchestras of the world, and equipped them with instruments the very handling of which would give pleasure to player and audience alike before a note had been sounded. And every one of these had been made by Christian Patt, with his own hands.

Some were of modern shape, though usually with wood of a lighter and more delicate hue than is customary today; some followed patterns he had found in old books or prints; some he had made to his own design, including a whole wall of lovingly and originally shaped violins, violas and cellos. In the twenty-five years of his new-found work he has made some four hundred instruments ('That's the first one I ever made,' he said, pointing to a lovely viola made from pine, without the waist of a modern one), and I have no doubt that if he had had two dozen pairs of hands he could have sold two dozen times the number of these precious *objets d'art* and *objets de musique*. And every one, every instrument of every family, he could himself play.

He led me downstairs, to his workshop, where there were the instruments he was currently working on (he also does repairs). There was a Steinbock horn (I think that is what we call a Capricorn), fully two feet long; it would have graced any performance of *Siegfried*, though I made a hopeless mess of trying to play the hero's horn-call. There was also an Alpenhorn, standing, twice as tall as its maker, in the middle of the room. On one wall there hung a bunch of bridges for the stringed instruments, which irresistibly brought to mind a bunch of garlic or onions on the wall of a kitchen; on the other walls there were diagrams, prints, half-finished instruments.

The workshop itself was a sight almost as wonderful as his creations. There were rows and racks and stands of chisels and gouges and bradawls and bits and knives and hammers and mallets and saws – scores upon scores of them, of different shapes and sizes and types, and they were all where they should be, each in its slot or niche or box – so lovingly ordered, indeed, that it might have been some rich man's pretence, kept for show not for use. A closer look would have at once dispelled the illusion, for the handles of these tools were comfortably worn, and the metal of them bright as only constant use would keep them, and every now and again I came upon one that was *not* in its proper place, whereat I felt greatly relieved.

Nothing was wasted; poking about, I came upon a cigar-box, labelled 'kleine Hornstücke' which means 'little bits of horn', and I opened it. It contained precisely that – little bits of horn; the box could have been labelled 'Might come in handy'.

Christian Patt was *homo faber* in person; and I, who can do nothing with my hands, writhed in envy even as I marvelled at, and saluted, this master of his art. But that was not the end of my marvelling and saluting, nor was it the end of the surprises the Patts had for me. Presently, we all got into a car and drove off up into the hills, and winding into a forest, we found a clearing, miles from anywhere, with a church in it. A beautiful church, called St Peter Mistail; the Patts vanished, and when they came back they had with them two more people, a man and a woman, and all four were dressed in lovely, authentic costumes of the sixteenth century, and all were bearing a variety of instruments, all made by Christian; they sat down and played a concert of pure, early music; we might all have been at the court of the Medicis.

I went away knowing that I had met a supremely happy man, doing what he loved and doing it with such art and beauty and understanding that it could transform the world. His art is beyond me; but his joy in it could be shared, and a golden afternoon turned, for me, into an evening of profound happiness.

3

For Those In Peril

THE NEXT VILLAGE, Passugg, started with a striking picture. On a building site, working alone at cutting and shaping wooden beams, were two young men dressed in a strange uniform – black floppy hat, delicately embroidered black velvet jacket, white frilly shirt and black bell-bottomed trousers, the whole ensemble set off by long, jewelled earrings. I gather that these days a single earring in a male ear denotes homosexuality, though I have also been told that it depends on which ear carries the signal, and unfortunately I have forgotten which it is. But each of these men wore a *pair* of earrings; whence, therefore, the jewellery, and the strange garb?

They explained, and the explanation took me back to a world that lived by the rules, attitudes and organisation depicted in *The Mastersingers.* These were journeyman carpenters, and for once the rank of *journeyman* made real sense, for these two had been apprenticed in Hamburg, and by the terms of what I suppose would be called their indenture they were obliged to go about in the world, in their vivid uniform, seeking work in any country but their own; they were ordered to get a testimonial from every employer they worked for, and their exile lasted for three years, at the end of which they would return to Hamburg and, if they had satisfied all the masters for whom they had worked while on their journeyings, they would be admitted as full-fledged master carpenters.

They seemed, as well they might, carefree; well, pursuing your trade and simultaneously seeing the world when you are nineteen or so must be an exciting life. And then, if the trade was that of the carpenter, how

8 Do not lean out of the window 9 The hospital beneath the hospital 10 The music-maker 11 With the oldest inhabitants 12 The journeyman carpenters

8

9

11

12

13

much more exciting it must be to any young man with imagination! The cutting and shaping of wood, for use or ornament or both, must be one of the very oldest and most fundamental crafts in the world; obviously, wood was worked long before metal, and when metal began it must have been used first to make tools for carpentry; only much later would metal itself be worked. Nor is it possible to imagine a world without wood, for all the plastic furniture, and if it *were* possible, the imagination would be a nightmare. These two young men are simple craftsmen in wood, and Christian Patt is a noble artist; but the wood gives them more in common than their trades give them differences, and I think that Herr Patt would agree that they were, in the most important sense, birds of a feather. That very English poet Richard Church once pointed out that wood has never done anyone any harm (cruelty employs metal, rope, leather, fire, water, stone, but not wood), except, he added, when once a carpenter was nailed to a tree.

Strolling about the village after this encounter I came to a tiny cottage with '1632' carved upon the lintel; as I raised my camera to take a picture, a tiny, grey-haired lady appeared in the doorway – not to shoo me away, but to welcome me into her garden so that I might admire her flowers, which crammed the whole patch and spilt over into joyous window-boxes. Presently, her husband joined us, and we sat on a bench in the morning sunshine and chatted. They were both well over eighty, and I assumed that they had been living in the same house most of their lives, if not since 1632. I asked, and was slightly disappointed when they said they had only been there for some fifteen years. Until then, they explained, they had lived in the village, and she made a gesture, at which he nodded, that could only mean that the village was an unimaginable great distance away. As it happened, the village was not more than 200 yards away, but no doubt removal day must have seemed like an endless voyage to a strange land. When I asked if I might take a picture of them both she protested: 'I'm not beautiful enough,' she said, while he bolted indoors as though I had been planning to shoot him literally. 'Don't worry,' she said, '*he's* gone to make himself look handsome,' and so he had, for he had changed his shirt and put on a smart flat cap.

Then I went on to Illanz, where the Rhine betrayed me, where, indeed, I thought more than once that he had done for me. Just outside the town – village, really – the sufficiently intrepid – or foolish – visitor can take a journey down the rapids. From my first sight of the

13 Rendezvous with destiny

High Rhine I had seen how the river rushed and leaped among the rocks, how the white water boiled and bubbled, how the spray was flung high in the air. A delightful sight, even an exciting one, from the bank or a bridge; what would it be like from the water? In the teeth of reason, I signed on for the voyage.

The voyage was made in a flat-bottomed rubber dinghy; it would hold about ten people, who sat on the plump sides with their feet on the floor. There were two professionals to a boat; one to steer and give commands, one as co-pilot and general factotum. On the bottom of the boat there were webbing straps, sewn at both ends; into these 'stirrups' we had to insert our feet, to ensure that we were not flung out of the boat as it pitched. Life-jackets were obligatory, and so were crash-helmets of the motor-cycle kind; I began to think that I had embarked on an enterprise considerably more hazardous than I had thought in advance it would be. Wernher, our captain, explained that the crash-helmet was necessary because if we did fall out, a crack on the head from a passing rock would probably put paid to us; he also pointed out that there was a stout rope running right round the outside of the boat, and urged us, should we be hurled over the side, to hang on to it. He further explained that he was in touch at all times with his base, by walkie-talkie, though I could not see how that would help me to hang on to the rope if I fell out, let alone to avoid being smashed to pieces on the rocks, crash-helmet or no crash-helmet. Nor was I enormously reassured when he said that there was a first-aid kit aboard, and even pointed to it.

It was when, a moment later, I discovered that it was the passengers who did the work, not the crew, that I wondered whether there was still time for me to change my mind, and proceed to Reichenau (where the voyage ended) by some less unconventional means of transport. I decided not to . . . in for a pfennig. We were issued with huge paddles, and given instruction in their use; we were also told that we must paddle in unison, for speed and safety. We set off.

Rapids are so named because they are rapid; so much I had deduced, but little else. I had not, for instance, guessed that within one minute of starting I would be drenched from head to foot, nor that within a few more the boat would have shipped some six inches of water. Nor, though this I should have guessed from the tiny junior rapids I had watched higher up, had I realised that when the rushing water hits a sizeable rock it turns into a massive wave which crashes over any lunatics passing by in a flat-bottomed rubber dinghy. Nor had I realised that continuous paddling with an instrument a yard long would very soon become exhausting. Nor was my dress quite appropriate for the experience; in fact, short of wearing tails and a top-hat, I could not have picked a more inconvenient outfit, consisting as it did of a woollen shirt, knee-breeches, long woollen socks and walking-shoes.

We are all familiar with the experience which, had we known in advance what it would entail, we would have fled from, leaving no forwarding address, but which, once undergone, we realise we would not willingly have missed for any consideration. This need not be a physical experience, and my record in that area had not been. It was my crossing of the Atlantic (both ways) in the *Queen Mary* on her final round-trip before she left the service for ever, to be parked off the Californian coast as a tourist attraction. Nothing would induce me to do it again; it was like falling through a hole in time and finding myself on her maiden voyage in 1938, and the boredom was so intense you could almost touch it. But in retrospect, with the feel of the awfulness long since forgotten (they made me judge the funny-hat competition on the last night), the bizarre nature of the whole enterprise, much enhanced by the fact that the Captain bore the unforgettable name of Treasure Jones, remains a memory surrounded by a glow of pleasure.

So let it be, one day, with the Rhine rapids. A hundred times at least I would have been thrown into the river with considerable force if it had not been for the canvas strips, beneath the water in the boat, holding my feet inextricably tight. A thousand times at least a wave broke straight over my head (I was up front on the starboard side); if I had had enough breath, I would have murmured, with Clarence, 'Ay me, what pain, methinks, it is to drown.' A million times at least I wished the boat, the organisers, my fellow-madmen and myself at the bottom not just of the Rhine but of the Pacific Ocean. And throughout the entire, awful endurance test, one thought kept recurring; in ancient times, great malefactors – murderers, traitors, coiners, blasphemers – were condemned, as a punishment worse than execution, to the galleys, yet here I was, and all the other passengers with me, having *paid* to undergo such dreadful condemnation.

Two mortal hours it lasted, two hours of strenuous labour and of being soaked, buffeted, terrified, pitched, tossed and exhausted; more exhausted, indeed, than I had ever been in my life. And yet, when I got back to my hotel, and really believed at last that the experience was over, I recognised my own feelings for what they truly were: unalloyed exhilaration.

I examined the feeling more closely; it was not only, not even mainly, the exhilaration of having successfully accomplished something I would not have believed I could get through at all. It was the exhilaration of the experience itself. There was, of course, *some* danger in the journey; a participant *could* be thrown out, the boat, though even when hurled high into the air it always seemed to land flat, with a catlike skill, *might* have capsized, say by getting a rock under one edge and a massive wave to follow it. But that knowledge was tempered by the more powerful knowledge that the people in charge were skilled professionals; neither I, nor, I afterwards gathered, anybody else, seriously believed that the trip might end in disaster. So that, too, could be ruled out as the cause of the exhilaration.

What was left to explain it? The clue was provided by a watcher on the bank, who was in position there opposite what was known as Das Schwarze Loch – the Black Hole. This was the hardest and most dangerous point of the whole mad voyage; the rocks were larger and more numerous, the water was faster, and the level involved a sharp drop. The boat was hurled between Scylla and Charybdis, the waves swamped us a dozen times, our paddles practically bent under the effort they demanded – and yet, I was told, everyone in the boat at this point, including me, was roaring with laughter.

I was reminded of a scene at the end of Hitchcock's *Strangers on a Train*, where the murderer, as a last desperate throw, has wrecked the machinery of a children's carousel in a fairground, so that it is spinning out of control. The whirling roundabout is surrounded by the parents, screaming, weeping, fainting, in panic for their children, begging someone to stop the machine and save them; the children, on their horses, are now going round so fast that they have merged into a blur; the adults' unbearable terror mounts still higher; and at that moment Hitchcock, the master, cuts to the *inside* of the runaway roundabout. Now it is the parents who form an indistinguishable blur; but the children can be seen clearly, *and they are having the most wonderful time of their lives*, spinning round faster than any roundabout has ever gone for them, laughing and cheering and screaming with joy.

When I had recovered, I had a bath, donned some dry clothes, and went for a gentle walk; I met a plump cat, black and white, with whom I had a long conversation about these matters. The cat indicated a lack of interest in my theories about fear and pleasure, and made clear that it would rather play. So we played, and I realised that nobody had played with it for a long time. It was sleek and well fed, obviously not a stray, but the purring happiness it exhibited at having its chin tickled, a stalk dangled in front of its nose for it to pat at, a seat on my lap offered, a head-to-tail stroking, a game of hide-and-seek in a nearby field of clover, was such that it was clear that I was rescuing it from boredom; clearly, it lived with people who did not realise that a cat needs entertainment.

I think the British are the only people who *do* realise this. The French are simply not cat-lovers, the Italians are indifferent, the Germans and the Swiss regard the beasts as strictly utilitarian, their function to catch mice or be cuddled by the children; only we have recognised that cats, for all their magnificent independence, seek pleasure as we do, and pine when they are denied it. I made my farewells; the cat was reluctant to give up so attentive a playmate, and followed me for some time. Another day had ended well.

Now, in Flims, I was only a short step from the point at which the Vorderrhein and Hinterrhein sink their differences, and the Rhine becomes one until it is safely across the Dutch border. Flims is a ski-resort, and like so many villages of its kind is split between winter facilities and summer ones; there are ski-lifts and tennis-courts, ice-rinks and swimming-pools, cable-cars and rowing-boats. Flims also offers 2200 beds in hotels, 5000 more in chalets and tourist apartments, and as many more as the camping-site will hold, together with a two-mile toboggan track, ninety miles of 'marked and prepared footpaths' (of which twelve miles are 'suitable for wheelchairs'), romantic sleigh-rides, horses to let, concerts from June to September and a 'fitness-track' suitable for everybody who wants to get fit, except for elderly people, who have their own 'Géricourse' track.

'The leisure industry'; what a phrase, and what a reality! Yet it is one of the biggest industries on earth, and there is hardly a country in the world which does not encourage it in the form of tourism from abroad. The money of other nations, in our strange world, is almost invariably preferred, and for good reason: not for nothing was the term 'hard currency' invented. In the end, international tourism will defeat and destroy itself, for the facilities provided will become entirely standardised throughout the world, and gradually people will come to realise that they may as well stay at home, since they will have the same experiences there without the trouble and expense of travelling. But by then nowhere will be worth visiting anyway, including the place we start from.

My hotel in Flims had a handsome restaurant with a vast panoramic window and a view outside it that justified the glass. All the same, I dined down the hill at the Adula Hotel; a perfect meal of *langoustines*, *foie gras* poached in raspberry vinegar, stuffed breast of chicken, fresh goat cheese and a sorbet, accompanied by a 1979 Lynch-Bages in perfect condition and priced a good deal lower than it would have been at a fairly moderate restaurant in London. What's in a view?

The only thing I know about Liechtenstein is that it has triangular postage-stamps, and even that is wrong, because it doesn't. Liechtenstein is an anomaly; it is a comic-opera state with a uniquely useful service. Its entire population amounts to no more than 27,000 people, and the capital, Vaduz, is referred to by the Liechtensteiners themselves as a village. It has existed almost as long as Switzerland; a traveller going from one to the other does not have to show a passport at the border, and anyway there is nothing to show that there *is* a border, in whichever direction he is going. But although it exists in the shadow of Switzerland, particularly in economic matters, Liechtenstein manages to make, nationally, a profit.

It makes, to start with, a good deal of money from tourism, because there is, at any rate from afar, a romance about these tiny states – they include also Andorra and San Marino, and even Monaco – that draws the curious to them. Somehow, they were forgotten by history, washed up on their bigger neighbours' shores and left there to demonstrate that not everything in the world is the same as everything else. They are figments of the imagination in one sense, of course, but there is a widespread and instinctive feeling that they are worth preserving, perhaps to remind us that small is beautiful, or at least that big is all too frequently ugly.

Liechtenstein also makes money – 10 per cent of its national income – from its postage stamps, though they are all relentlessly square or rectangular. But they go in for a vast variety of designs – pictorial, biographical, industrial, historical, scenic – all beautifully engraved and coloured, and the world, at any rate in its philatelic capacity, buys them in immense numbers. (No doubt the Liechtensteiners themselves buy the stamps to stick on letters, but remember that the Liechtensteiners number only 27,000 in all.)

Tourism; postage stamps; what else? What else indeed; 60 per cent of Liechtenstein's income is derived from the desire of individuals and institutions abroad to set up companies in a place which is the very definition of a tax haven, and a tax haven which asks no questions and keeps its mouth shut. Its symbol is high above the capital: the Prince's castle, which has walls twelve feet thick, and contains the Prince's personal art collection, rumoured to include the world's only Leonardo in private hands. But just as the Prince enjoys his twelve-feet-thick privacy, together with his Leonardo, real or imaginary, so at his castle's feet there is a whole army of accountants, lawyers, bankers, notaries, financiers and dealers, all devoted to the sacred principles of Liechtenstein hospitality: when money knocks on the door, usher it in with a smile, and look after it just as if it was your own.

I went to see one of these paragons of discretion; it seems that although there are indeed hundreds of firms specialising in looking after foreigners' business, there are half a dozen or so which are acknowledged leaders. The one I visited was one of this élite corps; it must have been, for it was the one that set up Mr Robert Maxwell's Liechtenstein operations, which have had the curious result of ensuring that nobody – or nobody outside Liechtenstein, anyway – knows who or what actually owns the Mirror Group of newspapers.

Dr Werner Keicher, young (he had not long succeeded his father as head of the firm), friendly and reassuring, received me in his smart, not over-luxurious office. And what could he do for me? Ahem.

The cough was mine. I wanted to know just how it was done, and in order to find out, I had to take it all seriously, to explain that I had funds that I wanted to protect, that I had earnings from countries other than my own that I wanted to keep out of Britain, that I wanted to use my offshore money to make more. What would he advise? Bearing in mind, I explained, that the burden of taxation I carried in my own country was too great for comfort, but bearing in mind also that I would not do anything contrary to British law. He replied, calmly, that his firm did not interest itself in its clients' relations with their own countries' tax authorities, nor indeed wish to know anything about them. I asked whether that meant that I could transfer massive funds to Liechtenstein without him concerning himself about their origins. He spoke with care, indicating rather than saying that some assurances might be required; I had a very faint impression that if I had turned up with a battered suitcase stuffed with a couple of million crumpled fivers, he would have asked me where I had got them from, and on being told that my grandma had put them in my Christmas stocking, would have said, in Liechtensteinese, 'Then that's all right.'

And was confidentiality assured? Really assured? His response was illuminating. I would have expected – did expect – a long and eloquent speech of assurance: please set your mind at rest . . . decades of experience . . . our whole business rests upon . . . no problem about that . . . first duty to protect our clients . . . Liechtenstein law has long recognised . . . I beg you to have the fullest confidence . . . no record of any breach . . . etc., etc., etc. Nothing of the kind: he simply said, 'Yes, yes, yes, yes,' and changed the subject. It was obvious that the matter of confidence was so deeply embedded in his firm's way of business that my question had no more weight than if I had asked whether it was permitted for a visitor to Liechtenstein to breathe. Of *course*.

I warmed to Dr Keicher; if I had spent any longer in his charming company I might have been tempted to use his services and his discretion for my own business purposes. But why, in fact, did I not?

This question is not nearly so easy to answer as I feel it should be. Let us first rule out breaches of the law; it is not now illegal for British citizens to have bank accounts and businesses abroad, to own companies registered in Liechtenstein and to buy and sell outside Britain. And it is well settled law that a citizen is entitled to arrange his financial matters, provided he is not breaking the law, in any way he pleases, in order to diminish the amount of tax that would otherwise have been levied upon him. And, obviously, I would not have been breaking any Liechtenstein law either. Why, then, would I not take advantage of Dr Keicher's skill, service and silence? After all, at home I claim every allowance against tax that the law offers me, I set off all expenses that may be properly deducted, I pay not a penny more tax than I am obliged to, and I feel no shame at all and would be surprised if I was told I ought to. Then what is the difference, assuming my imaginary Liechtenstein operations remained as firmly within the law as my real British ones?

It would, I think, be that the Liechtenstein operation would have *no* reality other than to enable me to avoid tax. To set up a foreign company, with articles of association and Liechtenstein directors on the board, and a company seal, and engraved writing-paper, and several bank accounts, and share issues and all the rest of it, solely for the purpose of lessening my tax, would be, in some vague but real way, to cheat.

I shook hands with Dr Keicher without availing myself of his professional abilities.

I went out into the street, and was rewarded for my probity by the delightful discovery of the world's politest parking-tickets. In Liechtenstein, they take the form of a yellow envelope, with the details of the offence on one side, and a quadrilingual (German, French, Italian and English) message on the other, to this effect:

> A check shows that you have exceeded your parking time. We feel that this is an oversight on your part, and so we ask you to pay a supplementary fee of 3 francs. Please put it in this envelope and drop it in the letter box marked 'Nachzahlgebühren' at the car-park exit. In paying this sum you will relieve us of the unpleasant duty of having to fine you. We wish you a pleasant trip.

Who could resist so courteously-worded a demand for three Swiss francs? Not I. Mind you, there was no excuse; if the Liechtenstein parking-tickets are the world's politest, their parking-meters are the most accommodating; they take, in three separate slots, three separate currencies – Swiss, German and Liechtenstein.

4

Dr Waldheim's Memories

LAKE CONSTANCE, or the Bodensee, has been my stamping-ground for many a year; I cannot remember just how many, but it must be more than thirty, because it figured on my itineraries in the days when I went walking, pack on back, in Bavaria and Austria. And I can remember very clearly the first reason for its inclusion; those were the days when I was discovering Baroque architecture, and one of the most glorious of that great gallery of Baroque churches stands on the northern shore of the lake, near the western end: Birnau. Not for a long time have I failed to make the pilgrimage when I have been within a hundred miles of it: *vaut le voyage.*

First, however, is Constance, my base for exploring the lake shore and the water itself, for I have to remember that the Bodensee is, strictly speaking, a bulge in the river; the Rhine enters it at the eastern end, hard by Bregenz, having by then marked the border between Switzerland and Austria for some miles, and leaves it at the western end, where the lake forks. The northern fork goes nowhere; it is just the end of the lake. But at the southern arm the water begins to gather speed, and as it leaves the lake behind, it will no longer brook any denial of its Rhineship; just where lake becomes river stands the little town of Stein am Rhein, the first time since its source that it figures in a place-name, and ahead is the journey to the Schaffhausen Falls, and, a little way beyond that thrilling cascade, Rheinfelden, where the Rhine becomes navigable, to remain so now all the way to Holland and the sea.

Constance has two claims on the attention of history, but first I must allow it to assert its claims on geography, botany, horticulture and even meteorology, for next to it is a short promontory running out into the lake and forming a tiny island, Mainau, which has a freak climate. Though it is in the heart of Europe, it has managed to persuade the heavens that it is in the tropics; it is covered with such very un-European produce as bougainvillaea and hibiscus, bananas and lemons, and the visitor to this peaceful little place (no cars are allowed, and visitors arriving on wheels must leave them at the landward end of the causeway) are constantly turning a corner and finding a grove of fruit and flowers and trees that are otherwise to be seen growing only hundreds of miles to the south.

But Constance's two slices of history must now be considered. The more recent was its curiously anomalous situation during the Second World War. The border between Switzerland and Germany runs, and ran then, right through the city, for the line of demarcation follows the southern bank of the southern fork of the lake, and then goes out, invisibly, into the water. Constance itself – or Konstanz, as I must call it while adjudicating on the border dispute – is the German half; the Swiss call their half, no doubt in accordance with their rigid principles of neutrality, Kreuzlingen, but it is all one town, and passing from one side to the other today involves only the most casual of formalities. When Switzerland, however, was manning her defences in the war, the border, on both sides, was to be taken seriously, not least because of the desperate refugees from Nazism who strove to cross it. I can never make that crossing myself without remembering the account of one of those who, destined for the gas-chambers, managed to escape to Switzerland; it told how the escaper, having got across, but knowing that he was liable to deportation, came face to face with a Swiss policeman, to whom it was obvious that the intruder had no right to be there and no papers to justify his presence. The policeman asked him what he was doing, and the man, who could only pretend, implausibly, to be a Swiss living near the border, said he had just gone out for an evening stroll and a beer. The Swiss policeman looked at him in knowing silence for a long moment, then said, 'Ja, schweizisches Bier ist gut,' and turned his back.

Constance's second slice of history takes us back to the fifteenth century, when the city (there is a legend that it got its name because it was founded by Constantine the Great, but alas, no evidence to support it, unless you count the discovery of a Roman fort) was for four years the centre of the world. The Council of Constance was convened to bring an end to the Great Schism of Christianity, when for a century there were two rival popes, and for a brief time three. It achieved its purpose, temporarily at least, with the election, as the one true pope, of Martin V, but in doing so it unwittingly laid the train of powder which was to blow Christianity apart so devastatingly that only in our own time, and a very recent part of it, have the pieces started to come together again.

The banner of revolt had already been raised; though Luther had not yet been born, his precursors had, and one of them, Jan Hus of Bohemia, carried the standard of reform to Constance itself, with a safe-conduct (he had already been accused of heresy) from the Emperor Sigismund. The Council, or the city of Constance while the Council was going on, must have produced one of the greatest gatherings in all history up to that date, and there cannot have been very many like it since. In Milman's *History of Latin Christianity*, the scene is described like this:

> For many months the converging roads which led to this central city were crowded with all ranks and orders, ecclesiastics and laymen, sovereign princes and ambassadors of sovereigns, archbishops and bishops, the heads or representatives of the great monastic orders, theologians, doctors of canon or civil law, delegates from all the universities, some with splendid and numerous retainers, some like trains of pilgrims, some singly or on foot, and, with these, merchants and traders of every degree. For the Council had come to be, it seemed, not only a solemn Christian Conference, but a great European Congress, a vast central fair, where every kind of commerce was to be conducted on the boldest scale, and where chivalric, historical and other amusements were to be provided for the assembled masses.

And another author* fills out the picture:

> Indeed, it is stated that, independently of those immediately engaged in the work of the council, no fewer than 100,000 persons were, through curiosity or hope of gain, attracted to the city at this time, among whom were mountebanks, buffoons, actors of mysteries

* L. G. Séguin, *The Black Forest* (1879).

from England – who, for the first time, introduced dramatic representations in Germany – and a vast number of women of doubtful reputation.

Hus marched into the lions' den; tolerated at first, among the seething multitude in Constance, he was abruptly accused of breaking his side of the terms on which the immunity had been granted. (It was said that he had preached, and celebrated Mass, both of which he had agreed to eschew.) He was arrested; so, almost simultaneously, was the third claimant to the papal throne, the false John XXIII (who had convened the Council). In view of the scandalous crimes of which John was accused, it was said of the two prisoners that 'the one was being punished for the very offences which the other was punished for protesting against'.

It is said that when Hus's condemnation was announced he said only, 'I came here freely, under the safe-conduct of the Emperor'; it is also said that at those words the Emperor blushed. Emperors rarely blush, but what is certain is that Sigismund did not lift a finger to save him, and Hus went to the stake, to be followed shortly afterwards by his colleague and friend, Jerome of Prague.

The Council of Constance healed the split in Christendom, but by burning Hus it ensured that the cause for which he died – a fundamental re-interpretation of Christian doctrine and the cleansing and renovation of the Christian Church – would rend asunder not just the papacy, but Christendom itself; from among the faggots which burned Hus, Luther snatched a brand with which he set the Christian world on fire. The ashes of Hus and Jerome were scattered on the waters of Lake Constance; they came back to the shore when, after the Reformation had begun, the city of Constance sided with the Reformers.

Constance is still Hus's town. There is a Hus Street,. of course; the Dominican monastery in which Hus was first confined while awaiting trial has been converted into the Insel Hotel (ironically, the most luxurious in the city); his effigy still stands in the Council House (a wonderfully proportioned building, with miniature watch-towers above two stone storeys crowned by a wooden one, the whole perfectly preserved and now used as a concert-hall); and the place, in the Cathedral, where he stood to hear himself condemned is marked with a slab. Even the house in which Hus first lodged when he arrived in Constance has survived; it stands beside the old gatehouse and is similarly half-timbered. It is a Hussite museum now, and a plaque in the façade records the details of his life and martyrdom.

There are other plaques in Constance; one, on the wall of the Hotel Hecht (it was built as a hotel in the early fifteenth century, bought in the eighteenth for a dwelling-house by Peter Thumb, who built the Baroque marvel at Birnau, then later turned back into a hotel, which it remains), records that Montaigne stayed there in 1580; another, just opposite the Insel Hotel, announces that Erasmus stayed there, with his friend Prebendary Bloxheim, in 1522. How nice, I felt, to have met both my greatest heroes in this charming and historic town.

Charming and historic: it is indeed both. But it has in addition a very different quality for me. I cannot visit Constance without being reminded, to the point at which I can feel the hair on the back of my neck prickle and rise, of what happened to me there on a visit many years ago. I had booked a room at a hotel in which I had stayed several times before, always in good weather. On this occasion, however, a day which had dawned fine and warm had changed its mind; a steep drop in temperature was accompanied by very heavy and persistent rain. I returned to the hotel after dining out, opened the door of the room and switched the light on.

As I finished writing the end of the previous paragraph, I had to pause and control my feelings, before I could proceed with this one. For what I saw, before fleeing from the room and the hotel, was a great concourse of spiders, which seemed to be as numerous as the crowds which had flocked to the Council of Constance; the walls and ceilings were crawling with them, *and* they were the big and hairy kind.

There are some people whom this sight would annoy, but not upset; there are even people whom it would neither annoy *nor* upset; but I am one of that unfortunate tribe called phobics, and my phobia is of spiders. I arrived in the lobby of the hotel, with no recollection of how I had got there, in a state of uncontrollable hysteria. When I could speak, I told the man at the desk what I had found in my room. 'Ah, yes,' he said calmly, 'you see, when it is wet and cold they climb up and come into the room'; I had a powerful feeling that he had much sympathy with the poor little things, liked nothing better than to offer them hospitality, and hated to think that they might have had to spend the night in the cold and the rain. I have never been back to the hotel; no doubt it would be safe for me in fine weather, but the thought of the weather abruptly changing for the worse, perhaps in the middle of the night, was too frightening to make the risk acceptable. (On this visit, for my Rhine journey, I stayed outside Constance, at Reichenau, in a furnished flat; I got in late, and there was nobody about, which wouldn't have mattered, but – unfamiliar with the domestic routine – I was unable to find any soap, however many cupboards and drawers I opened. Baffled, I suddenly had an idea; shortly afterwards, I found myself, for the first time, taking a shower in washing-up liquid. It was quite agreeable, too.)

And here is another plaque; Constance is as proud of its visitors as many cities are of their sons. This one records that Franz Mesmer lived here from 1812 to 1814, in what is now a handsome and well kept house originating in the fourteenth century. Mesmer is one of those who have given their name to a language, like the unfortunate Captain Boycott. (He has a second claim on immortality – he is mentioned in *Così fan tutte*.) But I wonder how many people today, using the participle form, mesmerised, in its figurative sense; remember where it comes from? (For that matter, how many people calling for boycotts remember where *they* come from?)

I took a final glance at the Rathaus, beautifully and gently painted outside. Painting the municipal offices is more or less standard in the Germanophone countries; indeed, some of the loveliest buildings in Europe are ancient town halls, and the continuation of the practice with new buildings means, apart from the pleasure they give to visitors like me, that future ages, with any luck, will have the same experience that we today have when we see, while travelling in Germany or Austria or much of Switzerland, an old half-timbered building, the colours of its decoration lovingly restored. In some of the smaller places, the Altes Rathaus is still the present-day Rathaus, the building having remained in the same use throughout the centuries. But the question it raises, which is why can Britain not do something similar, is easier to raise than answer. I don't know why, but the fact is that most municipal buildings in Britain are architecturally of the most unspeakable ugliness, so that painting them would be like slapping face-powder, rouge, mascara and lipstick on an aged and hideous crone. Somehow I do not think that our far-off descendants will gaze in wonder at the beauty with which, near the end of the twentieth century, the city fathers decorated the Town Halls of Reading, Basildon, Alloa, Merthyr Tydfil or Barnsley. And a tip to travellers in lands where they make much of their Rathaus; if you do not know where to eat well in the town, and every restaurant seems to you to be exactly the same as every other, try the Ratskeller, which will always be found in the immediate vicinity of the Town Hall (sometimes, indeed, in the very building), and you will have a much better than average chance that you have picked the best the town offers.

A few minutes later, thinking such thoughts, I found myself back at the harbour, which was covered in swans. As I watched, two pairs took off successively, on exactly the same flight-path, and the aeronautical image was irresistible, for their wingbeats were perfectly synchronised and both pairs looked as though they were not going to get off the water; just before the end of the runway, all four became airborne, and the clumsiness with which they had beaten their wings more and more furiously in the effort to leave the ground was instantly forgotten in the soaring beauty of their flight. Surely, for all their monochrome hue (and their reputation – I know not whether justified or defamatory – for bad temper), swans are the most beautiful birds in all creation. Where do we get the haunting legend that the swan, mute throughout its life, sings for the first and last time when it is on the point of death? Swift put the legend to deadly use in his epigram 'On an opera singer':

> Swans sing before they die; 'twere no bad thing
> Should certain persons die before they sing.

Going back to bed at Reichenau, I learned that on this scrap of land, like Mainau almost an island, there are no fewer than three Romanesque churches. It seemed unlikely, but why would my informant deceive me? I decided to trust him, and was rewarded for my faith; there they were, all three of them, in successive villages.

Romanesque architecture always strikes me as essentially innocent, unlike Gothic with its majesty, or Baroque with its self-consciousness. The three churches on Reichenau were perfect examples of what I see when I look at Romanesque buildings; it is as though a child, pure as an angel, has designed them. (And surely a child *did* design the old stone tower, with its pyramid hat, its arch in the base and its ten wooden shutters on each side, which was originally a gate to the Rhine bridge. But what child but a heavenly one would have had so instinctive and complete a sense of proportion?) The frescoes are done in a marvellously naïve style, with simple colours and an unsteady outline, but my feeling goes further; the structure itself exhibits the same spirit. That cap on the towers, for instance, is just what a child drawing an imaginary building would use to crown his drawing, but the result has

14 It is much worse than it looks 15 Dr Keicher: Now about my millions... 16 I always go to Liechtenstein to get my hair cut 17 A light breakfast on Lake Constance 18 Birnau: Nothing out of the ordinary 19 Birnau: The miracle within

14

15

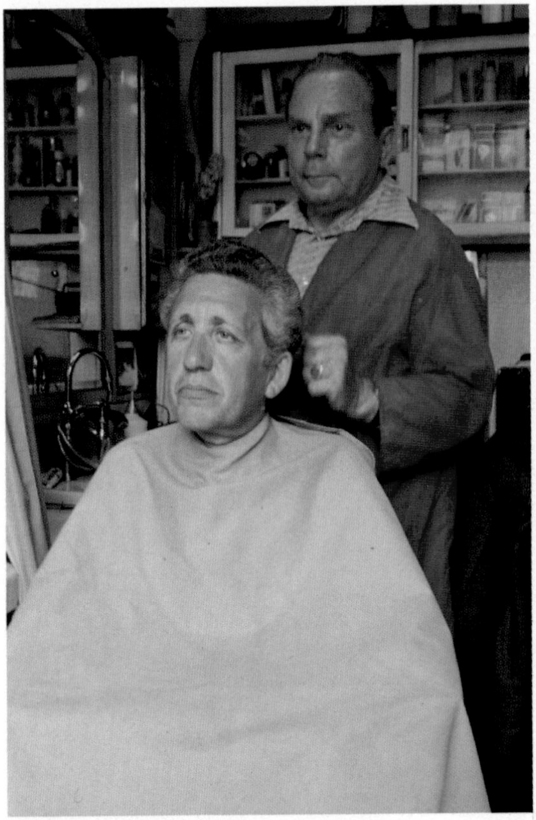

16

17

18

19

ABORTE

an overwhelming force, the same force that we feel when, in painting, we contemplate Italian 'primitives'. (This must be one of the most unfortunate terms in the whole history of art, suggesting as it does something crude, brutal and insensitive, whereas very many primitives have a beauty, in their innocence, greater than the noblest knowing masterpieces of the Renaissance.) And in the third, and finest, of the Reichenau churches I had a bonus. Sitting quietly and at peace as the last of the evening sunshine filtered in, I saw the chancel door open. In came a tiny, plump nun, wholly oblivious to me, or to anything but the task before her. There was a wood-carving, a simple, moving *Pietà*, in the nave, surrounded by pots and troughs of flowers, and the little nun had come to water them. Up and down the tubs and *jardinières* she went with her sprinkler watering-can, keeping the flowers fresh for Christ and his mother, while I held my breath lest she should notice me and break the spell of her rapt and loving service.

Next day I set out to explore the lake. That is not difficult; two ferries ply across it regularly, and many pleasure-boats make the circuit. One of the ferries does the short crossing at the Constance end; the other goes across the widest part of the lake, from the evocatively named Romanshorn to Friedrichshafen opposite. It was a day of pure blue sky, unwavering sunshine and the lightest of zephyrs, so I started early, but even as early as this the sailing-boats were out, scudding across the water as though they, like the swans, would soon take off.

Friedrichshafen, like every little town that needs visitors, sells its delights with vigour, but it is too busy, too serious, too commercial (its skyline, particularly round the harbour, is dotted with modern office blocks), to pose as a true holiday village. It has a fine relic of the days when it was the capital of Württemberg and had its own king (whence its name – Frederick's Harbour): a massive, twin-towered Baroque church with a palace attached. But its most powerful claim on a lake-visitor's time is its aeronautical history, though at first sight it looks as though it couldn't have had any. It had, though, and a twofold version, moreover. First, it is the city where the airship was created; Graf Zeppelin was born across the lake, in Constance, but he set up his revolutionary business in Friedrichshafen, and the first of those extraordinary, silent, vast, slow, beautiful creatures of the air was launched there in 1900.

The story of the airship resembles that of the prehistoric creatures which once roamed the earth; they were like nothing before or since, they flourished mightily but briefly, they were destroyed by a fatal flaw and disappeared for ever, and when, today, we see a pictorial representation of them, we must have a poor imagination if we do not catch our breath in wonder at their majesty, their absurdity and their tragedy. Nobody knows for sure what wiped out the Brontosaurus, the pterodactyl and *Tyrannosaurus rex* (if you want to know what a prehistoric monster looked like, catch a common lizard and look at it close up), but the airship died because the terrible inflammability of the gas with which it was filled led to a succession of disasters. So much is common knowledge; but many of those who know it do not know of the irony with which the story is accompanied; the airship was abandoned at the very moment when a safe, non-inflammable gas was being developed.

At the Zeppelin Museum, the Count stares down haughtily at the visitors, looking alarmingly like the Kaiser; the museum itself is full of lifelike models of his strange creation, but no museum would be big enough to hold a real example, and for all the meticulous proportions of the miniatures, they cannot convey the mysterious, other-worldly appearance of the airship that haunts anyone old enough (I just am) to remember.

Friedrichshafen, having tasted glory in the air, was not content to retire as the former home of the airship; a second birth followed, though Friedrichshafen is not quite so energetic in telling the story. The Dornier aircraft were developed and built here in the 1930s, and added greatly to the achievements of German arms in the Second World War. The Dornier started as a seaplane, and there is a model, with photographs, in the Zeppelin Museum, a sight almost as uncanny as the Zeppelin itself, for above the giant wing from which the fuselage is suspended there is a row of *six* huge engines. I thought again of the swans and their take-off; when this ungainly thing lumbered down the harbour for the first time there cannot have been many among the bystanders who believed that it would ever be airborne.

The town's Information Office, in producing its guide, has to pick its way delicately through the susceptibilities of its visitors; the British might not like being reminded that the land-based Dornier contributed notably to the Blitz, and the French could well have a double embarrassment, for the Zeppelin works in Friedrichshafen were comprehensively looted by the French occupying forces ('removed' is the word the town employs, adding that 'After long years of negotiation with the French authorities some of the exhibits were returned').

Outside the museum, as well as the bust, there is a monument to Graf Zeppelin; a simple and beautiful basalt obelisk, with a no less simple and beautiful legend, which, translated, says, 'First we must wish, then we must believe, then it will happen.' Not far away is a more practical memorial; the Graf Zeppelin House, which is a huge complex of conference and cultural rooms (sooner or later the world will fly out of its orbit under the weight of conference and cultural 'centres'). The Graf Zeppelin House is particularly exact in offering its facilities; they start with the Hugo Eckener Hall (Eckener was one of Zeppelin's two closest collaborators in developing the airship), which holds 1300 people, and continue with the Ludwig Dürr Hall (Dürr was the other of Zeppelin's partners), which holds 450. Then there is the Alfred Colsman Hall (300), the Count Soden Room (140), the Claude Dornier Room (120), the Captain Lehmann Room (90), the Karl Maybach Room (80), the Captain Flemming Room (60), and finally the Captain von Schiller Room (30). There cannot be many organisations of any size which, wishing to meet, could not be accommodated somewhere in the Graf Zeppelin Haus, where between sessions they could try the restaurant, the café, the pub, the bowling-alley and the underground garage. And if there is a long enough break between sessions, or they feel like playing truant from the next one, they could do worse than leave the town and stroll up the hill to the Haldenberg Chapel, a tiny, whitewashed church with nothing to commend it except the peace it radiates.

Here is Meersburg, a beautiful little town but bestrewn thick with souvenir shops of the most depressing kind. After a time Meersburg itself begins to feel like a souvenir; it reminds me of Rothenburg-ob-der-Tauber for its extreme self-consciousness (it is not as bad as Oberammergau, but *nothing* could be as bad as Oberammergau). Still, it does have a formidable castle, begun (or so it boasts) in the seventh century, and added to, over the centuries, by such misty figures, half legendary and half historical, as Dagobert, Charles Martel and Frederick Barbarossa. I could well believe it, for the whole thing had a powerfully barbarous and primitive feel; the walls must be at least eighteen feet thick, and the castle is perched high up above the town, dominating it and the surrounding countryside (which was presumably the point); the view from the castle suggests that Dagobert, Charles Martel and Barbarossa must have felt quite pleasantly satisfied with its situation, particularly as the moat is so huge that several full-size houses have now been built in it. It was not difficult to think of bearded warriors jousting, quaffing wine from goblets of horn, clashing their shields together for love of din and occasionally splitting each other's heads open with a two-handed blow from a giant sword.

A little further along the German shore is Überlingen, as unspoilt and innocent of self-knowledge as Meersburg was eager and knowing. It has nothing in the way of a castle to compare with that of Meersburg, the very name of which means 'Sea Castle', and it has just as many tourists crowding the streets, but it has clearly found the secret of accommodating visitors, and even catering for their apparently insatiable need for souvenirs, without being damaged.

It starts well, for the Information Office is housed on the lake's edge in a fine red eighteenth-century building, originally the Corn Exchange, with lofty arched doors. Not far away is the Old Town, full of gnarled half-timbering, the houses carefully and painstakingly restored, all except one, a little apart from the rest, which needed no restoring because by some miraculous dispensation of time it is perfectly preserved in the condition in which it was built, in 1495. It belonged to a wealthy burgher of the town, Clemens Reichlin, but the point is that any stage designer working on a production of *The Mastersingers* would simply pick it up and put it down on the stage for Act Two, without wanting to change anything at all; even the date – 1495 – is right. (It couldn't be Beckmesser's house, though; it isn't tidy enough.)

Überlingen retains no fewer than seven of the old town's gates and towers, together with a good deal of the original walls; such places give a convincing idea of what life must have been like there in the fifteenth century, with the gates shut at night, the watchman making his rounds, ready to sound the alarm if brigands or enemies were trying to get in, and the churches dotted about all over the sleeping town, offering their protection of the things of the spirit while the stone towers and heavy iron portals protected the things of this world.

But the greatest sight in Überlingen, perhaps the greatest masterpiece anywhere on the lake (not even excluding the church at Birnau), is the Münster, the Cathedral of St Nicholas. From the outside (like so many of the finest Baroque churches) it gives no hint of the glory within, but as I stepped inside, the afternoon sun illuminating everything from the Gothic roof to the gigantic, quintuple nave, I could hardly believe that this tiny town, which even now has fewer than 20,000 inhabitants, could be the site of such magnificence. There is a series of a dozen or so side-chapels, each with a handsome altar, richly carved, and paintings and statues to match, but it is the High Altar, created only in the seventeenth century by Jörn Zirn, which makes a visitor silent, breathless and unable to move for fear that it should vanish. It is four storeys high, and at first sight appears to be carved out of a single block of ivory, though after a moment the white sheen can be recognised for a trick of the light; the mighty altar is of wood. The exuberance, profusion and intricacy of the carvings – it includes scores of figures, many of them life-size – defeat comparison; I could think of nothing like this anywhere I had ever been, and I left the building wanting to dance my way out.

A cup of tea before going on to Birnau; after the Münster's glory it had to be in the old town. I found a café, suitably authentic-looking, though the half-timbering on some of the neighbouring buildings was depressingly straight and new, and in some places the builders hadn't even bothered to fake the beams; they had *painted* them on the walls, a spectacular example of missing the point.

I found myself at a table with a group who were plainly locals. To them, I was no less plainly a foreigner, and when they had elicited just what kind of foreigner, they wanted to know what I was doing in Überlingen. 'And what do you think of the town?' I spoke of the old houses, of the towers and walls from the ancient fortifications, of the Cathedral. And here I discovered something strange and sad. These things meant nothing to them. They knew of their existence, of course, and had been inside the Cathedral; then why the lack of enthusiasm for the treasures of history, art and beauty with which they were surrounded? As far as I could understand, with my German and their English, the explanation was that these had nothing to do with their lives. It was not just that Clemens Reichlin was nothing but a handful of dust five centuries old; it went deeper than that. The way they lived had no connection, however remote or tenuous, with the sights and richnesses of Überlingen, or at least they did not *feel* any such connection. I had sought out the café because it was in the old part of the town; they had chosen it because it was the nearest. I found myself, to my own surprise and alarm, arguing with them, though my most telling point was blunted by my inability to remember the German for 'imagination', which I was trying to accuse them of lacking; they took it all in good part, but plainly thought I was half mad.

The German for imagination, in the sense I had in mind, is *Einbildungskraft*. But I did not remember that until long after I had left Überlingen.

The Pilgrimage Church at Birnau surprises me every time. I think I know it very well indeed, but whenever I return I realise that I haven't taken the full measure of it at all. When I am away from it, I see a white ceiling rich with paintings; in fact, the *whole* ceiling is painted. I also forget the three beautiful clocks – blue with golden hands – that are set in the ceiling amid all the other beauty. But above all, though I do always recall the great explosion of light and air that rolls over me as I step inside, I never recall the full force of it. For me, Birnau is second only to the Wieskirche for beauty, and it is even more profuse and rich in its decoration. It also has the 'Honigschlecker' (the honey-sucker), the gold and white stucco cherub who has just put his finger into a beehive and is sucking the honey. This is supposed to be a pun; the figure stands beside an altar dedicated to St Bernard of Clairvaux, who was known as 'The doctor whose words are sweet as honey', but anyone who will believe that Feuchtmayer, who carved the 'Honigschlecker', was trying to point a religious moral with it would be capable of believing that Bernard Göz, who painted the ceiling, and for that matter Peter Thumb, who built the church itself, experienced nothing but holy thoughts at the sight of the completed masterpiece, and anybody who would believe *that* would believe that God, as the week of Creation went on, looked upon his handiwork and saw that it was good, but failed to see that it was also beautiful.

A brief glance at Lindau, almost the last point to the east on the northern shore. Lindau is a handsome little town, with a fine harbour; the stone gate of it makes me think of the similar sea-portal at Bombay. It has a strange claim on a visitor's attention; the largest model railway in Europe. This was constructed by one of those madmen without whom the world would not only be duller, but would hardly get on at all: a Herr Simmoleit. He started it in 1939, and it has been growing ever since. Now he has 500 metres of track, 40 points, 55 signals, 15 locomotives and 10 trains. The main station in the system is called Modellstadt – Modeltown. There are 11,000 metres of cable, 8000 soldered points and 300 signal lamps. The making of it demanded 250 kilos of gravel, 30 kilos of glue and 1000 square metres of chipboard and hardboard for the base of the whole thing. Lunacy on this scale must be commended; besides, since Herr Simmoleit started it in 1939, it must have been very useful in helping him to while away the war.

Lindau has one vivid memory for me. Years ago, staying at the Bayerischer Hof, I had gone over to the station (it is right opposite the hotel) to get the English newspapers, which come in, or used to, on the evening of the day they are published. As I turned away from the paper-kiosk with *The Times*, a young man approached me, put out his hand, and said 'The Reverend from Abingdon?' I goggled at him, and he repeated the question in exactly the same words, whereat I continued to goggle. The first doubt began to rise in him; he dropped his hand and re-phrased the question, more tentatively: 'Aren't you a clergyman – from Abingdon – in England?' There was only one answer to that question, and I gave it: No. He apologised, assuring me that I looked exactly like this mysterious Abingdonian man of God, and turned away. He walked off across the station, and his back was as eloquent as his front had been; it was saying, every step of the way until he disappeared through the far door; 'Why on earth did the vicar of Abingdon deny his identity? What *can* he be up to, that he should insist on being incognito?' It occurred to me that when he got home and met his reverend friend, he would ask him precisely that question, to the great consternation of an innocent clergyman who would deny everything, and be disbelieved by the young man at home as he had been abroad.

Just a little to the west of Lindau is the only real luxury resort on the lake: the Hotel Bad Schachen. Just a little to the east is Bregenz, clinging on to the tiny stretch of the lake shore that is Austria's. Just a few miles away is Hohenems, where every year in the second half of June I go to steep myself in the music of Schubert, to whom the Hohenems Schubertiade is consecrated. I have elsewhere written a great deal about the Schubertiade*; here, where the Rhine runs into the Bodensee, is the Bregenz Festival. This year, I am visiting both, and I shall be staying, as I always stay for the Schubertiade, in a hotel up in the hills above the next village to Hohenems, Dornbirn. From the balcony of my room – no. 314 – I can see the end of the Bodensee, as the Rhine enters it. For the moment, I have nothing more to say about the Schubertiade: instead, let me talk about the hotel.

What makes a hotel outstanding? One answer is: great and unfailing luxury. Many travellers, and I among them, would say, by this test, that the greatest hotel in the world is the Mandarin in Hong Kong. Its comforts are indeed remarkable, its staff are trained to the point of complete faultlessness, its guests want for nothing – *nothing*. If the Hong Kong Mandarin is the world's finest, then I think Europe's best

---

* In *Conducted Tour* (Jonathan Cape, 1981).

is the Brenner's Park at Baden-Baden, and for the same reason: the luxuriousness of every aspect of it wraps a guest round from the moment he walks in. I salute these two great resting-places as having approached as close to perfection as is given to mortals to achieve.

But there are hotels which do not aim at the Parnassus of these great palaces, and seek to make their guests happy by a different route. And I know two which manage, in their own way and with their own perhaps subtler methods, to make *their* guests entirely and perfectly happy throughout their stay. One of them is where this book, like several of my previous books, was written: it is Homewood Park, near Bath. The other is the hotel in which I stayed, on my Rhine journey, while I enjoyed the Schubertiade and the Bregenz Festival and where I always stay for the former: it is the Hotel Rickatschwende.

What makes these places what they are – havens of peace, happiness, warmth, laughter and a deeply felt therapeutic invigoration? In all human endeavour, it will be found that any enterprise, be it a family, an industrial or business concern, a sporting ensemble, a church, an army, a political party or a band of criminals, is given its character, its essential nature, its aims and its wherewithal to pursue them, by those at its head, and from no other source; an army led by an incompetent will be defeated, a church directed by a leader without faith will decay, and a firm whose managing director is indifferent to its success will speedily decline.

But a hotel run by people who are deeply and consistently concerned to make their guests happy will succeed. It will succeed, obviously, in attracting customers; but it will also succeed – and as a hotel guest rather than a proprietor this naturally interests me more – in making their customers' lives more peaceful and more content.

Homewood Park and the Rickatschwende do achieve just that. Stephen and Penny Ross at the one, and Herr and Frau Mandl at the other, strive to make their hotels happy places, and succeed in doing so. And because they are the people they are, they communicate the feeling to their staffs.

The test is simple: I defy any human being of understanding and sensibility to visit either for more than two or three days, without feeling *at home* – that is, feeling as though the place is the home of a friend of limitless hospitality who has extended a truly heartfelt invitation to come and stay. The hard work that goes to make these two oases what they are is, as it should be, invisible; but as one who is familiar with the backstage areas of both, I can testify that it is immense. But I insist that no amount of hard work would make Homewood Park or the Rickatschwende such glorious caravanserais without the unwavering determination on the part of everybody at both to see that their guests are happy.

In saying that the Mandarin and Brenner's on the one hand, and Homewood Park and the Rickatschwende on the other, mark the highest standards of the two varieties of hotel comfort and happiness, I think I have thereby implied that a third aiming as high does not exist. That is very nearly true: but I know of one hotel which stands midway, on the most slippery and dangerous ground of all, yet succeeds both in keeping its balance and in providing much of the luxury of the palaces with much of the intimacy of the at-homes. It is Pflaum's Posthotel at Pegnitz, known to all wise Wagner-lovers as the place to stay when going to Bayreuth, which is half an hour away by the bus that Herr Pflaum provides for his Festspiel guests. Pflaum's has been in the same family for ten generations; as its name suggests, it was originally a coaching inn, and it is easy to tell from outside where the original building ended and where the extensions began.

Chez Pflaum, there is the same devotion to the cause of making the guests happy, the same faultlessly trained staff (mostly girls so pretty that they would make St Ignatius Loyola's knees buckle beneath him), the same anticipation of the next request, the same feeling that nothing is too much trouble, indeed that nothing is *any* trouble. Andreas Pflaum (his brother Hermann is the chef) shows his capacity for thinking of his guests in countless ways, but there is one tiny symbol of his thoughtfulness that I have always felt sums it up; when he boards the bus to tell us what time the opera ends and what there will be for dinner when we return, he never fails to beseech us, in German and in English, to look once more in our pockets, wallets or handbags to make sure that we have our tickets safely stowed. (Every now and again, his injunction is followed by a scream of horror from half-way down the bus, and a red-faced patron is seen leaving it hurriedly, to return a few minutes later looking simultaneously embarrassed, relieved, shell-shocked and grateful.)

Not long after the conclusion of this Rhine journey, I made my quinquennial pilgrimage to Bayreuth, and stayed, as I have invariably done since I discovered it, at Pflaum's. When the *Ring* and *Mastersingers* were over, I had to catch a plane from Nuremberg (anything up to an hour away, depending on the traffic) which left at 6.55 in the morning. That meant a departure from Pflaum's at 5.15, an hour which made me long for Siegfried's potion of forgetfulness, or better still for Mime's poisoned soup. At the door of my room, despite my insistence the night before that nothing should be done, I found an enormous, richly laden breakfast tray, with a massive thermos of coffee; the last of the *brigade* to go to bed had been detailed to provide it.

I tiptoed down the stairs to the taxi that had been ordered by Herr Pflaum. In the hall, I found Frau Pflaum, not only dressed but impeccably coiffed and made up, to speed me on my way.

The Schubertiade often has two concerts in a day, sometimes three. But when there is only an evening one, the day can be spent walking. I went up to one of the nearby peaks in a cable-car, trembling with vertigo. (The day before, I had seen a picture in *The Times* of a man cleaning Nelson on his column, with a *Times* photographer himself snapped, presumably by the cleaner, as he came up the last steps of the ladder. The picture, therefore, was taken over the photographer's shoulder, and showed the entire length of Nelson's Column, right down to Trafalgar Square and the lions. Even from the photograph, I thought I was going to be sick.) Safely on the ground, I walked down, following the red and yellow markers, to the valley, being doubly rewarded when I got there. First, I came upon a house which sported an amazing array of what I suppose were the equivalent of the garden gnomes of England. They were wooden heads, more or less life-size, on posts, a vast avenue of them stretching right across the front of the house and the garden at both sides; there was an Arab in his head-dress, a beekeeper with veil, a Viking with horned helmet (together with a Vikingess in a suitably modified helmet and a tunic in a most fetching shade of blue), a cardinal in his red hat, a bride, a wizard, a society beauty, the Devil, a sailor, a yokel, a postman, a professor, a Chinaman, a railway guard, a French soldier (with *képi*), a tramp, and a variety of less clearly identifiable other figures. They were all plainly home-made, which I suppose is rarely if ever true of the gnomes; who had taken so many hours out of his life to entertain the passers-by? I shook my head in wonder and passed on, to find just round the next corner a wooden bench in a most inviting patch of shade. But it was no ordinary bench; it was painted in the colours – red and yellow – that I had been so faithfully following down the mountainside, and said as plainly as if it could speak that my toiling was over, and my rest was well earned.

For some years, the Schubertiade has been acquiring the alarming habit of transferring some of the concerts to a larger hall, thus dangerously disturbing the perfect intimacy and charm of the performances in the two rooms of the Hohenems Palace: the Rittersaal upstairs, which holds only 300, and the courtyard downstairs, with 500. This time, the overflows were in Feldkirch, which stands on the Ill, just before that handsome river flows into the Rhine. Though the concert-hall at Feldkirch is singularly lacking in both intimacy and charm, it must be forgiven; it was where Janet Baker gave her recital – Schubert, Mahler and Schumann. I have rarely heard even her in such radiant form; after the performance I could hear the word 'artistry' in six languages, including Japanese. But once again, I had to rebuke her for allowing her importunate schedule to oblige her to flee as soon as she had sung. Is it not monstrous, I thought, a crime against heaven, that this rare and precious spirit cannot spend a few richly earned days in the peace of these hills and woods? But what about the rest of the world, which wants to hear her as much as I do? The rest of the world be damned, say I.

Gidon Kremer played in Feldkirch too; the Beethoven Violin Concerto. But when he got to the cadenza in the first movement, I thought I had been struck mad; instead of either the familiar Joachim or one of its more rarely played rivals, he embarked on a gigantic digression quite twelve minutes long, *with full orchestra*. It was said to be based on the cadenza Beethoven wrote when, the concerto having failed at its first performance, he transcribed it for piano, but the sounds coming out of Kremer's fiddle suggested Schönberg, and Schönberg played backwards, at that. He got back finally to the trill which ushers in the orchestra (except that in this version they had never been ushered out) from a key so remote that I thought my teeth would fall out, and he added to the *bizarrerie* by playing two more such cadenzas, though these, mercifully, were unaccompanied.

In the interval, I ran into Elisabeth Schwarzkopf. 'You look well,' I said – rather superfluously, because she looked radiant – but she said, 'Actually, not at the moment.' I said I hoped it was nothing serious, and she rendered me speechless for some time by saying, 'I've just fallen off my bicycle on my way to play tennis.'

Away from the music, things threatened to turn serious. Three beloved friends had arrived, and we dined in a tiny restaurant at a table in the garden; they proceeded to read me a long and severe lecture, full of loving friendship, on my refusal to grow old gracefully; not that they put it that way, but that is indeed what the problem is – my resentment of ill-health, my refusal to accept any limitations on my life governed by the fact that as I grow older I can no longer do the things I did without thought when I was younger, my anger (and, I suppose, fear) at the thought that my body was no longer instantly and fully obedient to my commands.

Next day, John Julius Norwich and Molly arrived. They had planned to come a few days earlier, but his mother had died on the previous Saturday. He had rung to tell me the news within a few hours, and he had said, very wisely, that this was not an occasion for mourning. Diana had been almost 94 and – as she put it – she was raring to be off. What a life she had had! Of course, we can't mourn such a passing, any more than that of Robert Mayer, who was little short of 106 when he died. Diana had finished her life and there was nothing to add; why, then, should her friends go round wringing their hands and wearing black?

Why indeed? She was buried at Belvoir, and John Julius said 'We gave her a splendid send-off.' He added an enchanting story about her that I had never heard; when she was the young beauty, dazzling Society, the *Tatler* started a series of Profiles called 'People We Would Like to Meet'. She was to kick off the series, and the headline said 'First, Lady Diana Cooper', and underneath in smaller type, 'Next Week – Mussolini'.

I am glad I knew her, even if it was only for the last fifth or so of her life; as I said to John Julius, she lit up the sky for us all. I wouldn't have missed her for the world.

Back to the Rittersaal, this time for a brilliant recital by Andras Schiff. There was a boy – he looked about sixteen to me, but these days that could mean anything – who sat in the window-seat, right beside the pianist; he was there for Arrau and also for Brendel. He was sandy-haired, bespectacled, and looked a serious young man, with a firm set to his mouth; he clearly had character. But the extraordinary thing about him – he was directly in my eye-line from my regular seat, just behind the pianist's shoulder – was the way he sat, his eyes fixed on the pianist's hands, without moving, without blinking, without his concentration slipping or declining for a single moment. Nothing else existed for him; it was one of the most astonishing feats of total concentration I have ever seen. I guessed that he must be a budding or aspiring pianist; if so, and if watching great models will help his career, he has made a fine start.

A final, strange sight to end the 1986 Schubertiade. Outside the

Hohenems Palace runs a tiny stream; it was low this year, because the weather had been consistently fine, and in a patch where the gravel was showing through was a woman's shoe, caught by the stones, bright red and high-heeled. I speculated as to how it had got there. Had she thrown it at her lover in a quarrel, and missed? Or had he caught it when she threw it and then thrown it in himself to punish her? Or had she tried to wade across the stream when the water was higher, panicked when it came off and the water threatened to sweep her away, and so abandoned it and hopped to the shore?

And after the final sight, the final thought, provoked by all those friends. The truth is that, more and more, I do not want any company other than that of the people I love. Of course, I could not live in a way that made such an aim possible, but the closer I can approximate to it, the happier I now am. With the friends of Hohenems I don't have to make the particular effort required to engage with someone who is virtually, if not altogether, a stranger; I can be depressed if I *am* depressed, I can make silly jokes or launch on a discussion of the most serious things, knowing that such friends will accept me in any mood or key, as of course I will them. Perhaps – no, surely – it is another recognition that I am growing older, and becoming more and more reluctant to spend time without being certain in advance that it will not turn out to be wasted. Not long before, I had shocked another friend by saying that I would be perfectly happy if I never, for the rest of my life, met anybody I did not already know. I thought it was true, and I think so still.

After Hohenems, Bregenz, and *The Magic Flute*. (Q: Is there any other part of the world where two international music festivals take place with only some ten miles between them? A: Yes. Santa Fé, where they are both in the same town.) The Bregenz Festival's great magnet is the floating stage; it is moored at the edge of the lake, and from the landward edge the auditorium rises in a sweeping, fan-shaped amphitheatre. I have always longed, at Bregenz, for someone who has recently seen *The Marx Brothers at the Circus* to perform the same trick as is played at the end of that film; there, too, a floating stage is the main attraction, with a symphony orchestra on it, but someone (Harpo, presumably, though I have not seen it for a long time and cannot be sure) has cut the ropes, and the film ends with the orchestra floating out to sea playing the Prelude to Act Three of *Lohengrin* for dear life (literally, I suppose). I had heard great things of this *Zauber-*

flöte; it was said to be exceptionally spectacular; well, the spectacle could only be improved if the stage set sail for the open waters of the Bodensee.

It was not to be; apart from the lack of a saboteur, the tethers are of stout metal. Before the opera, though, there was another, and very different, spectacle to be considered. I was standing in the foyer, with ten or fifteen minutes before the performance was due to start, when there was a discreet commotion, and men with walkie-talkies appeared. A few moments later, the cause appeared: Kurt Waldheim, President of Austria, and former Secretary-General of the United Nations.

'There's no art,' said Shakespeare, 'to find the mind's construction in the face.' Shakespeare was right, and no one with any pretensions to logical thinking, let alone fairness, would judge the character of a man he had never previously met from the countenance alone. I accepted that; but it so happened that as the Presidential party was shown to the seats reserved for them, I – for my seat was approached by the same staircase and entrance door – was swept along with the distinguished tide. I was, therefore, for a few unbroken minutes, in a position to examine Dr Waldheim's countenance from a distance of only a very few feet – indeed, once or twice I almost bumped into him.

O Shakespeare, must you? Am I bound by your wise judgment? Very well, I am; but if I had not been, if I had been allowed to trust an instinct based on no more than a few minutes of proximity, I would have said, without even a shadow of a moment's uncertainty, that the charges brought against Waldheim during the campaign for the Austrian Presidency – charges of conduct in the Second World War which, if true, would have rendered him unfit for any responsible post in any country, let alone in Austria – were all too soundly based, so furtive, restless, calculating, shifty and haunted did he look.

Let us be clear what those charges were. They did *not* include any serious suggestion that he had been guilty of war-crimes or atrocities for which he should, or might, have been tried and condemned by the War Crimes Tribunal. They were twofold: one, that he had known far more about what was happening to the Nazis' victims than he had ever admitted, and that units to which he had been attached *had* been involved in unforgivable crimes; and two, that throughout the Austrian election campaign he had repeatedly lied about his wartime career. The second of these charges had, during the campaign itself, been amply proved.* His mendacity, indeed, had started years before; he had deliberately falsified the autobiographical details required for the summary of his life and career that the United Nations distributes to those who want to know more about its senior executive. (He claimed that after being wounded he had left the army for good; it transpired that he had in fact returned to active service.) The first charge, of guilty knowledge amounting to complicity, is less certain. Certainly he insisted repeatedly that, say, he had never been at a specified place where terrible things had been done; when evidence showing that he *had* been there was discovered, he gave a start of surprise at this lapse of memory. Well, any man may have a poor memory, and many do; but his faults of memory – certainly more than one – all went in the same direction only, tending to free him not just of taking part in crimes but of knowing anything about them.

If Kurt Waldheim had been prosecuted for doing evil things in wartime, and I had been on the jury, with only the evidence that the election campaign had brought to light, I would have voted 'Not Guilty'. But I would have been happier if the trial had been held in a jurisdiction that allowed a verdict of 'Not Proven'. And if President Waldheim's supporters would reply that I am being unfair, and even allowing my irrelevant judgment from his appearance to influence me, I would ask them: whose fault is it? Does a man with nothing in his wartime soldiering to be ashamed of knowingly set his hand to a document which says plainly that his wartime soldiering was other than it was? If his defenders say 'Yes', then it is for them, not me, to explain.

Perhaps it was just as well that it was the *Magic Flute* that was on the bill. Suppose it had been *Fidelio*! For there, at the heart of that sublime work, is the Waldheim Question laid bare for all to see. It is Pizarro who had come to murder the innocent man; but it is Rocco who obeys – *Befehl ist Befehl* – the order to dig the innocent man's grave, and who is quick – a great deal too quick – to turn State's Evidence in the final scene of the opera. Yet we must be fair to Rocco/Waldheim. When the trumpet of liberation and victory is heard in Florestan's dungeon, and the messenger – *deus ex machina* indeed – comes clattering down the stairs to announce the news that goodness has triumphed at the last moment over evil, and that Florestan is saved, Rocco emits (some productions have him falling on his knees) a spontaneous cry of 'Praise be to God!'

---

* Further lies have come to light since.

I settled into my seat with a final thought about President Waldheim; it was that my 'If I had been on the jury . . .' was doubly speculative, for the failure of Austria to search out and try the countless Austrian war-criminals has been inexcusably disgraceful; while the Germans, for decades now, have never ceased to sift that bloodstained sand and pursue justice wherever it may lead, the Austrians have taken refuge in the black lie that there were no Austrian Nazi war-criminals other than those tried and condemned at Nuremberg. The truth is that even if there had been real evidence of real complicity on the part of Kurt Waldheim, he would never have been brought to trial. But the overture to the *Magic Flute* had begun, and

In diesen Heil'gen Hallen
Kennt man die Rache nicht.
Und ist ein Mensch gefallen,
Führt Liebe ihn zur Pflicht.

Shakespeare was right, and so was Mozart. And the production was quite as spectacular as had been promised, with volcanoes splitting in half to emit the Queen of the Night, and fireworks *ad libitum* throughout.

*21 The Schubert gateau (*mit Schlag*) 22 Rehearsing the Octet 23 Where is Harpo now that we need him? 24 An awful lot of water 25 Not quite Venice 26 Basle honours Erasmus of Rotterdam 27 Go on, have another*

21

22

23

24

25

26

27

28

29

5

Erasmus of Basle

APART FROM MY trip down the rapids, which didn't count (except, perhaps, to relieve me of several thousand years in Purgatory), and the ferries across Lake Constance, I had not so far embarked upon the bosom of the Rhine. The next stretch of the journey seemed to call for a progress on the water, and I signed on, therefore, from Kreuzlingen on the Swiss side of Constance, for the voyage to the Schaffhausen Falls, where I trusted that the boat would stop safely short of the drop. (It is from the bridge across the Rhine at Constance that the river is measured; from there to Rotterdam there are huge boards on both banks, marking the progress of the Rhine, measured off in kilometres, with smaller boards marking the tenths. At the Constance bridge the first of the boards says defiantly, 'o'.) I was not to know that this placid stretch of water, strewn on both sides with tiny villages, castles, churches, monuments, inns, towers, meadows and life, would prove to be among the most beautiful and enchanted stretches of the entire river. The Rhine at Basle, Strasbourg and Cologne is more imposing, at Mainz and Worms more historically significant, at Bonn more political, at Duisburg and Düsseldorf more powerful in their role of purveyors of goods and services to the twentieth century, along the Route of Seventy Castles more enrapt in legend; but from the moment the Rhine leaves Lake Constance, via the southern arm at the western end, until the traveller hears the roar of Falls downstream as he approaches his journey's end, there is no part of the Rhine more powerful in the heart's-ease and delight that it provides.

The boat bustles back and forth across the river; dizzy, I speedily lost

28 Art can be fun (and should be)   29 Market day in the village

count of the number of times I had crossed from Switzerland to Germany and Germany to Switzerland (for along the High Rhine, as it is called here, the border runs down the middle of the river). An odd comparison occurred to me; the boat tacking back and forth resembled nothing so much as the progress of the *vaporetto* on the Grand Canal, and for Gottlieben, Ermatingen, Gaienhofen, Steckborn, Wangen, Mammern, Kattenhorn, Burg and Stein am Rhein, I began to murmur Ca d'Oro, San Samuele, Accademia, Ca Pesaro, San Marco. The difference was that on the Grand Canal all is magnificence; on this stretch of the High Rhine the magicked traveller finds himself in Toytown.

It started with a handsome bonus in the form of Gottlieben Castle; now early nineteenth-century mock-Gothic (C. S. Calverley, asked by a sightseer on a first visit to Oxford of what period the recently completed additions to the Quad at Christchurch might be, replied 'Early Bloody, I believe, though some say they are from the Late Disgraceful'), the original had been built in the middle of the thirteenth century, and during the Council of Constance *both* the great prisoners – the deposed Pope John XXIII and the accused Jan Hus – had been imprisoned in it. But that is ancient history, and the Castle at Gottlieben today is home to someone far less forbidding, earth-shaking, controversial and harsh. As the boat glides past, the wise (and well-informed) passenger will cock an ear not for theological disputation but for sounds and sweet airs, that give delight and hurt not, for the chatelaine of Gottlieben Castle today is Lisa della Casa.

Has there ever been an opera company of such glory as the constellation that filled the heavens above Vienna in the years immediately following the Second World War? I think not – not even the Caruso era in New York – and even if another company could be found to rival them musically, it would never be able to compete also with the beauty of the company's ladies. In Salzburg, in the early fifties, I heard a *Figaro* which included Schwarzkopf, Seefried, Fischer-Dieskau, Kunz, Dermota and – a young newcomer, in her debut as Cherubino – Christa Ludwig. The same company, at the same time, included also Jurinac, Welitsch, London, Schöffler – and della Casa. It was before the Reign of the Producer had begun (that era is just ending now, in bloody revolution from booing audiences, and not before time, despite the memorable evenings it has provided, from the Visconti *Don Carlos* to the Tarkovsky *Boris*), and the voices, watched over by such conductors as Böhm and Furtwängler, were supreme. I was fortunate to hear them all, again and again, in the springtime of my musical enthusiasm, and I shall not hear their like again in this world.

Alas, strain as I might, I heard no song, carried by the wind, floating over the river from Gottlieben Castle, but I raised a hand in salute and gratitude to its beautiful tenant, and went on my way downstream.

Back and forth the boat sped – no, moved unhurriedly, for there was time to take in each frontage, with its brightly painted shops and hotels, its church standing guard, its castle or its ruin, its soft, green fields rising from behind the houses, with more gentle castles dotting the hills. If this is Toytown, it is also a *Boutique fantasque*, without self-consciousness, without, as far as I could see, any signs of eagerness for tourists, without a truly ugly building anywhere. (Nor any sign of a customs official demanding the sight of a passport, though most landing-stages had at least a hut marked Zoll.) I disembarked, temporarily, at Stein am Rhein, the most picturesque town in all this lovely gallery of the picturesque. The word itself has become suspect in our world, a synonym for something false or artificial, a painted façade behind which is only a void. But Stein am Rhein, picturesque though it is, is no Potemkin Village.

It is a perfectly preserved sixteenth-century town, and that 'perfectly' does not mean only that the buildings are intact. The buildings *are* intact, and their paintwork is kept clean, bright and fresh, but the work of restoration has been done with such unobtrusive delicacy, such fineness and understanding, that a paradox at once arises: these buildings look as though they *were* built yesterday, but as though yesterday was a day in July 1540, not July 1986.

Half-timbering abounds, of course, but here it is only part of the construction, not of the decoration; it is the painters who rule in Stein am Rhein, not the builders. Along the whole of the High Street there is hardly a building which is, or at least looks, less than four centuries old, and almost every one is a glory of delicate reds and greens and golds and blues and whites. There are oriel windows everywhere, their lines picked out by the paint, there are façades painted with the narrative of a local legend, and one, the Hotel Adler, which seems to record the entire history of the town, if not of all Europe. The shop-signs alone would make the place magic; they are of delicate wrought iron, painted in black or gold – here is one, for instance, above a little restaurant, which is a fish curling back upon its tail, and here is a sheep standing guard, rather inappropriately, over a greengrocer's. And here is the Rathaus, with its four-faced clock, its dormers, its all-round painted walls, and its modern windows, on the ground floor, bright with geraniums; before it stands a fountain, with a fierce-looking knight, unhorsed, on a column in the middle. And here is the old town gate with its watch-tower, and here a lovely, untouched courtyard which looks as though no human foot has disturbed its peace for hundreds of years, and which values its privacy so much that it has even worked out a way of preventing its visitors from taking photographs; the angle of the walls and of the outside staircase, and the placing of the tree, and the shape of the archway by which it is entered, are all such as to frustrate those who want to find a spot from which the whole thing may be taken in. And here are the town swans; a fine pair of them rolling like drunken sailors (strange that a bird as graceful on water and in the air should be so clumsy on land) through the streets. And *here* is a simple restaurant with *raclette* on the menu, and it is time for lunch.

A love of fun is not the very first quality that comes to mind when contemplating Switzerland; how, then, did they come to invent not one but two dishes that are at least as much sport as food? The *fondue* is one of the pleasantest board-games ever invented (almost any number can play), and *raclette* – which is, after all, only melted cheese with various relishes – is even more of a comedy. At least, it is if it is done properly, but the waitress, to my regret and indignation, deduced that I was nothing but an ignorant foreigner (I *was* a foreigner, but I was *not* ignorant) and simply put the melted cheese on a plate, whereas the pleasure of *raclette* lies in the diner slicing off the cheese and watching it melt before him. Meanwhile, a thought struck me; do you suppose that for the Swiss *fondue* and *raclette* are not fun at all, but merely meals, to be taken in the same spirit as any other dish? I hope not.

It was time for a last stroll through the town before getting back on the boat. I was glad to see that, although they had long since come to terms with the knowledge that every summer their home town would be invaded by thousands of visitors, the people of Stein am Rhein had not lost their feeling for the place. This was their native ground, and they were very plainly proud of it. But they were not proud of it as a man (or a town) might be proud of possessing a famous painting or statue or even library; they were conscious of the unspoilt beauty around them precisely because it was what they were used to in their daily lives. (What did they know that the people of Überlingen had forgotten?) A kindly *Hausfrau* stopped for a chat when I asked her for directions, and I gently asked the obvious question: how did she feel about living in a beauty-spot? She waved an arm at one of the half-timbered buildings, plainly authentic; 'Look,' she said, 'I *live* in a house like that.' The only word I could think of in reply was 'Congratulations', so I said it, and she smiled me on my way.

One more pause was necessary before the final stretch to Schaffhausen; Diessenhofen is an ancient little village, well preserved, its tower guarded by a splendid stone gnome, but its treasure is a covered wooden bridge across the Rhine. On the other side is the German town of Gailingen, and the river is very narrow here. I went back and forth because of the trick the bridge plays; from either end the bridge looks like a tunnel (which, literally, it is), and peering through it brought the town on the other side so close that I felt I could touch it. But just beyond the bridge, on the Swiss side, is the strange anomaly of Büsingen, a German enclave entirely surrounded by Switzerland. Some time ago, a referendum in the area produced a very large majority for becoming Swiss, but both countries were too embarrassed (though for different reasons) to accept the verdict of the electorate, so to this day it remains German, with a most curious state of affairs in the post office: though Büsingen's official currency is Swiss, the post office sells only German stamps.

The traveller can hear the Schaffhausen Falls long before he sees them. From some miles away there is a continuous, rolling thunder to be heard; then there are three bridges, very close together, and then there is the perpetual rainbow shimmering in the perpetual spray. But before the first bridge is sighted, there is a sight upon the shore well worth lingering over; an extraordinary circular fortress, called Castell Munot, perched above the town. It reminded me of Edinburgh Castle, not in its architecture, but in the sense of impregnability that it gives; just as the visitor to Edinburgh is convinced that the castle could never have been successfully assaulted (as indeed it never has been), so the first glimpse of Munot suggests that it could never be taken. (I don't know whether it ever was; if so, the assault-force must have been not only brave beyond the call of duty, but probably invisible as well.) But the most remarkable thing about Munot I learned only later; it was designed by Dürer, who I have never thought was an architect of castles. (I can well believe that Leonardo was.)

And then the spray. Schaffhausen's falls do not, of course, compare with Niagara or Victoria; they are the biggest in Europe, but that means little – well, it means some 75 feet. Yet they are undeniably impressive. The Falls are split in two; the higher side consists of a series of rock slabs descending like a staircase, over which the water crashes;

it is possible to imagine a superhuman canoer going over the Falls on that side, in effect sliding down the banisters. On the other side, though, the drop is sheer, and nothing could survive it. In the middle of the fatal half, a huge, jagged rock sticks up well above the water, parting the torrent, which throws itself past as though with a greater fury at being thus checked.

It is possible to get up on the rock, and I did. A boat, with a *very* skilled hand on the tiller, steered right under the cascade, which hits the water a few feet off the base of the rock; there is thus a gap, into which a slim boat can just fit, as the water crashes down, barely missing its riverward side. At the foot of the rock a little landing-stage has been built, and the visitor steps gingerly ashore, soaked to the skin within a few seconds because of the spray. Then he scrambles up the rock, which has had steps cut in it, and finally arrives at the peak, where a Swiss flag damply flies. On both sides, the water hurtles by (seven hundred cubic metres a second, they say), and the familiar illusion – which works here in the form of a conviction that the water is still and the rock moving – becomes not only plausible but terrifying; I felt as though I was rushing through the boiling madness of the water at the speed of a bullet. When the boat returned for me, I squelched down the steps and into it with a sense of relief, though not before I had noticed something which puzzled me mightily, and puzzles me still. Right in the middle of the roaring water, a few feet upstream from the crag and therefore just before the waters divide, a metal pole is sticking up, obviously embedded in a rock below the surface, or conceivably in the river bed. But who fixed it there, and how? If the Falls could be switched off, it would be possible, but I could work out no method by which the pole (which looked like some kind of marker, and may well have been) could otherwise have got where it was.

No one could tell me, but I learned something else about Schaffhausen, a tiny curiosity of history. The town was bombed by American aircraft in 1944; the Americans insisted that it was a mistake – a bombing force had lost its way and, thinking it was still over Germany (which is, after all, only just the other side of the river), had jettisoned their bombs – but the Swiss were convinced, not without reason, that the bombing had been deliberate, for Schaffhausen was (and still is) a centre of the Swiss arms industry, and Switzerland, at that time, was still constrained to make weapons for the Germans. (Some time earlier, a British force had bombed Zürich, with no excuses; Zürich was another armaments town, and there was no pretence that the raid had any other purpose than to cut down Swiss deliveries to Germany.)

I have always loved Basle, ever since, going to Switzerland, via France, by train, I arrived late at night at the Franco-Swiss border and, having had my passport inspected without problems by the French, I was told that I could not proceed further until daybreak and, on enquiring the reason for this, was told 'The Swiss are asleep.' But it is a beautiful city, strikingly situated at the junction of three nations, set on the Rhine at its finest, alive and modern, and with one of the richest art galleries in Europe. Some years ago, on holiday in Italy and about to return home, I picked up an English newspaper a week or two old and found in it a review of an exhibition, devoted entirely to the work of Lucas Cranach, at the Kunstmuseum in Basle. It sounded so splendid that I immediately changed my travel plans and went home via a few days in Basle. And days were needed, not hours, for the exhibition was vast; the organisers had scoured the world for Cranachs, and must have laid hands on practically every one in existence. And then, turning a corner, I found myself face to face with my cousin Clive, with whom I had shared the discovery of music in our youth; he, too, had been drawn to Basle by that newspaper article, and he greeted me – for it was with him I had been travelling across France all those years ago – with what had become a standard cry for both of us: 'The Swiss are asleep!'

I stayed at the Drei Könige, also known (reasonably enough in so multilingual a city) as Les Trois Rois, and my room was 119. At the Three Kings they tell you that not three but, over the years, anything up to *thirty* kings have stayed there, and I can well believe it from the ornate splendour of the building and the luxuriousness of the fittings. But the significance of Room 119 was not that a crowned head had lain upon my pillow; a very different kind of occupant had stayed in it in 1897, a man who lacked not only a crown but a country, or at least a country which he could call his own. He was Theodor Herzl, and he was in Basle for the World Zionist Congress, which he dominated from beginning to end – by all trustworthy accounts, he seems to have been one of the most powerfully charismatic figures in history – and which ended with the historic decision to campaign for a Jewish national home. No more would the goal be assimilation and equal rights; from now on, Jews would strive for a land which they could call home, and live in it on sufferance from nobody. Fifty-one years later, the dream came true, and it is pointless to wonder what Herzl would have thought of the modern state of Israel, and of the irony inherent in the fact that Israel has become not much more than another modern state, whereas the dreamers of Basle saw her as a unique enclave, showing the way to the world.

There are ironies much greater than that in the story of Herzl and the renewed foundation of Zionism as a crusade for a Jewish state. In the first place, Herzl himself was about as assimilated a Jew as had ever been seen. His Austrian family (he was born in Hungary, then still part of the Empire) had long since liberated themselves from the ghetto; they were prosperous, enlightened, liberal in politics, sceptical in religion and German in culture. All these attitudes he adopted as he grew up, but the anti-semitism of Vienna on the one hand, and his sympathetic but contemptuous feeling for the Jews of the ghetto (or the ghetto mentality) on the other, led him gradually to the conclusion that the anti-semitism of the world would never cease, and the Jews' final liberation from the ghetto never take place, until there was a Jewish state.

His ideas for a Jewish state seem strange today. The flag was to be white with seven gold stars, but the number had nothing to do with the seven-branched candelabra of the Jews, the holy *menorah*; the seven stars were to symbolise the seven-hour working day, which would be established in the new Promised Land. Nor would Hebrew be its language; every Jew who settled there would retain his own native language, and the *lingua franca* would be Yiddish. And throughout the Jewish state the English ideal of the aristocrat, and the English attitude to sport, would prevail.

Well, whatever Theodor Herzl's ideas for a Jewish state, and whatever the nature of the state of Israel, he had a fine view of the Rhine from the balcony of Room 119 in the Drei Könige Hotel. And not only he; there has been a hotel with that name here since 1026, and among the uncrowned heads who have stayed in it are Voltaire, Dickens and Picasso. Napoleon, who was an Emperor but did not care for a crown, passed through, and so did Metternich. So, for that matter, did the young Princess Victoria. Later on, as the hotel's Golden Book records, there was Montgomery, and General Guisan.

The river is very fast at Basle, also very grey and opaque. (Basle is also, astonishingly, the last town straddling both sides of the river, for from here to the North Sea there is no other.) For me, however, Basle is the city of Erasmus. Erasmus of Rotterdam is only one of the many figures in history claimed by the cities of their birth but whose opinion of their birthplace is quietly forgotten. Erasmus left Rotterdam as soon as he could, and never went back there, just as Beethoven fled Bonn for Vienna at *his* first opportunity. Erasmus, though he was at home in all Europe, including England, settled in Basle; he left it after twenty years, only when it began to lose its tolerant nature under the pressure to take sides that was exerted by the Reformation. Erasmus himself felt the pressure, and resisted it as long as he could; but when the great trimmer could resist no more, he came down, quietly and calmly, against the Reformers: 'Christ I know. Luther I know not.' Alas, quiet and calm were qualities prized by almost nobody in the struggle, and Luther himself, who had admired Erasmus and wooed him long and passionately, fired off thousands of words of the foulest abuse at him. But Erasmus returned to Basle to die, and is buried there. As it chanced, while I was there Basle was staging a vast and comprehensive exhibition of his life and achievements; the occasion was the 450th anniversary of his death, but no city, least of all Basle, should need an excuse to honour Erasmus, particularly today. In an age of fanaticism he preached tolerance, when all around him were going mad he preached sanity, and adrift in a sea of hate he loved, and was loved by, thousands (as his correspondence alone demonstrates). This age in which we live is perhaps the most fanatical since his own, and it is his timeless values and spirit that we need most. And we can have them for the taking; there is nothing remote or ancient or classical about him; you cannot read his letters without feeling that you are listening to the voice of a friend. May his wisdom, his tolerance and his wit be with us yet.

The exhibition did him proud. There were hundreds of books, of course, including a first edition of *The Praise of Folly*; it was in a glass case, but immediately below it was a very fine facsimile that the visitors to the exhibition could handle, and I turned the pages enchanted with his marginalia, including some tiny comic sketches. The walls were covered with drawings, paintings and etchings (including the Dürer portrait which hangs above my desk), a whole section was devoted to *The Complaint of Peace* and its editions, and all the people with whom he was most closely associated – and not only in friendship – were amply represented: Dürer, Holbein, Luther and, of course, Froben. There was a beautifully made mock-up of Froben's print-works, with the old presses and type-faces and fonts and machinery and tools; and a visitor with even the smallest imagination must have felt that Froben was actually in the room. Even more strongly felt was the fancy that

Erasmus himself was present, for there was another reconstruction, this one of his study, with him in his characteristic pose (he wrote standing up) at a tall desk. The room was full of Erasmian memorabilia, and the figure was cunningly placed so that the passer-by could not quite see his face, or not more than a glimpse of his profile.

And here, at the end, was his will. His writing was clear and firm to the last; I had forgotten that he had died in Froben's house, though I suppose if Erasmus had been asked in advance where he would wish to die he would have said, 'In the house of my friend who has been publishing my books for more than twenty years.' Just outside the exit of the exhibition, in the next gallery of the museum in which it was laid out, there was a bookstall with a vast array of books – books by him and about him, books about his time, about the Reformation, about Luther, about printing, about Basle, about Switzerland – the whole background and foreground of Erasmus. I left the building with a cry of 'Bravo, Basle!' heedless of the startled look on the faces of the burghers I was complimenting.

Why do I love Erasmus so much? For the same things that make me love Montaigne; they were both teachers and philosophers and scholars of the greatest understanding and wisdom, but they were entirely and recognisably human withal, in their strengths and weaknesses, eccentricities and timidities, vanities and generosities. Erasmus could confess to a hangover; Montaigne revealed that radishes sometimes gave him indigestion; Montaigne, after writing some of the world's greatest stoic philosophy, ran for the hills when the plague approached his home; Erasmus, faced with an almost unavoidable choice between the Church and the Reformers, took refuge in the claim that he had not read the lesser Reformers' books and had only leafed through one of Luther's, though history reveals that he made the claim just after writing a private letter to a friend discussing the Reformers' works in great detail, and particularly Luther's.

Erasmus and Montaigne are mirrors in which ordinary, fallible human beings may see their own faces; in those mirrors we see our faces not only as they are, but as they might be – human, weak and sinful, yet capable of being godlike, tremendous and holy. I defy any man to read Erasmus or Montaigne without vowing to live better thereafter.

Basle is not all Erasmus; Basle can unbend. It unbent for me by serving me breakfast on a tram. Basle is one of the cities – I found many more throughout Germany – that still keeps its trams; the regular ones do not serve breakfast (though, like the ones in Amsterdam, they do have postboxes fixed to their sides), but Basle has a special tram that can be hired for a private tour of the city; it is of the 1914 vintage, but lovingly restored and kept up, and off I went in my solitary splendour, as it clanged its way in and out of the traffic, managing with great ingenuity not to get perpetually stuck behind one of the regular trams by turning off at junctions and finding an empty stretch of track to whizz along. On the front of this strange vehicle, where the ordinary trams have their numbers, this one had a board, in the same shape and style, bearing a crossed knife and fork.

Basle can unbend still further; the Rathaus, on the Market Square (a real market, incidentally, thronged with buyers and sellers, as though this was some little country town to which the farmers bring their produce every Wednesday and the townfolk flock to buy), is painted a screaming red inlaid with gold, and fantastically decorated all over, with a wonderfully irrelevant, multi-coloured tower on the roof, the whole thing encrusted with mad gingerbread decorations. It looked like something run up by the Brothers Grimm in playful mood. (But the Brothers Grimm were *never* in playful mood, as poor Hans Andersen discovered when he met them. Thinking that they had in common their love of fairy-tales and genius at telling them, he began to chatter, only to find that they regarded themselves as grave literary historians, mythographers, archetype collectors, philologists, psychologists and scholars, but certainly not tellers of beautiful stories for children; Andersen fled, taking his despised imagination with him.)

Still further. The Kunstmuseum houses one of the world's greatest collections; in the forecourt, striking the right note of high artistic seriousness, is Rodin's *The Burghers of Calais*. But on the first landing of the massive staircase there stands Jean Tinguély's masterpiece of fun-sculpture. Certainly it is the biggest work of his, by far, that I have ever seen; there are two in the Tate which are tiny by comparison. This one is fully thirty feet wide, and high and deep in proportion. It had hundreds of pieces – made out of bits of old bicycle, alarm clocks, musical instruments, bells, pokers, spades, hammers, buckets, dolls, motor-horns, chains, gongs, plates, Meccano, truncheons, umbrellas, tin-cans, light-bulbs, dustbins, tyres, spoons – everything in creation that an artist with a totally liberated imagination combined with a rigorous sense of construction could press into use in a machine which, when it was switched on, would clang and bang and whistle and flash and gyrate, without ever losing the mad surrealist logic with which it was made, so that a movement started in one corner – say by a hammer falling on a fire-iron – would continue right across the entire contraption, as the banged fire-iron tripped a plate which tilted a wheel which squeezed an accordion which knocked over a doll which tightened a wire which pulled a handle which opened a flap which emitted a piston which drove a cart which jogged a ball which rolled down a keyboard which . . . well, which entertained and enthralled me to such great effect that I could hardly be dragged away from it.

Why shouldn't art provide fun? The world, particularly the art world itself, has only grudgingly and to a very limited extent admitted that, at specified periods under strict supervision, it may be allowed to. But Tinguély goes further and makes art that not only *gives* fun, but *is* fun. For this, he has been repeatedly warned off from attempting to join the company of the Elect, but since he has never shown any interest in being admitted to that fraternity, this probably does not worry him as much as it worries them. And Basle – Basle, of all places! – not only offers his mightiest work a home in the most central spot in its mightiest gallery, but thumbs its nose at the Elect by installing – and right outside Basle's new opera-house, too – a huge pool crowded with a set of water-sculptures by the same artist, with the same dazzling imagination, the same classical attention to form, and the same quality of being, as well as offering, fun. And even the amateurs have been allowed to make their contribution; there were long stretches of pavement, in the pedestrian precincts, given over to (or possibly taken by) young artists in chalk. I was surprised to see that the pictures were not like the usual pavement-artist's work – romantic woodland views, portraits of pop-singers and terrible abstracts – but very elaborate biblical and historical scenes, in a style which might be called a long way after Tintoretto. (Possibly the presence of the Kunstmuseum inhibits the artists from being more playful, or possibly, even, the city forbids it.)

There are, however, limits to Basle's fun. My hotel room at the Drei Könige had the now usual extra television channel which offers a choice of films, at a modest charge, for those who want to watch something other than the programmes of the local television stations. The instructions card offered films in five categories: Action, Science Fiction, Thriller, Comedy or Blue Movie. Though Basle has offered its handsome hospitality to Tinguély to demonstrate that art can laugh, and though half a millennium ago it gave even greater hospitality to Erasmus of Rotterdam, to whom nothing that human beings can do was without interest, yet the thought of a Swiss-made Blue Movie was so far beyond any possibility of belief – so unimaginably implausible, macabre and bizarre – that I forbore even to try it for ten minutes, and instead fell asleep dreaming of chocolate.

But the story of Basle's fun and Basle's art gallery is not quite finished. A wealthy Swiss industrialist and art-collector, Rudolf Staechelin, had lent some twenty paintings to the Kunstmuseum on permanent loan; the loan was continued by Staechelin's son when Rudolf died. In 1967, however, financial catastrophe overtook the firm, when a plane belonging to an airline in which the Staechelin family were principal shareholders crashed, with the loss of 126 lives. The legal claims for compensation bankrupted the airline, and Staechelin was compelled, because of his massive losses, to sell some of the art collection built up by his father.

A Van Gogh – *La Berceuse* – was sold in Paris for the equivalent of 3·5 million Swiss francs. It was decided that two Picassos – *The Two Brothers* and *Seated Harlequin* – would follow. From America came an offer of 12 million Swiss francs; Staechelin said that if the City of Basle could raise 8·4 million, he would sell them the pictures for that sum. The Parliament of Basle Canton voted 6 million francs towards it; that left 2·4 million to be raised. At this point, a citizen of Basle who objected to the use of taxpayers' money for such a purpose called for a referendum on the question, and collected the number of signatures which make the holding of a referendum in Basle obligatory.

The referendum was to be held on December 17th, 1967. A twin campaign was launched by those who wanted to save the Picassos for Basle: it was to raise the extra money, and to defeat, in the referendum, the proposal to forbid Basle to pay over the 6 million francs. On November 25th, the 'Beggars' Festival' opened.

For three weeks, something like Saturnalia raged in Basle. Politicians and actors, writers and bankers, celebrities of all kinds, were to be found acting as waiters in restaurants or giving banquets, to raise money; the streets ran with outdoor theatres, puppet-shows, musicians, all collecting for the Picassos; a soup-kitchen with a difference (the soup was charged for) was set up in front of the main post office and dispensed Picassosuppe day and night; antique and art markets sprang up all over the town, the proceeds to go to the fund; schoolchildren marched in processions; art students drew the two Picassos on every pavement in the city; a local composer wrote a march for the campaigners; one of the Burghers of Calais was provided with a museum attendant's cap to hold out for donations, and another of them wore a lapel-button saying 'Give your shirt'; at midnight on the eve of the referendum, the President of Zürich Canton led a torchlight procession of drummers and pipers to hand over a cheque for 260,000 francs. When the money was all in and counted, it emerged that there were 2·5 million francs in the kitty, 100,000 more than the target.

Then the vote; the turnout was the highest for any referendum in Basle's history, and the proposal was defeated by 32,118 to 27,190.

Two days later, a journalist and a photographer were invited to call on Picasso at his home in the South of France. He told them that he had been so touched by Basle's action that he was going to give the city four of his paintings to add to the rescued two. On January 5th, 1968, a banner was strung right across the front of the Kunstmuseum: it bore the words 'The Picassos are here'; there they were, and there they have been ever since. Who could fail to love a city which sheltered Erasmus from the winds of the Reformation and which, centuries later, rose so notably to the occasion on behalf of the genius of Picasso?

My last action before leaving Basle was to cross the Rhine by the ferry. It is called the Chain Ferry, and has been plying back and forth across the river, in much the same form, for centuries. A cable has been strung across, high up, and another cable, attached to the boat, is coupled to it, sliding along it in the manner of the old trolley-buses; it looks like a safety-chain, and that is exactly what it is, for the Rhine current here is enormously powerful, and if the ferry-boat's motor failed it would be swept away. It was a charming little vessel, with an enclosed awning at the back for foul weather and a giant tiller for the boatman to keep his craft steady against the current. All ferries have something in common, and this one reminded me of the Venetian ones ('the common ferry that trades to Venice,' Shakespeare calls it); even, with the awning, in appearance.

The next stop was at Mulhouse, which shares an airport with Basle. But Mulhouse has also a Museum of its own; it was a Museum the mere thought of which made my heart sink, yet the reality of which so stunned me with what it contained and how its contents were displayed that I realised it had passed the ultimate test: a visit to a collection of objects which are of no interest whatever to the visitor, yet which nevertheless keep him in a state of rapt excitement for hours on end.

A Car Museum has nothing to offer me; I do not own a car and indeed cannot drive; apart from a Rolls-Royce and the old Volkswagen

'Beetle' I cannot put a name to any of them (well, if I notice the 'logo' on a Mercedes I can name that); how they work is naturally a complete mystery to me; and I have never felt the smallest thrill at what car-lovers call the 'romance' of motoring, and least of all at seeing and handling veteran and vintage cars.

The Mulhouse Car Museum is housed in one gigantic shed, some 200 yards square; it holds more than 600 cars, in date ranging from the very earliest types made late in the nineteenth century to the late 1950s. The hall which holds them is diagonally criss-crossed by walkways, broad avenues bordered by lovingly copied replicas of old *fin-de-siècle* Parisian lamp-posts with globe lamps atop; the cars themselves stand in neat rows parallel to the diagonals, on gravel. They are, as even I could see at a glance, lovingly tended; their paint is impeccable, and highly polished, as are all their outside fitments; peering into them, I saw that the same was true of the inside, where dashboard, door-handles, upholstery and carpets were all, even though faded or worn, clean and unbroken.

The cars are arranged, so far as is practicable, in groups, maker by maker. The largest group is composed of the Bugattis, but there are Ferraris, Delahayes, Hispano-Suizas, Alfa-Romeos, Panhards, Rolls-Royces (a complete chronology of these, starting with one that had no resemblance at all to a Rolls-Royce of today except that unique bonnet), and scores more makes that meant nothing at all to me. But what fascinated me was to see the entire history of the motor-car before me in one room, and – even more fascinating – to see the extra-ordinary quality of the old designs, beside which almost all of today's cars look ugly, clumsy and meretricious.

I climbed into the prize of the collection: a Bugatti, made for the Chairman of the Company, in the 1920s. I sat in the back and fingered the speaking-tube that communicated with the chauffeur. The upholstery was covered in floral brocade, and was still luxuriously comfortable; when I emerged, I learned that it had cost, new, £70,000. By today's monetary values, that means not far short of a couple of million. Surely even the richest and most extravagant millionaire today would not pay that much for a car? Indeed, how *could* he? Surely nobody is building cars as expensive as that? (I think I read not long ago that the newest model of Rolls-Royce cost, with particularly luxurious fittings and every imaginable kind of extra, something like £150,000.)

The mystery remained as I left. So, for that matter, did the mystery of how I came to be so suddenly and so deeply interested in motor-cars.

And there was a third mystery. The cars were collected, as a hobby, by a man called Fritz Schlumpf; he and his brother (now dead, though Fritz lives on in Basle) were French, and ran a successful business in Mulhouse. Then the business ran into financial difficulties, there was a strike, the strikers 'impounded' the cars as security for their wages, torrents of lawsuits began to flow, prosecutions were mooted, and in the end (this is Schlumpf's story) he was forced to sell the entire collection to the French government for a small fraction of the millions it had cost him to put it together. He is, understandably, an embittered man; and the torrent of lawsuits flows still.

I never saw, though I looked eagerly for it, the motor-car that gets stuck in the snow in Orson Welles's *The Magnificent Ambersons*.

30 I think I'll use the Bugatti today   31 No, I won't – home, James

30

31

32

3.

34

6

A-Hunting We Will Go . . .

THE LITTLE TOWN of Breisach is dominated by its Münster, St Stephen's. It is approached by a handsome old square tower which was presumably the old gate to the town, but Breisach, no doubt wishing to demonstrate that it has a life of its own and is not wholly dependent on the Münster, has placed near the mighty cathedral a number of very modern and striking sculptures in doorways, on street corners and – the most striking of all – right beside their Gothic glory. This last is of two figures, modelled in clay and cast in bronze, a girl and a boy, both looking like students, though neither, to judge by their dejected appearance, about to burst into 'Gaudeamus igitur'. The girl seems to hurry on, the youth slouches half a dozen paces behind her, his hands in his pockets. I thought it forceful, but could not tease out a meaning (and why should it have a meaning?), and went on into the cathedral. Up on its hill (there were lovely views down to the Rhine from its terrace) it looked more castle than cathedral, and in its turbulent history (the whole town had been razed by the Army of the Revolution in 1793) may well have played the role right through. But today the pilgrims come from afar to see one incomparable treasure within; the High Altar, in the form of a carved wooden triptych, by a master of whom the only thing known for certain is that his initials were H. L. (Some say they stood for Hans Loi, but since nothing, apparently, is known about him, that does not extend the knowledge very far.)

The central panel depicts the Coronation of the Virgin; each of the wings holds two saints, St Stephen and St Lawrence on the left, St Gervase and St Protasius on the right; behind the centre rises a tower of

32 Grünewald's masterpiece 33 Equipped for the Black Forest 34 Across the river and into the trees

wooden filigree, carrying angels; in the predella at the foot of the altar are the four Evangelists, all hard at work writing, though St Matthew, his arm outstretched in an imperious gesture, points to the page while glaring haughtily at St John as if to show him, not for the first time, how a Gospel should be written. (John takes no notice at all as he concentrates on his own work, with the beginning of a smile round his lips.)

Ready to assure the German customs officers that I was not part of the revolutionary army rejoining my unit, I re-crossed the Rhine into Alsace. I was making for Colmar, and when I arrived I went straight to a tiny restaurant beside the Musée d'Unterlinden, which houses the greatest altarpiece of all, the Isenheim Altar of Matthias Grünewald. I went upstairs to wash my hands; my route passed through a room that was being used for a private family lunch-party, a dozen or fifteen of them. I guessed it was great-grandmother's ninetieth birthday; at least, there was a tiny matriarch, lace over her head, who was clearly the centrepiece of the occasion. I greeted the company as I went through the room, and when I emerged (by which time they had presumably agreed that I was a foreigner) they returned my greeting and offered me a glass of wine. They were from a farming community nearby; one volunteered the information that it was going to be a good harvest this year. The ignorant British townee asked them how they knew, so early in the year and the corn far from ripe (that much even I had noticed), and they laughed as though they would never stop, to think that there was a man in their midst who couldn't tell what kind of harvest there would be simply because it was the beginning of July.

Lunch had been almost finished when I appeared; they had clearly eaten and drunk well, to judge by the empty dishes and bottles. Nobody was tipsy, though all were merry and rubicund; as always in France, the children, even the youngest, were of the party, and had clearly eaten and drunk of the same things as the adults. Once again, I was reminded of that extraordinary quality of *savoir vivre* that the French have to a greater extent than any other people, even the Italians, who have it in a slightly different and less powerful form. The French not only enjoy their food; they make it clear, visibly and audibly, that they enjoy their food. It is not a matter of the quality of their *cuisine* or even of their relish for it. It is their enjoyment of life itself, and therefore of the good things of life, and thus of food and drink, which are indeed among the good things of life. This happy band no doubt had as many problems and mutual dislikes as any other family, but they were united in the feeling of well-being the meal had provided. I bade them farewell, and wished them a good harvest, and their laughter rang in my ears as I went downstairs.

And then, once more, back to Grünewald. It never fails; on the contrary, it grows every time. I had been here only a few months before, but now, again, I noticed details I had never seen before, one small, one great. Since my last visit, I had read a scholarly book on Grünewald, which naturally devoted a great deal of space to the altarpiece. The author said that St Anthony, in the Temptation, is emitting 'a wail of terror'. Now I had always believed that St Anthony, in spite of the hideous demons that are tormenting him (and they out-Bosch Bosch in their dreadfulness), is as serene in his faith as was St Lawrence on his grid-iron, telling his torturers that they could turn him over because he was done on one side. I approached the Saint with some nervousness, fearing that I would be convinced by the expert, and I peered at him, with his great bushy white beard, demanding his secret. His secret was what it had always been; Anthony feels the horror of the devils and the nightmare, he feels the pain as they pinch him and pluck at him, trample him and scream at him, but, like Bunyan, 'He knows he at the end, Shall life inherit.' There is, of course, the further evidence for the scholar's view provided by the inscription in the corner of the panel, in which the Saint cries out, 'Where were you, good Jesus, where were you, why did you not come to heal my wounds?' This may seem conclusive, but it is not, for two reasons; first, God and an angel have responded at once to the Saint's plea, and their demeanour is one of rewarding him for his steadfastness, not of shoring up his tottering faith. Second, and much more important, the Saint is echoing, almost word for word, Christ's great cry from the Cross: 'My God, my God, why hast thou forsaken me?'

Of the two things I had not previously noticed on any of my visits to the painting, the lesser was the fact (which strengthens my argument about the Saint's faith) that he is clutching his rosary, indeed clutching it the tighter because one of the devils is trying to prise it from his grip. That, surely, is a powerful symbol of St Anthony's untroubled faith; added to the look on his face, terribly beset but confident in Christ, it seems to me conclusive.

But the other newly observed aspect of Grünewald's masterpiece is more significant. Hitherto, looking at the panel with Christ on the Cross, I have seen the figure through eyes mainly used to the Crucifixions of the Italian masters. Most of them, and indeed most artists from elsewhere, paint or model the crucified Christ as the god-man who has passed, or is passing, through pain and earthly care, into his Kingdom. Grünewald, as I fully realised for the first time on this visit (so powerful and hypnotic were the images already in my mind with which I had formerly approached it), will have none of that. He paints precisely what the watchers at the foot of the Cross would have seen; a man being tortured to death in the most horrible and gruesome manner. Christ's face and body register *pain*, pain beyond all human bearing, and as I took in the implications of it in a way which I had not done before, I realised that this work – with which there is almost nothing to compare in all the works of Christian art apart from, say, the Sistine Chapel and the B Minor Mass and only one or two more – was even greater than I had supposed. For when, after that ordeal, we arrive at the culmination of the work, the panel with the Resurrection, we can see the risen Christ plain (while the sleeping soldiers look not just asleep but stunned), with the earth and its cares now truly left behind, and with nothing but the nail-holes (the palms are turned towards the spectator) to show for the ordeal, unbearable but borne.

I strolled out into the afternoon sunshine, and looked in at the Dominican Church, and was greeted with a sound so nostalgic for me that I felt the tears prick. The organist was practising (there was no service going on) and what he was playing was that Toccata and Fugue by Widor which I used to hear at least once a month in chapel at school, because the organist was very fond of it for a Voluntary (for which it is indeed most fitting); I stood transfixed by music and memory, and the Widor rumbled to its end as the bass came in. And I had a second reward in the church: a painting by Martin Schongauer, set just inside the chancel gates, called 'The Virgin in the Rose Garden'. There she is, in a huge red robe, with the Christ-child on her lap; behind her is an array of roses, trellis roses of many different kinds. But what is so charming about the people of this church is that there is a handwritten notice tied to the chancel gate, giving the correct names of each of the roses. I couldn't help feeling that the Virgin would have been pleased.

Colmar repaid exploring. The old Corps de Garde building, previously an ossuary chapel, has had another and even stranger transmogrification: it now houses the headquarters of the Committee for Action for the Economic and Social Progress of the Department of the Haut-Rhin: I forbore to push the door open and ask them how they were doing. Lovely old houses; the Maison des Têtes, named for the curious gargoylish figures on its façade; the Maison Adolph, from the fifteenth century, and the Maison Pfister, from the sixteenth, both looking as though they were proposing to topple into the street immediately (but I suspected that they had looked like that for some hundreds of years); the Maison Bartholdi, birthplace of the sculptor who designed the great Lion of Belfort and later the Statue of Liberty; an even older house, dating from the fourteenth century and later the dwelling of Martin Schongauer's family. I have always wondered what it would be like to live in a house previously occupied by someone who has left an indelible mark on the world; how I envy John Morgan, who owns the house in which Mozart stayed on his visit to London.

Then there was the Quartier des Tanneurs, fronted by the most perfect carved stone staircase, overhanging eaves and decorated roofs; the Tanners' Square is now occupied mainly by antique shops, and right in the middle there reared up a handsome fountain with a tanner atop; he looked very self-confident, perhaps too self-confident to be a tanner, particularly since he was holding a sword. I have never seen a tanner with a sword, but then I have never seen a tanner at all, and the only thing I know about them is that according to the First Gravedigger buried tanners rot more slowly than other corpses.

And here, after I got lost several times trying to find it, was Colmar's Little Venice. Petite Venise turned out to be rather impressive; not just – like London's – a brief glimpse of an old waterway, but a network of canals, giving a surprisingly Venetian feel. There wasn't a boat of any kind to be seen on any of them, let alone a gondola (surely there cannot be a mock-Venice from which water traffic is excluded?), but whoever designed it was determined to make it as authentic as possible, for a good deal of the area is without pavements of any kind along the frontage, so that the only approach would be by water.

Strasbourg loomed; but first, something much stranger loomed. I recrossed the river to Freiburg, where I was greeted by a monster cloudburst; within a few seconds I was more completely drenched than I had ever been in my life with my clothes on; the rapids themselves were a light sprinkling compared to this. Soon, though, the sun, ashamed of its inhospitable partner, came out fiercely, and I dried off in no time. I sat at a café for a while, contemplating the experience before me – an experience quite unlike the one at the rapids, which had been purely physical; this dilemma was going to be moral, and I was by no means sure how I was going to manage. Well, first I had time to see Freiburg.

Freiburg has a fine and handsome Cathedral (just around the corner from it there is a plaque on the wall of a house in which Erasmus lived for a year after he had left Basle to the tumults of the Reformation, in search of somewhere more peaceful, and in which he wrote *De civilitate morum puerilium*, or 'Good manners for boys'); the town also has a most charming cooling system, consisting of a series of water-channels that run down the main streets – presumably they follow the lines of the old open sewers, though now they contain only clear, fresh water. The Cathedral is a handsome building, as I have said, but it is also a difficult building to photograph, because its height and the surrounding buildings mean that there are very few points from which it may be snapped in its entirety. Backing away, step by step, as more and more of it could be seen in the viewfinder of my camera, I finally stepped straight into one of the gutters, the water in which runs some six inches deep. If I had been trying to take a picture of a restaurant, a military monument, a smoking chimney, a traffic-jam or even a pretty girl, I might have accepted my ducking as a punishment; but a man who wants to take a picture of a Cathedral should surely be granted some dispensation.

I sought a simple restaurant for dinner, and found it in a tiny hotel called the Markgräflerhof. The meal was excellent, and beautifully served, but it was not that that made the experience so memorable. Consider: Freiburg is an old and attractive town, with a good number of noble buildings, and its University is ancient, and justly renowned, but it is small in population, and no one would claim that it was a great centre for anything, a place to which all Europe beats a path. Nor, even if all Europe did, would Europe necessarily find the back street in which this outwardly unremarkable little restaurant stood. Yet it had a wine-list that could stand comparison with most of the greatest and most famous temples of gastronomy anywhere in the world. It had something like a hundred and fifty clarets, including a huge selection of *grands crus* in a vast variety of vintages going back to 1936, and the burgundies were hardly less considerable; and that was only the French section, which was followed by pages and pages not of German wines in general (they came later) but of Baden wines. Who would have thought that behind the innocent face of Freiburg such unexpected treasure would be lurking?

Next day, I found myself drinking Kirsch, and a particularly potent variety, too, at nine o'clock in the morning. My ordeal had begun.

I was dressed for the ordeal, not to say the Kirsch, in a green shirt and tie, twill breeches, a jaunty hat and a green Loden jacket with a badge on the shoulder; I began to feel rather as though I had been inducted into the SS, though the insignia was only that of the Forest Association. But the forest in question was the Black Forest, and the Association was an association of huntsmen. It had never occurred to me that I would ever find myself hunting in the Black Forest; for that matter, it had never occurred to me that I would ever find myself hunting anywhere. But before the moral question came to be considered – should I be hunting at all? – the surrounding circumstances had to be considered.

We were making for the hut where we were to stay. The Kirsch is the traditional start to such an expedition, and is drunk with a formal toast: the glass must be held in the left hand (nobody knew why), the leader of the party cries 'Waidmanns Heil!' ('Hunters' luck'), and everybody repeats it before downing the firewater. The hut was just beyond the highest point in the Black Forest, some 4000 feet; not surprisingly, it was both misty and cold, and on the way we had even passed some snow beside the path. The hut, though, was very welcoming; cramped, of course, with double bunk-beds, but pleasantly and fittingly decorated. It had no electricity, but it had a wood-burning stove which gave out waves of welcome heat; welcome, particularly, because the hunting expedition was going to start only in the afternoon. It seemed that the prey have regular hours; they can be stalked only at dawn or teatime, and since we had missed the early shift for today, we would have to concentrate on the afternoon one. Meanwhile, I was to be instructed in the use of the gun, and it was most noticeable that the holding, the breaking, and the correct method of walking with it, were gone into with very considerable thoroughness before I was allowed to see a cartridge, let alone put it into the breech.

These hunters were serious men, and the seriousness was of a particularly attractive kind. They were amateurs, in the sense that they hunted for sport, not pay; but they were not amateurs in their hunting methods, and I soon discovered why not. No one is allowed to hunt in Germany without a licence, and the licence is granted only after success in an astonishingly rigorous examination, which follows a year-long course of two evenings of instruction a week, and demands not only a high state of proficiency in shooting, but the completion of a series of papers on zoology, biology, botany, ecology and several more such disciplines. The consequence is that there are no more than some 3000 licensed huntsmen in the whole country, and there is nothing like the carnage – human as well as animal – that invariably accompanies the hunting season in Italy and the United States. (A farmer in the latter took to painting 'COW' on the sides of his cattle, in a vivid red, to persuade the eager but unskilled stalkers that the beasts were not rhinoceroses or grizzly bears; I never learned whether the device cut down the casualties among his herd.) Even in Britain, where the close seasons are well observed, there is no test of proficiency for a gun-licence, even proficiency in shooting straight; if the budding sportsman can satisfy the authorities that he genuinely wants a licence for hunting, he simply pays the fee and walks away.

The seriousness of my friends the huntsmen was only partly due to the examination they had passed; they were serious men, and knew that to take life, even animal life, was a serious business, not to be embarked upon lightly, and still less with a feeling of indifference to their prey. They would shoot deer, hare, rabbit and boar (though there are not many of the last left), but as they talked about the game, I began to discover the nature of their attitude to the animals, and the word reverence was not too strong. They regard their prey as, in some curious sense, their equals. True, there is sport and pleasure in it for them, and they do not seek to deny that. They eat their game – or somebody eats it, anyway – but they do not pretend that they would otherwise starve. But to think of English fox-hunting, with the nastiness of the hunting itself and the infinitely greater nastiness of the people who do it (and most particularly the greatest nastiness of the lies they tell about doing it for conservation purposes), the contrast with these grave, honourable hunters – one of them a civil servant, one a woodman, all plainly hardworking men – could not be greater. They are bound by a duty, which, as they described it, resembled nothing so much as a religious oath, to follow and dispatch any animal they had wounded but not killed outright. (I asked whether, if I had my gun to my shoulder when a deer came into sight, I would be permitted to pull the trigger; Herr Lauterwasser said, regretfully, no. In the first place, I had not passed the examination, so I would be breaking the law; in the second – and he made clear that this was even more important – if I wounded an animal and it could not be found, why then, he said, he would have to start packing his bags to leave the region for ever.)

We drove some way to our rendezvous with the earliest of the means of survival that human-beings have practised; the cave-drawings of

Lascaux are 20,000 years old, and hunting was already ancient when it was depicted there. The last part of our journey was a march through the forest itself; in a clearing there stood a tall, strange wooden structure, appallingly reminiscent of the watch-towers of a prison camp. This was our 'hide'; we scrambled up the rough ladder into a miniature cabin in the sky. My comrades explained that strict silence had now to be observed, for the prey had sharp ears; sharp noses, too, which also ruled out smoking.

Now there was nothing to do but wait; they told me that the wait might last for hours, and still end in failure, but beginner's luck held, for only a few minutes after we had taken up position and fallen silent, a slim deer emerged from the edge of the clearing and made to cross it. It was brought down, killed instantly, by one of the marksmen. There followed a ceremony in which some of the most ancient and primitive feelings of mankind were touched upon. First, the beast had to be gutted, otherwise it would swell up horribly almost at once. Then a twig was dipped in the blood and touched gently to the face of the huntsman who brought down the animal. Then a sprig of leaves was placed, carefully and reverently, in the mouth of the deer. This, they explained, was its Last Supper; the parallel was explicit and without doubt intended, but there was not so much as a hint of jest or irony or contempt, let alone blasphemy. On the contrary, it was plainly the hunters' way of honouring their fallen foe, and the ceremony was completed when a sprig of the same leaves that had provided the deer's symbolic consumption of the Host was placed in the hat of the man who had killed it.

That night we feasted well in the hut; my new friends would not let me lift a finger, even to help with the washing-up, but I pleased them by making a speech in my best German to the effect that the nations of the earth have a vast variety of phrases to accompany the downing of a mutually taken drink; thus the French say 'Santé', the English 'Cheers', the Jews 'L'chaim', and the Germans, of course, their traditional 'Prosit'; but today I had learned much from my companions, and not least the huntsmen's toast. So, I said, I take the glass in my left hand, and give you the huntsmen's greeting: 'Waidmanns Heil!' They responded in chorus with the same toast, and we fell to.

'We' included the three dogs that had come with us on the hunting expedition; they were a setter, a spaniel and a long-haired dachshund (the last variety being one of the very few kinds of dog I actually like, not that there are many more in the category of those I can just about put up with, before getting to the great majority which I detest). The dachshund was called Alfie, and we had become firm friends in the course of the day; when I gave the traditional toast he thumped his tail in furious approval. But the dogs provided me with a bonus so unexpected and delightful that when I crawled into my bunk for the night I could hardly sleep for pleasure. I asked the huntsmen why they did not use Alsatians (creatures I loathe as much as I fear them, which is very much indeed), and the answer was succinct and, to my ears, the most beautiful music imaginable: 'They are too stupid and too vicious.'

Next day we parted; one of the hunters, the woodman, had left early, and on the way back to Freiburg I met him, following his trade. He had cut down a tree, and was chopping it into logs. I thought of a line of Chesterton's: 'The woodman cherished what he smote, And honoured even the chips'; this man clearly did, and he was as serious about his work as he had been about his sport.

A little further on I came to a village with the splendidly ridiculous name (ridiculous to English ears, anyway) of 'Aha'. I at once imagined a traveller, gone astray, asking for the name of the village he could see in the distance and being told 'Aha!'; he then stumps off in a fury, cursing people who won't even tell him the name of his next stop. Then I got lost myself and all attempts to discover where I was ('Aha!') were unavailing. I cursed as my timetable slipped, but Providence knew what it was doing, for it was saving for me a sight which I would otherwise not have seen, or even suspected the existence of. Miles off the route, I found myself in a village called St Blasien, and at first could hardly believe what I saw as I reached the centre of it. St Blasien has a cathedral with a dome that measures forty yards across and forty yards high, the world's largest after St Peter's, Rome, and St Paul's, London; turned upside down it could easily accommodate the entire population of the village. Inside, the church is almost completely white, and the ground plan is so vast that it could accommodate the population of most of the countryside for miles around. Its history is as amazing as its size; it has been repeatedly destroyed by fire, and in its present form was completed in 1983. Cobbett, of all people, came to mind; *Rural Rides* is full of one of his most engaging obsessions, which was his belief that all claims that England's population had once been very much smaller than when he was travelling must be false, because the huge size of the churches could only be explained if they had been built for huge congregations. What would he have said if he had seen the cathedral of St Blasien, and then looked at the size of the village?

Thus rewarded, I soon discovered where I was, and made my way back to Freiburg, where I carried on my Freiburg sightseeing; there were handsome burghers' houses round the Cathedral square, a very severe but not unhandsome complex of modern university buildings, the St Martin's Tower, with its effigy of the Saint sharing his cloak with a beggar, and one fiery particle of history. It was from Freiburg that Marie-Antoinette set out for Strasbourg in 1770, where she was met by Cardinal de Rohan and conveyed to Paris for her marriage to Louis XVI. A few years before, at Schönbrunn, she had had another, much stranger, proposal of marriage; a musical infant prodigy, then aged eight, had sat upon her knee after performing miraculously at the harpsichord, and looking up at the Princess, he had solemnly said, 'You are very beautiful, and when I grow up I am going to marry you.' The Princess, and all the company, laughed; I have always wondered whether, on the scaffold, she had remembered that occasion, and thought for a moment that perhaps it would have been better, despite the disparity in their ages and circumstances, to have become Marie-Antoinette Mozart.

But for all the charm of Freiburg, the moral question that had been at my elbow all the previous day had now to be considered. What was I doing on an expedition to kill animals (in the case of the deer undoubtedly more beautiful than I am), whatever the attitude of the hunters and whatever the care they took over their killing?

I have heard, but can find no lexicographical evidence for it, that, in duelling with pistols, a duellist who did not want to kill or even wound his opponent, and who would therefore fire harmlessly into the air, was said to have 'deloped'. I am almost certain that if I had been permitted to draw a bead upon the deer, I would have deloped; I could not have brought myself to kill it. Let us leave aside the fact that the deer was beautiful and graceful; what if it had been a boar, which is neither (or an Alsatian, suppose they were legitimate prey, and I am sorry they are not)? Would I then have fired? If so, why? If not, why not? Give your reasons.

No, I would not have fired; but I am not sure that I *can* give my reasons. It will be easier, I think, to work it out if we concentrate on the deer. I eat venison, and enjoy it. Somebody has shot the deer I dine off; am I then not a hypocrite? If I would eat it, why wouldn't I kill it? I don't eat battery chickens, though on gastronomic rather than humanitarian grounds, but what about white veal, which many very good restaurants serve? If I understand the system, the calves are treated as inhumanely as are the battery chickens. For that matter, what about caviare, which I believe invariably involves cruelty? But suppose I ate no poultry but free-range, no beef but what had been lovingly reared and humanely killed, no venison except from deer shot and saluted in the manner of my friends? Are we *all* hypocrites unless we are vegetarians? Indeed, are we the greater hypocrites for refusing to kill but being willing to eat? The vegetarian might say that we have no right to take animal life to sustain our own, and it is true that a vegetarian diet can provide as much nourishment as a carnivorous one; this takes me further than I am willing to go, but the sharper question is whether we have the right to take animal life *for our sport*. Nobody eats a fox, but, to do the fox-hunters justice, the distinction cannot be between sport which ends in dinner and sport which is sport only. It is true that the opposition to meat-eating (and meat eaten without being hunted, or cruelly reared) has turned into a fanaticism so mad, violent and totalitarian that even the fox-hunters have begun to evoke sympathy, let alone the butchers whose shop windows have been broken by these crazed avengers, and the workers at the meat-processing factory which was burned to the ground by them, with the loss of hundreds of thousands of pounds for the owners and the loss of their jobs for all the employees. But that doesn't affect the question; have we the right to take an animal's life, or to have someone take it on our behalf? I don't know; or rather, I think the answer is yes, but I am very far from being sure that I can rationally argue the case. It is not an answer to say that my German huntsmen were honourable men; they could still have been doing wrong while thinking they were doing right. Certainly these men combined the ancient German character of teutonic chivalry and seriousness, together with the modern German character of hard work and hard play; in other words, they have combined the old German virtues and the new German virtues and left out the bit in the middle.

I recall that I ate fish for dinner that night; possibly my choice was dictated by my wrestling with the problem of meat, but what about fish? Assuming that it was not caught by inhumane methods . . . and then there is the question of lobster . . . and how far do you go – as far as whitebait, for instance . . . and I don't like the taste of frog's-legs, but if I did . . . I fell asleep thinking about these matters, but happily did not dream of being pursued by all the animals I had ever eaten. But I awoke knowing that Strasbourg was my next stop, and knowing also what much greater moral dilemma awaited me there.

7

. . . to Catch a Goose

THE BOAT FROM Lake Constance to Schaffhausen might be likened to a bus; from Freiburg to Strasbourg, the ship was more like a huge limousine. The Köln–Düsseldorf Line, which dates back to 1826, now runs a vast fleet of vast ships, which ply between Basle and Rotterdam. The one I boarded was as much a floating hotel as any Cunarder, and at first glimpse, not much smaller; I learned that it could hold (though not sleep) 3000 people. It was a pleasure-cruiser – for speedy business other vessels are used – but it reminded me vividly of my vow, sworn after my one transatlantic sea voyage, never voluntarily to go on a cruise, and if compelled to, to hang myself from the yard-arm (whatever that might be) in the course of my first night aboard. (I have said that I would not willingly have missed the experience of the Queen Mary; but I have also said that in no circumstances would I repeat it. Going aboard the *Queen Mary*, I recall the two emotions, the second pressing hard upon the heels of the first, that I felt. The first was that the ship was enormous, gigantic, vast; so indeed she was, *for a ship*. But then I realised, with rising panic, that if she were a village, she would be the smallest village in the world. An hour later, having explored the ship, the truth struck me; three times round the boat-deck and the *Queen Mary* had been exhausted in its capacity as a *place*. Another truth struck me soon after, when the ship had sailed and land been left behind; unlike all other places, it was impossible to call a taxi and go somewhere else.)

That evening, in Strasbourg, the French were at their best. I telephoned, around ten o'clock, for a table at Valentin-Sorg, one of the

Strasbourg restaurants with a star in the Good Book. They said they regretted, it was too late, the kitchen was just closing, *nous sommes désolés*. I pressed them; I said I would come instantly in a taxi; I threatened to create an international incident by dying of starvation on their doorstep. They gave in, and said they would serve me if I arrived soon.

So far, it was like a restaurant in any country, possibly even Britain. But when I got there, *vive la différence*. Did they greet me with rebukes, with sour faces? Did they look at their watches? Did they urge me to choose my meal quickly? They did none of these things; it was as if I had booked my table a week before, for 8.30, and arrived exactly on time. The *apéritif* was enquired after and the menu proffered. The *apéritif* arrived, and the head-waiter followed it at a discreet interval, with a run-through of the *Spécialités du jour*. He then vanished, to return only when I signalled that I was ready to order. Long before I had finished, every other table had emptied, but there was not the smallest pressure on me, not the slightest sign of irritation on the part of any member of the staff. And when I had finally finished and paid the bill, the head-waiter, his deputy and the *sommelier* formed an honour guard, all smiles, to escort me to the door. I do not even believe that the episode was based on a commercial consideration: well, he's here now, let's serve him, it's another slice of income after all. No, it was yet another example of that *savoir vivre* which is at once the mystery and the saving grace of the French.

Strasbourg is a very strange place, and I very much doubt that it was as strange as this before the European Parliament arrived, though it is true that I cannot work out any reason for the strangeness to have been caused by the arrival. For a city with a population of a quarter of a million (400,000 altogether in 'Greater Strasbourg') it seemed astonishingly lacking in sophistication. Such a city, with such international political significance, ought surely (this is France, after all) to have at least an arcade or two of elegant shops, selling fashion, shoes, jewellery, confectionery, leather goods and the like. Strasbourg sells all those things, of course, but very much in the mode and quality of London's wretched, ruined Oxford Street. Quality goes hand in hand with design, especially in France, but the shops themselves, almost without exception, looked dull, crude and old-fashioned, the fascias cheap, the lettering without elegance. The conclusion was that this town had been left behind. But that only left another mystery; how could Strasbourg have been left behind, with so international a character imposed on it by the European Parliament?

Never mind; there were other qualities to Strasbourg, as a walk round and through it amply demonstrated. The walk, I may say, took place in weather so cold that I would not have been in the least surprised if it had started to snow, and after a time the misery grew so great that I plunged into a department store and emerged with a huge quilted overcoat.

That was my second attempt; I had tried a men's outfitters first, with a request for something along the lines of a Burberry. As it happened, they had a Burberry *même*, and draped it over me; the only drawback was that it was at least four sizes too large, and looked on me like a giant tent. It came down to about three inches above my ankles, and the sleeves dangled several inches beyond the tips of my fingers. I pointed all this out to the assistant, but he overdid the business principle; 'Ah, non!' he cried, and explained that this season one was wearing such coats longer, it was the fashion; last year, *vraiment*, it would have been somewhat on the large side, *mais aujourd'hui, vous savez, c'est très à la mode*. I risked being laughed at for my ignorance of the fashionable length for *le Burberry*, made an excuse, and left.

Strasbourg's canals, unlike Colmar's, are more reminiscent of Amsterdam than Venice; there is a hint of the Dutch city's concentric rings of canals, and Strasbourg has a kind of watery *boulevard périphérique*. In *Petite France*, which is the oldest quarter of the city, I could have reached up and touched the eaves of almost any of the crooked, handsome little houses. As in all these old towns, the streetnames reflect the trades that were once followed here; there is a Street of the Tanners, of course, the window-sills of its houses groaning under the weight of geraniums but otherwise clearly unchanged for four centuries and more, and I began to look about (because they must be there) for the Goldsmiths. There is always, in old French towns, a quai des Orfèvres or a rue des Orfèvres, and here there was a tiny impasse des Orfèvres.

I wandered on, caught in a wonderful time-warp from which I had no wish to escape. Four handsome, square, capped towers loomed up, the old watchdogs of the river approach, and a covered bridge, not of wood this time, but of massive stone; from its windows I watched the glass-enclosed tourist-boat glide beneath, crammed with English visitors, and I wondered what the less historically-minded ones among them made of the boat's name: *Rouget de l'Isle*. Anything less appropriate than the composer of the *Marseillaise* for such a comfortable, bourgeois craft on such a comfortable, bourgeois errand could hardly be imagined. (Oh, but it could be, and in Strasbourg is. Rouget de l'Isle first sang the Revolution's marching-song in this city; it is not clear whether he was accompanied by some kind of band, or indeed making it up as he went along, but there he was, on the pavement, no doubt to the astonishment of the *citoyens* and *citoyennes*, striking up the now world-famous song. But the point is that the spot on which this historic première took place is now occupied by the Banque de France, which is, of all the French banks, the most conservative, not to say stuffiest. I suppose we could say that the Banque de France has had the last laugh.)

On the other side of the bridge was a glimpse of the French, not at their best, or their worst, but at their most French. Two little boys, perhaps nine years old, were chatting by the water's edge; a moment later the third of the musketeers arrived, the same age. And what was the first ceremony of their meeting? A solemn handshake, accompanied by a bow. It seemed perfectly natural, and no doubt, to them, was.

And here is the rue Martin Luther, and here the Church of St Thomas, the chief ornament of Lutheran Protestantism, as a plaque on it announced proudly, adding 'in the whole of Alsace'. Luther was one of those figures who were necessary for the historical process, and were ready to history's hand when the time came. The Reformation had to happen, on the grounds of the Church's corruption alone, even if there had been no theological basis for it. But as with so many historical events, it is possible to wish that another instrument had been chosen, instead of this uncomfortable, fierce, implacable, intolerant, roaring, God-intoxicated man. I had not long since been in Basle, rubbing shoulders with Erasmus. (Who was it who said 'Erasmus laid the egg that was hatched by Luther'? Whoever it was, he was better at epigrams than history; Luther would have gone the same way, step by step, if Erasmus had never been born.) It was only fair that I should now come face to face with Luther, even though I was going to do so more appropriately when I got to Worms. He could never be a friend and counsellor; he is one of those figures – Savonarola is another, and so is St Athanasius – to whom it is impossible to deny sanctity, yet who make us shiver.

Still, St Thomas's church is a noble edifice, a massive thirteenth-century building with a series of compartmentalised naves, and an altogether more happy association in the fact that it was here that Albert Schweitzer devised the ceremony of an annual organ recital on

35 What am I bid? 36 Successful bidders

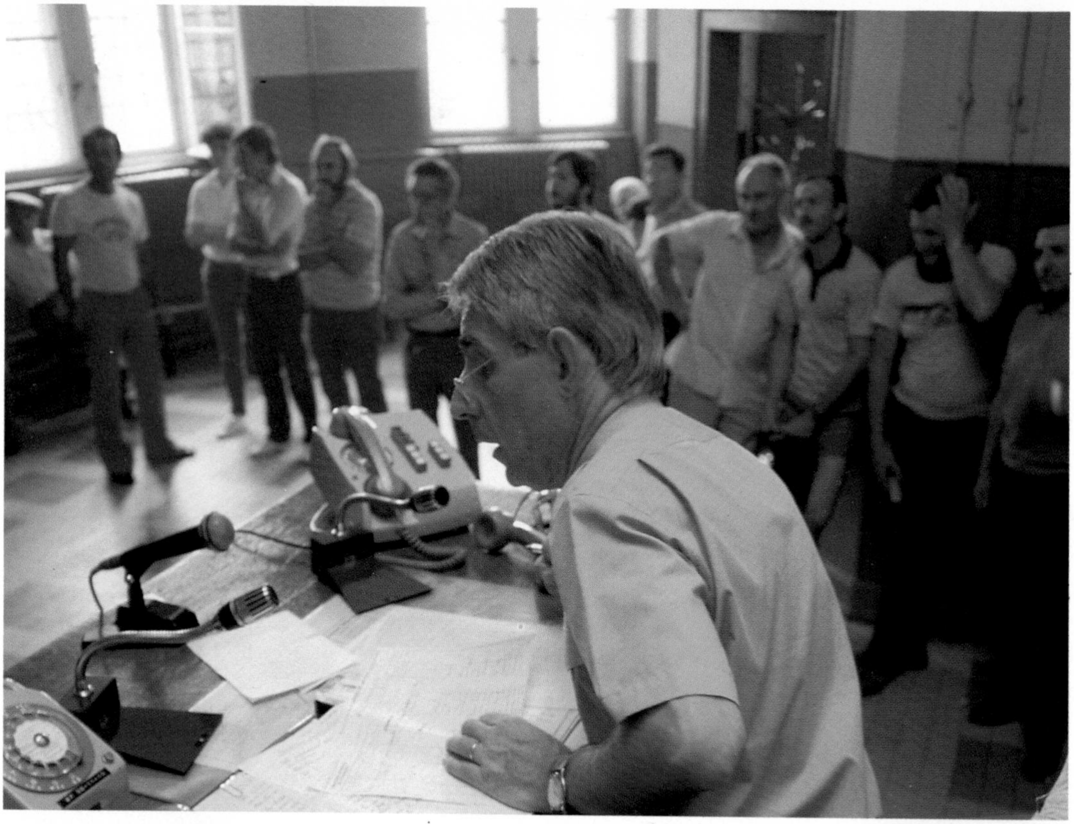

35

36

37

38

the anniversary of Bach's death, and inaugurated it by playing the first of these himself in 1908. The organ was being played when I entered the church; it was a sonorous mid-eighteenth-century one – not, happily, playing Luther's *Ein feste Burg*, which, apart from reminding me to shiver at the thought of Luther, would have sounded most inappropriate on this mellow instrument.

As I got nearer the chancel, I began to think I was suffering from hallucinations, because, in the place where the High Altar would normally be, stood what was apparently a replica of that unspeakable thing in the Frari, at Venice – the hideous marble pyramid which Canova designed for the tomb of Titian (who is in fact buried in a monument quite ugly enough as it is, while Canova reposes, fittingly, in his own creation). As I got closer still, I could see that the similarity to the Canova monstrosity was only superficial, but the hallucinatory feeling became stronger when I discovered that the marble slab I had seen was in fact a monument to Maréchal Saxe, designed, at the behest of Louis XV, by Jean-Baptiste Pigalle (who presumably gave his name to the Parisian thoroughfare). What they actually do for an altar in this church I never managed to discover, though I presumed that they do not worship Marshal Saxe, Louis XV or Pigalle (or Canova, for that matter). But I did discover one other fact about St Thomas's, which is not to be found on a plaque in the church. It originally had a set of five great bells, four of which were destroyed in the Wars of the Reformation; the remaining one, a tenor, still hangs in the church, and tolls the hours. But for four hundred years it has been kept four minutes fast, in order to announce the time to the people of Strasbourg before the Catholic Cathedral (which stays on to the right time) does so. I could only conclude that it is no wonder at all that Northern Ireland is in the mess it is.

All the same, glorious Protestant Gothic (with a bit of Romanesque) though St Thomas's is, the Cathedral of Notre Dame loses only on time-keeping. At the west end, there are two columns on either side of the nave which must be quite twenty feet in diameter, and the rest of the nave pillars, looking rather like liquorice allsorts in their alternating stripes of yellow limestone and reddish sandstone, are not much slimmer; marching beside these is the glow from some of the most marvellous ancient stained glass outside Chartres. What Catholicism never lost, but which Protestantism after a time began to be half-hearted about, was *tremendousness* – not, of course, solely in size. Strasbourg Cathedral, like all its kind, breathes a giant self-confidence,

37 The barge park 38 The happy sailors

and if it were not for the fact that this one, again like all its kind, was built *ad maiorem Dei gloriam*, it and they would be the most appalling examples of *hubris* in the world. If the architect of one of the places like this stepped back when he had finished, rubbed his hands in pleasure and satisfaction, and said words to the effect of 'How very clever I am', he would have risked being damned in the deepest pit of Hell.

Also, in such buildings, it is easier to understand why the iconoclasts smashed so many English cathedrals, or at least the interiors. The Second Commandment does say 'Thou shalt not make unto thyself any graven image', which Puritanism, at any rate, took literally (the Jews and the Muslims have never broken it), but which Catholicism has always ignored.

Just outside the Cathedral, I bought some soap at the Pharmacie du Cerf, which must hold the European record for antiquity, old though so many chemists are: it has been on the same spot, in the same trade, since 1268.

Another Alsatian meal, this time in the most fantastically decorated building in Strasbourg, the Maison Kamerzell; the outside, which is of wood, had been carved in extraordinarily great detail; building and decoration took from the late fifteenth century to the middle of the sixteenth. Upstairs, it was a warren of interconnecting rooms (like Lapérouse of old). And in the middle of dinner there was a visitation from the Salvation Army. A man and a girl, in the traditional uniform, with nothing but a tambourine for accompaniment, went through each room singing quite pleasantly (though the hymns had rather mournful tunes), while another Salvationist followed with the hat, very gently and diffidently.

They made a good haul, and certainly nobody objected. I don't know what the Salvation Army's reputation is like in France today; for that matter, I don't know what it is in Britain, but I know that it used to be enormously high. For all its narrowness, fundamentalism and restrictive rules, anyone involved in work with the fallen would tell you that the Sally Ann would go into homes and conditions that no one else, not even the hardiest social worker, would touch; the organisation had an unrivalled record, in its social work aspect, of selfless help for those who had sunk as low as it is possible to sink in a civilisation like ours. I sometimes think that the Day of Judgment is going to be very interesting indeed.

Strasbourg was holding its forty-eighth annual Festival while I was there (one might think that in nearly half a century they would have learned to indicate in the concert programmes where the interval comes, but they haven't). I went to two recitals; Beethoven sonatas from Yehudi Menuhin and his son Jeremy, and a mixed programme, mostly Beethoven, from Ashkenazy. (The Palais de Congrès, where the music took place, was simultaneously playing host to two conferences, one of urologists and the other of taxi-drivers, though what the latter found to talk about I couldn't think.) The concert-hall itself was designed in the most tired and unimaginative style, with functionless bulges on the walls like the messy wooden screen behind the platform in our Barbican Hall, and poor acoustics.

Ashkenazy, though, was in fine form, and he exuded, as he always does, the serenity and benignity of his character (very like Yehudi, in some ways). A stormy 'Waldstein', followed by an even more stormy 'Appassionata', and a splendidly colourful performance of Schumann's *Carnaval* to finish; not a work close to my heart, but he played the twenty-one episodes with a lightness of spirit, and a wit and gravity wherever they were respectively required, and rollicking tempos for the waltzes.

His serenity of character was tested, however, by an audience that appeared to be under the impression that professional coughers were to be engaged at very high salaries, and had therefore come to audition. A more temperamental pianist – Michelangeli, for instance – would have walked out, and even Ashkenazy, when a photographer crawled round the front of the platform and raised a camera for a flash picture just as he was about to begin the 'Appassionata', waved the man away. But the waving itself was pure Ashkenazy; not angry, not irritable, not upset, but done in a manner that said as clearly as words, 'I don't want to offend you, but I had rather you did not take pictures now, so would you mind not doing so? Thank you.' Even the consumptive Strasbourgers applauded the gesture.

For the Menuhin recital, somebody had had a charming idea, and a long memory too. Tucked into the programme were miniature reproductions of two pages from the local newspaper – *Les Dernières Nouvelles de Strasbourg* – from, respectively, the issues of December 4th and 5th, 1933. This was Yehudi's debut, aged seventeen, in Strasbourg; on the 4th there was an interview-profile, and on the 5th an account of his performance ('Yehudi Menuhin a fait sensation . . . devant un auditoire subjugué, conquis, ému, il a joué du Beethoven et du Bach . . . cet inoubliable concert . . . ce prodigieux garçon . . . la sonorité de Yehudi Menuhin apporte à l'oreille la plus délicate une satisfaction suprême . . . '). Well, time has touched the prodigious boy, and the satisfaction this time, fifty-three years on, was not quite supreme, indeed the performance of the 'Kreutzer' was almost slapdash. But he can still draw forth from his Lady Blunt Stradivarius sounds that few other violinists, though they are half his age or less, can produce. And the performance ended with a gesture that I had never seen before, and my astonishment was not for the gesture, but for the realisation that it had never been done, though it seemed, on the instant, both fitting and perfectly natural. Normally, the page-turners for accompanying pianists have the demeanour of ghosts, tiptoeing on and off the platform as though they are, or would like to be, invisible. But Jeremy Menuhin's page-turner, a bespectacled girl, at the end of the performance, was to be seen clapping as vigorously as anyone in the audience. And why not?

Les Dernières Nouvelles de Strasbourg is still being published, under the same title, and I had been glancing through it each day. The more I glanced, the more impressed I had become; many of the smaller provincial newspapers in France seem to report nothing of greater importance than the death of a rabbit, run over by a car on the D 457, but *Les Dernières Nouvelles* was several cuts above the usual thing. Indeed, compared to almost all of the American provincial press, apart from the few great ones that still hew to the old traditions, *Les Dernières Nouvelles* is far better. And there was a signed leader on the Waldheim affair, by Claude Moniquet, which was as tough as anything I had read on the subject anywhere. The subject, he said, was not closed. Nor is it.

My first encounter with the European Parliament was appallingly symbolic. Entering the building (not quite as ugly as photographs had suggested), I found, immediately inside the plate-glass swing door, a security scanner of the type familiar from airports; there was a table beside it, again of the kind used at airports for the hand-searching of bags. A security official sat beside it, glancing up with manifest indifference as I approached the scanner; I swung my briefcase towards him, expecting him, according to standard practice, to indicate that I should put the bag on the table and walk through. Much to my surprise, he waved me on, bag and all, with the same air of indifference. The scanner (my briefcase held my tape-recorder and camera) shrieked its suspicion for all to hear; I stopped, awaiting the inevitable frisking and equally necessary examination of my briefcase. The security man waved me on again, hardly even glancing up this time.

Later, I was equipped with a pass and a lapel-badge, but at this first entry I had nothing at all to indicate what my business in the Parliament building might be, or whether I had any kind of security clearance. I was a stranger, and they took me in; the only conclusion possible from the astonishing laxity of the security arrangements was that those in charge of them had long since decided that nobody would want to blow up the European Parliament, for the very good reason – good but sad – that nobody would think it worth the trouble. And the reason nobody would think it worth the trouble is that the European Parliament is in truth no Parliament at all, its powers meagre, its actions empty, its very name a reproach to the countries – every one of them a constitutional democracy with a real Parliament – which make it up.

The popular view of the European Parliament, certainly in Britain (though I cannot believe that it is very different elsewhere), is that it is a splendid wheeze for the members of it, who get a handsome salary, together with lavish expenses, from their taxpayers, but that nobody else, least of all the taxpayer, gets anything out of it other than the knowledge – the more bitter for the more ecologically aware of those who are providing them with their ample income – that many tall trees must be cut down daily to provide the immense quantity of paper distributed by the wagon-load to the members, who throw it unread into the nearest waste-paper basket.

That, as I say, is the popular image; unfortunately, the caricature corresponds with uncomfortable closeness to the reality. The European Parliament is cruelly and misleadingly named; it cannot be a Parliament, because it would have to be supra-national in its powers, and none of the High Contracting Parties are willing to give up any significant part of their own Parliament's powers to a body not elected by their own voters. Within this crippling limitation, the European Parliament has, as a matter of fact, done a great deal of quiet good, but a glance at the Council of Europe, which is where the power lies (it is not directly elected), is enough to show that if the members of the Parliament really tried to crack the whip it would be taken out of their hands and broken over their heads. (It is interesting that the only one of Europe's overlapping circles of authority, power, influence and play-acting to have established itself among the member publics as a real entity doing real things is the European Court of Justice; this is partly because the legal principles by which it operates are drawn tightly and carefully – as any legal principles have to be if they are to be effective and respected – and partly because the Court takes care only to pronounce judgments on the cases that come before it rather than making grand but empty statements about justice, rights, human dignity, liberty, equality, fraternity and the weather.)

Take a single, remarkable fact about European co-operation. Throughout the Community, there is complete freedom for the nationals of any member state to seek employment in any other. Only a few years before that measure was agreed upon, anyone proposing it would have been thought mad, *fou*, *verrückt*, *loco*; it has now been operating for some years, and the heavens have not fallen. But does anybody suppose that, whatever the European Parliament did or said, it would have been passed into the national law of all the member states if those who actually wield the delegated power they get from their electorates had not worked out an agreement on it?

The truth is simple; all the member governments are elected to be selfish on behalf of their own people, to get as much as they can out of the Community and to give as little as possible. If eleven of the twelve nations in the Parliament combined, across party borders as well as national ones, to demand that the French government should cease to subsidise the most inefficient farming community in the West, the French government would go on exactly as before. The point is that that must be so; the Community is not a United States of Europe, and people not yet born will grow old and die long before it becomes one.

The Chamber is handsome enough to be taken seriously. It is built on the continental model rather than our two-sided version; each Euro-MP has his or her own desk, a section of one of the concentric circles. Members vote from their seats, by putting a card into a slot – it identifies the member and at the same time records the vote: yes, no or abstain. (It looks exactly like a credit-card, which may also be symbolic.) There is one microphone between every two seats; it is on a flexible stand and can be bent to the left or the right. Members speak from their seats, and many of them do not get up to do so, which looked very strange to British eyes. It was also strange, for one used to the spontaneity of Britain's Parliament, to see that practically all the members *read* their speeches; I remember a similar shock when I first went to a debate in the United States Congress, and again when I went to a Presidential Convention. And considering that the debate I heard was on the subject of violence against women, and that the women members were naturally given priority in speaking, it was frustrating to hear them tonelessly reading a speech on a subject that by its very nature demanded a living argument, and passion in the presentation. (One mystery remained unsolved. There were unofficial meetings going on elsewhere in the building, some of them organised by committees and organisations working in the same field as that of the debate in the Chamber; a notice in a prominent position invited those interested to come to just such a meeting, where there would be discussion of rape, wife-beating, harassment at work and other brutalities and indignities visited upon women, including *nightcaps*. The poster was obviously composed by someone whose native tongue was English – it was perfectly idiomatic – yet there was no explanation of the inclusion of nightcaps among the sins of men against women, and I could find nobody who could explain it.)

The translation booth ran right round the back of the Chamber; a strange mathematical problem had arisen. The first members of the European Community were France, Germany, Italy, the Netherlands, Belgium and Luxembourg. The Belgians and the Luxembourgers agreed to speak French, which meant that there were four official languages – French, Dutch, Italian and German. But that meant *twelve* translations, for each of the four would need translations from *and into* the other three. The next batch of accessions were Britain, Ireland and Denmark; when they joined, the Irish declared themselves willing to speak and understand English, which meant that there were now *six* official languages – the original four plus English and Danish. But this meant that although the number of languages had risen by 50 per cent, the number of cross-translations had risen by 250 per cent, and the number required was now *thirty*. And each of the most recent new entrants – Spain, Portugal and Greece – required its own language to be translated to and from all the others, so that although the total of languages had risen by only another 50 per cent – from six to nine – the number of translations had leaped to a monstrous *seventy-two*. It can be expressed in a mathematical formula: where x is the number of official languages, the number of translations required is x squared minus x. (If the Swedes, the Norwegians and the Finns all decided to join, the number of translations required would be 132. Then if the Poles, the Romanians, the Turks, the Yugoslavs . . .)

That, however, was not the only problem encountered when the Community had last been enlarged. When the Six had become the Nine, the Chamber was full; the last circle of desks went right to the back of the hall. Where could the next three, now that the Nine were about to become the Twelve, be accommodated? The balcony was used for spectators, and was therefore, reasonably, regarded as sacrosanct. And the new members could hardly be suspended from the ceiling. How was the trick done?

It was done, as an official put it to me, by 'shrinking the bums' of the existing members. The seats and desks were all taken out, and replaced by new ones two inches narrower; that gave them just enough more space to accommodate the three newcomers. (Now if the Swedes, the Norwegians, the Finns, the Poles . . .)

I left the European Parliament a sadder but a wiser man. I, too, had once dreamed the dream of a Europe without frontiers, without rivalries, without tariffs, with a common currency, a common law, even a common nationality. The dream never became, as it might have done, a nightmare, but there cannot be many people left asleep. The awakening was caused by the realisation that the Wicked Fairy had not been invited to the christening, and was now making her presence felt. She was the force of nationalism, perhaps the most powerful conviction that mankind can have now that the imperatives of religion have been so widely abandoned. Nationalism need not be aggressive, though it often has been; it need not even be insular or inward-looking; in its essence, I now believe, it is not only necessary but admirable, for it is the integument that holds a people together, that gives them an identity and a pride to go with it, and no amount of international co-operation will provide those qualities. But it means that the idea of a United States of Europe is now further from realisation than ever, and it also means that the European Parliament is doomed to go on talking largely to itself.

With that melancholy but inevitable reflection I went off to Strasbourg station to book some tickets. Since my itinerary was complicated, I went first to the information counter, presided over by a smart young woman who spoke fluent English. If she had had a signboard on her desk, the text couched in all the languages of Europe, saying, 'I don't propose to be helpful in any way, so you are wasting your time in seeking help from me, and if by any chance I should help you, I quite certainly do not intend to be in the least pleasant while doing so,' she could not have made her meaning clearer. After a few minutes trying to get her to do the job she was presumably being paid for, I gave up and worked out my own timetable.

Part of me was glad that I had encountered what I now thought of as the Cow of Strasbourg; for my secret vice is timetables. If I have a hobby, that is what it consists of. Airlines, railways, buses – none of

39 The European not quite Parliament   40 First catch your goose   41 Batten down the hatches   42 Even the river must sleep

41

42

43

44

their timetables, however complex and esoteric, has any terrors for me. I can find my way across the most heavily mine-strewn tables ('Does not run on September 25th', 'Stops here only to set down passengers', 'On Wednesdays change at X as well as Y') to my goal, and a dislike of flying long distances at night has even led me to crack The Great Pacific Code. (It is impossible to fly all the way from California to the Antipodes by day. Or rather, it is impossible to those – almost all of mankind – who lack my skill with timetables; *I* have found not one way, but a variety of ways, in which the trick can be done.)

I don't know what my fascination with timetables means for my character. The obvious answer is that it represents an obsession with the passage of time, which grows stronger as I grow older; but the obvious answer is wrong, for I have had the obsession since I was a youth to whom the very idea of growing older was an absurdity. Let us just say that I enjoy timetables, from the vast world-comprehensive airline volume (four inches thick) to the pleasant fictions of the British Rail version, and leave the subject there.

And leave it for a much more uncomfortable subject. Some way from Strasbourg, in Duttlenheim, I had an appointment with a goose-farmer, and *he* had an appointment with the man who does the *gavage* – that is, the force-feeding of the ducks and geese which produces *pâté de foie gras*. And here I was, at the farm (a handsome farmhouse, incidentally, I guessed from the very best part of the nineteenth century). The first preconception to fall was the popular belief (which I had anyway suspected was a legend) that Strasbourg geese are nailed through one webbed foot to the floor; so horrible is their ordeal, the story goes, that otherwise they would seek any means to escape. There was not a nail to be seen, nor a nail-hole in any webbed foot, and when I raised the question directly, the farmer smiled as one who had been asked if Father Christmas really comes down the chimney.

I started at the beginning, with a peep into the incubator, where the chicks were actually popping out of their shells. (I learned that the temperature of the incubator was the same as that of the human body – are we now to be told that we are kin to the geese as well as the Great Apes?) Then, moving from shed to shed, I saw them at all stages, from infancy to maturity. At the shed containing the geese which were no longer chicks but not yet fully grown, I moved gently in among them, and they responded with a kind of surrealist ballet; there were about

43 *The Lutine Bell: rung when someone breaks the bank* 44 Rien ne va plus? Geht's nicht mehr!

300 of them, and they moved in a single mass away from me, towards the back of the pen, like an army marching in step and doing, without doubt, the goose-step. When they came up against the back wall, with me still in careful pursuit, they turned about (I half expected to hear the word of command), and flowed down the pen, parting to go round me, as the water of a river flows round a rock. They were plainly very nervous creatures, whence, I take it, the implication of one who is reported to be unable to say 'boo' to a goose; a goose being the most extreme form of something it is not difficult to say boo to.

The goose farmer was gruff in his manner, but clearly a sympathetic figure. He told me that *pâté de foie gras* had been invented for Louis XIV, by his chef (possibly another legend, though he swore it was historical), and that the French and others had been eating it ever since, as indeed I knew well, for I must have consumed many kilos in my time.

Geese, I discovered with surprise, will come when they are called, though not by me. The farmer's colleague, bidden to demonstrate his powers of goose-summoning, knelt down in a field at the end of which was a substantial gaggle, a hundred or more, and embarked on a strange chant, which sounded like rapid repetitions of (pronounced as French, of course) 'gon, gon, gon, gon, gon, gon'. To my astonishment they came trotting up in a body; I was by then squatting beside him, and the geese surged all around us, entirely ignoring the stranger, presumably because the familiar figure was there to give them reassurance. He picked one up and gave it to me to hold; the creature simply sat on my lap as though it was a cat (it was warm like a cat too), and submitted without struggling to being stroked; I even stood up, cradling it in the crook of my arm, and it did not seem to mind that either, though there was no sign that it was enjoying it as a cat does when it is tickled under the chin.

He surprised me further, when I enquired about the exact nature of the call he made to bring the geese running; he said that it didn't matter what words he pronounced, they responded only to the sound of his voice, and he demonstrated it by chanting various forms of gibberish, which proved as magnetic as his original call. But all this entertainment constituted only the curtain-raiser to the real drama. And the curtain was about to rise, because the *gavage* man had arrived.

The *gavage* is now mechanised, but the principle presumably goes back to the chef of Louis Quatorze. The *gavageur* (or *gavagiste*?) entered the first of a row of pens, each of which held some twenty or thirty birds. He shooed them all to one end, then seated himself on a chair, forming a barrier enclosing them. Then he plucked one forth from the mass, and held it firmly between his knees. Then he reached up to a contraption hanging from the roof on a swinging arm (it ran along on a rail, so that he could continue to use it as he moved from pen to pen across the shed), and as he did so he extended the bird's neck. Pulling the contraption, which ended in a kind of funnel, set it going; as it began to emit corn, he thrust the narrow, spout end of the funnel deep down the bird's throat, and the machine did the rest, because at the open end of the funnel a paddle was going round and round, pushing the corn down the funnel, through the spout, and into the bird. When he judged that – there is no other way of putting it – the bird was full, he slipped the funnel-spout out of its throat; the funnel sprang up and the machinery cut out. The full bird was pushed to the other end of the pen, another bird was pulled out of the gaggle and held between his knees, and the process began again.

It was not a sight for the squeamish, not even the slightly squeamish. The birds did not struggle while the *gavage* was actually going on; nor did they seem to be choking. When they were released, however, and pushed away from the gavaging-stool, they looked stunned – as well they might, I suppose. But it was noticeable that when they had recovered somewhat, there was no sign of their trying to eject the corn from their gullets; on the contrary, they were clearly gobbling down the last grains. All the same, the question had to be asked, and I asked it of the farmer: is this not cruel, indefensibly cruel?

He said, firmly, that it was not. What happened to the liver was not a disease, like cirrhosis, and was not in itself painful. I pressed him on the point, saying that in England they will never believe it, and he thereupon embarked upon a spirited and very robust defence of the whole thing, not saying that it is an ancient custom and the result is delicious, thus implying that the feelings of the ducks and geese were of no significance, but insisting, in detail, that it was not harmful, and castigating those who pronounced on the subject without knowing anything about it. (He didn't point out, which he might have done, that we kill and eat ducks and geese, irrespective of the condition of their livers, and the distinction between the carcase and the liver is too fine to be seen.)

I was back to the dilemma first met with on the deer-hunt. Is there room to stand between vegetarianism and eating *pâté de foie gras*? I marked time by saying to the farmer that there was a great deal of hypocrisy in the argument (not all on one side), that at any rate we could presumably agree that we could either complain about *foie gras* or eat it, but not both (to which he readily assented), and that it seemed to me that even if the processes of *foie gras* are inexcusably cruel, they are only more cruel in degree than raising living creatures (however humanely) to be killed (however humanely) for our tables. (The vegetarian, incidentally, can call *me* a hypocrite or a brute – though not, I think, both – but he would spoil his case by calling the huntsmen hypocrites.) And of course we can see only through our own eyes and feel only through our own feelings; what was happening to the birds in the *gavage* seemed horrible and painful, and so it might have been, but it does not at all follow necessarily that something that would cause us pain and revulsion would do so to another kind of creature; if we condemn, as I do, the fox-hunter for saying that the fox enjoys being hunted, we must nevertheless keep in view the possibility that the goose doesn't mind being stuffed.

At the end of the afternoon's *gavage*, I was no nearer resolving my dilemma than I had been at the end of the hunting. I *think* we must be vegetarian or carnivorous; that is, I do not think we can defend meat-eating by saying we do not eat battery chickens or battery calves, or caviare or *foie gras*, but we nevertheless do eat meat, provided our qualms are allayed. That argument seems to offer only the worst of both worlds. But where we can find, or even seek with hope of finding, the best, I still do not know. A feeble answer, no doubt; but all I can manage.

Early in the morning, I went to the Strasbourg barge auction, which is an auction not of barges, but of barge cargoes. A room full of bargees might be a rather forbidding sight, but these men were as jolly as could be, all of them straight out of the Marcel Pagnol Marseilles trilogy. The system used by the auctioneer combined ancient ritual and modern technology; a marker climbed up a ladder to chalk progress on a blackboard, and at the same time an amplified telephone hook-up with Mulhouse kept everybody informed on how the bidding was going up-river.

Talking to these weather-beaten men, I quickly discovered that they are a very independent breed. Almost all were the owners of the barges they piloted, but even the freelances, skippers for different firms, make their own timetables. They will not be constrained by anything but the wind and weather, and clearly love their waterborne life. The little bar across the road was thronged with them when the auction ended, with shake-hands obligatory even among men who half an hour ago had been standing side by side in the auction room and chatting to each other between bids. Nobody seemed particularly put out or overjoyed at the failure or success of his bid, but I suppose that the placid life of a barge breeds a philosophical type of bargee, and anyway the auctions take place every other day, which gives plenty of opportunity for a bidder beaten today to succeed the day after tomorrow. I asked one of the bargees if it had been a normal day, and he said no, it was busier than usual.

In one of A. P. Herbert's *Misleading Cases*, a bargee is prosecuted for not sending his children to school, and is triumphantly acquitted; the magistrate says that living on the barge, and helping in the work, the children will learn such valuable skills as navigation, and they will have instilled into them such admirable precepts as the duty of any sailor to go to the help of a vessel in distress. Such knowledge, together with the healthy outdoor life that being on a barge entails, is far better and more useful, and far more of a real education, than any amount of knowledge of the dates of the Roman Emperors.

I thought of this as I travelled, slowly, evenly and majestically, on the *Fleurie*, the barge of M. Myriam Bouret, who was plying from Strasbourg to Rotterdam with a cargo of grain and tobacco. I had met him at the auction; he had loaded swiftly, and set off at dawn; shaking the sleep out of my head, I went aboard. On the way, with only the first glimmerings of light in the sky, I was pursued through the streets of Strasbourg by the delightful smell of baking, and particularly of baking croissants; French bread gets stale notoriously quickly, but it is equally notorious that that doesn't matter, because they bake it freshly several times a day, starting, evidently, at six in the morning.

'Batten down the hatches'; this nautical injunction is what ships' captains are supposed, by landlubbers like me, to shout to their crew when bad weather impends; that, too, came to mind when I saw the hatches, for they were battened down with impenetrable neatness against anything the weather might send, not excluding a hurricane. The barge was not only shipshape, it was also meticulously clean, yet in answer to the very first question I asked him – 'I suppose you wouldn't take coal or cement, or any kind of dirty cargo?' – he said that he would take anything at all, and that he had frequently taken coal, adding (and it was clearly a matter for pride) that he banked on cleaning the holds for the next cargo, even if the exchange was coal to corn, in a single day. And he demonstrated that principle, together with the independence bred by the bargee's *ad hoc* existence, by saying that whatever there was at Rotterdam that needed taking to Strasbourg, he would take it: 'C'est le métier.'

I had plenty of time, as the *Fleurie* chugged along at a steady fourteen miles an hour, to get to know the life of a bargee and his family. The Bourets had four children, a boy of perhaps seventeen, a girl a year or so younger, a second girl of eleven, and a third, Sophie, who was six. (Sophie and I became good friends, the ice being broken at the outset when she invited me to play with her remote-controlled pick-up truck.)

The first surprise was the discovery that the Bourets had no house or apartment anywhere on shore; the barge was their home as well as their factory or office, and the living quarters immediately testified to the fact. Mme Roseline Bouret was a placid and motherly soul; she had organised and decorated the family's miniature dwelling – pot-plants on the shelves and cacti on the windowsills – with no concession to the water that for ever surrounded them, other than the essential task of ensuring that everything was stowed away when not in use, and that all cupboards were firmly latched shut lest whatever they contained should emerge in bad weather and roll about the floor.

This was a land-based home that happened to spend its time going up and down rivers and canals, but into it she had crammed everything that any French housewife on shore would, starting, naturally, with the dining-table and the kitchen, and continuing with the gingham curtains. It reminded me, particularly the low ceiling, of the old 'prefabs', those portable boxes that were hastily constructed at the end of the Second World War to replace, temporarily, some of the housing stock that had been destroyed by bombs. (They were supposed to last for only a year or two, until the public housing programme had ensured that the entire nation had a permanent roof over its head. Alas for good intentions and politicians' distant horizons – 'If wishes were horses, beggars would ride' – for many of the prefabs were still in use decades later.)

Sitting in the wheelhouse, watching the river go effortlessly by, I picked up the book of charts from which the boat was navigated. It was an extraordinary volume; the route was described in exhaustive detail, sometimes foot by foot; the tone was that of someone giving instructions to a blind man negotiating a minefield. Surprised, I questioned M. Bouret on the hazards of the Rhine, having convinced myself that all he had to do was to avoid hitting another vessel and to shut his ears to the Lorelei's temptations. 'Pas du tout,' came the firm reply; it seems that the Rhine is a particularly difficult and dangerous stream; the currents, the rocks, the depth – all must be charted and followed with the very greatest exactitude, and although the huge, slim wheel was never turned more than a few inches at a time, there was hardly a minute when it could be left alone, and hardly a second when the concentration could be allowed to flag. I wondered whether the Rhine ever became really rough, and if so whether the barge did much pitching and rolling – M. Bouret's thousand tons did not seem very much to me, compared to the huge triple-decker pleasure-steamers. Again, 'Pas du tout.' M. Bouret's pride and joy, I discovered, sat far lower in the water than the pleasure-boats (and there was no mistaking the contempt in his voice for these idle triremes, bobbing like elegant corks in the water of life, and afraid of rolling up their sleeves and getting their hands dirty, while the real business, of real life, was carried on aboard his barge).

The first lock loomed up. If anything summarises and typifies the life of a barge, it is the locks. For there is no way of hurrying a lock; the water-level outside must match exactly the level inside, and the water pours in (or out, depending on which way the boat is going) at its own speed, which is the speed of the river or the canal on which the lock stands. The massive gates, holding back the waters of one of the world's mightiest rivers, let go slowly and reluctantly, then wait patiently until they can swallow another vessel and digest it at the same, unhurried pace; the ritual symbolises the barge life itself, and gradually I began to understand why such a life can appeal so powerfully to those of the appropriate temperament. I thought of Siddhartha, Hermann Hesse's Everyman, passing through every variety of experience, from the heights to the depths, discovering that they were all vanity of vanities, and ending his days with the old ferryman who has never stirred from the spot, watching the river – every drop of water eternally different and eternally the same – roll on, ever unchanging and ever changed, to the distant sea.

After lunch, I volunteered to share the washing-up with Cindy, the eldest girl. The younger two went to school in Strasbourg and lived there *en pension*; the boy worked full-time on the *Fleurie*; Cindy herself went to school at Dunkirk and lived there with her grandparents. Would her brother follow in his father's footsteps, as M. Bouret had followed in *his* father's? 'Absolument,' she said, 'c'est certain,' then, clearly feeling that she had committed her brother too far, added, 'je crois.' But was this the life for her, too? 'Ah, non,' she said, 'absolument pas,' and this time there was no qualification.

Yet they seemed a contented and harmonious family; the children at school while the parents are for ever cruising the rivers might seem an odd arrangement, but it is no odder than the life of an English family with the children away at boarding school. And in fact the Bouret children, at least the younger two, must see more of their parents than English boarders of theirs, for although M. Bouret's determination to follow the cargo wherever it goes means that he and his wife never know when they will be back at Strasbourg, they are certainly there more often than English parents would be likely to visit their children at school.

Even in the middle of a river, and the river Rhine, too, there is no escaping one familiar fact of modern life. Suddenly, a little green cutter materialised at the side of the *Fleurie*, flying the German flag and the symbol of the German Customs, and the revenue man skipped nimbly aboard from his mobile Customs Post. I was taken aback; I had supposed that if the Customs had been interested in the cargo of a regular Rhine barge, the interest would be perfunctory, and confined to a friendly exchange of shouts and an occasional shake-hand at a lock. *Pas du tout*; the Customs' visit to the *Fleurie* involved a long and detailed conversation, the production and examination of many papers, the ticking and stamping of the same, and more questions to finish with. The cutter finally came alongside, the Customs officer leaped as neatly off as he had on, with a parting call of 'Bon voyage,' and the motor-boat sped off after their next quarry.

I asked M. Bouret if he had ever thought of real sea-faring, across a real sea; he said he had often thought about it but in the end never put his thoughts into action, though he surprised me by saying that the *Fleurie* had been built in Canada, so at least *it* had crossed the Atlantic even if he had not. Besides, he said, the *Fleurie* was not licensed for any but inland waterways: 'Même la Manche?' I asked. 'Même la Manche.'

In parting, I asked him what he did in his own holidays. 'Je cherche le soleil.' I asked whether he liked to get his feet on solid ground, and he said he did, but when he gets into his car and drives off he feels that he is only really easy in his mind if he can see water; if there is nothing but fields, 'Je suis perdu.'

Here was another happy man, with an equally happy wife. The slow crawl along even water plainly soothed and calmed them; the

45 Europe's finest

5

46

47

unceasing vibration of the engines was their music; the changing cargo and the changing seasons gave them all the variety they wanted. M. Bouret's life is not quite the life of Christian Patt, but his, too, is a life spent in doing what he likes to do and what he does well, which must be the secret recipe for contentment. And the Siddhartha symbolism is rounded off; M. Bouret is a happy man because he is doing what he likes, but I felt sure, as I went towards the gangplank and shook hands with him and his wife, and – very gravely – with little Sophie, that his happiness is completed by the fact that he spends his life on the slow, flowing, perpetually renewed water of the Rhine.

46 Without whom this book would not have been written 47 Fleet Street's newest technology

8

Rhinemaidens In My Sauna

IF I HAD nothing else to show for this journey, it would still have been worth making for my discovery, in the course of it, of the solution (which had eluded me all my life) to the problem of how Baden-Baden got its tautological name. It was not because it once had a mayor who stuttered, nor because a deaf traveller had stopped to ask the way, nor because some medieval scribe had a hangover so fierce that he was seeing double. The answer is simpler and less romantic: Baden-Baden took unto itself a hyphen in order to distinguish itself from the lesser resort of Baden.

The obvious comparison is with Bath, not only because they are both spa towns, but because of the grace of the buildings and streets, the easy, civilised atmosphere, the visible and invisible links with a greater past. Just as it is possible, in Bath, to conjure up the days of Beau Brummel and Beau Nash, so it is possible in Baden-Baden, to conjure up the era of its greatest *réclame* – roughly 1870 to the First World War – and imagine that the future Edward VII and his raffish crew were still prodigiously eating and drinking and gambling and wenching and then sweating it all off in the baths, preparatory to starting it all over again in the evening.

I may as well begin with the baths. I had never had a sauna before, nor even a massage; I have never troubled the attendants in the 'Fitnessraum' which is now standard in German and Austrian hotels (and, more and more, elsewhere too); I have never seen the appeal of plunging alternately into hot pools and cold pools. But when in Baden-Baden . . .

I had an ample variety of baths to choose from: the Roman-Irish Baths, the Baths of Caracalla (in the arena of that name in Rome they perform outdoor opera, their speciality being *Aida* with real elephants in the Grand March), and the Friedrichsbad, which is, I gathered, the oldest and, in Baden-Baden's heyday, the most fashionable too. Well, if it was good enough for Tum-Tum, it was good enough for me.

I confess that I hesitated when I discovered that it was a mixed sauna; the Prince of Wales was certainly partial to naked ladies, but only in private, and I have always thought that that was the right attitude. However, the Friedrichsbad saunas are mixed, and I could hardly demand that they should abandon decades of the custom solely for me.

Before I got to the naked ladies, I became convinced that I would not live to see them. The massage, a vital part of the experience, would have made the Gestapo torturers envious of their ingenuity with which it had been devised; what feels like boiling water is flung over the victim, who is lying face down on a bench, and he is then assaulted by a man with a scrubbing-brush that seems to have nails instead of bristles; not only was it designed to rip the skin whole from the sufferer's body, but it is plonked down on him with such force that several times I was convinced that my spine had broken under the impact.

Then there was a succession of hot rooms, the hottest registering 140 degrees (Fahrenheit, though it felt like Centigrade), and after that a series of pools, which is where the naked ladies came in – five of them (even Wagner specified only three Rhinemaidens), and some of them were certainly pretty enough to sport with in the waves. Unfortunately, only one of the pools was suitable for sporting; one contained water that would have had Professor Kurti, at Cambridge, pricking up his ears excitedly, because it felt as though it had already attained what the scientist had been seeking for decades – Absolute Zero, or minus 273 degrees. The next pool was tepid, but after the Kurti version it felt as though it would have had a lobster ready for the plate in ten minutes. Only in the last pool, which was – and, after the other two, felt – pleasantly warm, could I feel relaxed, though the naked ladies, who were used to all this, seemed to have been relaxed throughout.

The final stage was the best; the condemned man is reprieved at the last moment, and led to a cubicle with a comfortable couch in it, where he is wrapped in luxurious towels and permitted to sleep. I awoke feeling – well, feeling what? Exhausted, certainly; stretched (as in rack); genuinely exercised, in the sense of the muscles feeling less tense than usual; but for me, at any rate, there was not what sauna devotees proclaim as its greatest boon, the feeling of blissful contentment, of having shed all the cares of the outside world and been armed against them for the moment when the outside world must be re-entered. It had certainly been interesting; but I left with no great wish to repeat the experience. In that attitude, however, I found myself in a minority, for I learned that fully half the adult population of Baden-Baden has a season-ticket for these baths, and if you consider the range of other baths in the town, and the number of visitors who still go there to 'take the waters', it would seem that the whole town spends its time, day and night, splashing in and out of pools hot, cold and tepid, and being assaulted, without hope of a successful prosecution of the assailant, between pools.

The Casino, I decided, was more my style, and so it proved. Baden-Baden's gaming rooms must still be the most elegant and luxurious in the world. The whole place seemed to be made of chandeliers, gilding, painted ceilings (covered in the varnish of a century's nicotine), lavish murals, dinner-jackets and mink wraps.

Not much has changed; Edward and his cronies played baccarat, also known as chemin-de-fer ('Never stand on a five' is said to have been His Royal Highness's only contribution to philosophy), but roulette is now by far the most popular of gambling games in European casinos, and probably in American ones, too, though gamblers there are much keener on blackjack and dice than are European ones. Now, as then, the management of the Baden-Baden Casino are as discreet as deaf-mutes; now, as then, the croupiers watch ruin and triumph with the same impassive faces; now, as then, those in whose blood the fever runs swear that they will linger only for half-a-dozen turns of the wheel and bet not more than a tenth of the money in their pockets; now, as then, they break both halves of the vow. The German for 'Faites vos jeux', incidentally is 'Bitte das Spiel zu machen', and for 'Rien ne va plus', 'Nichts geht mehr'.

A stroll round Baden-Baden was instructive. It is a backwater, certainly, but not *only* a backwater, not even only an elegant backwater. The place is, again, like Bath, fully alive. You can always tell by the shops; in Baden-Baden they are genuinely distinguished – designed and stocked with good taste, the goods (jewellery, furs, carpets, clothes, antiques) of the best, and the shoppers clearly at home in them. (One shop was called Münchner Moden, or 'Munich Fashions', an interesting reflection of the fact that Munich has long been thought of – rightly, I am sure – as Germany's smartest and most advanced city.)

Baden-Baden clearly has a life of its own; the throng in the pretty pedestrian street were not just sauntering, and the greengrocer in the middle had laid out his boxes of tomatoes, cucumbers, onions, avocados, oranges and lemons as a giant's palette – and a giant with an artistic bent, too. Nor was entertainment missing; a real hurdy-gurdy man wandered down the street, with a real monkey on his shoulder.

In the Cloister of the Holy Grave there is a monument to a Crusader, in whose commemoration the monastic order who tend the Grave was founded; a local lad made good. His name certainly rings down the centuries as one of the greatest figures of that strange, magnificent obsession with the recapture of the holy places of Christendom, but the name itself – Gottfried von Bouillon – could hardly have been more unfortunate. I had always felt that a man called Godfrey Soup, though he might make a devoted husband and father, and in his profession a conscientious minor civil servant or expert on *incunabula*, could never aspire to lead a Crusade. Yet Godfrey Soup he was, and as Godfrey Soup he donned the red cross and inspired his men to heroic feats by doing heroic feats himself. What's in a name?

Baden-Baden is plainly terrified that its visitors may think the town insufficiently exciting; I collected half a sack of bulletins, leaflets, town programmes, invitations to seminars, conferences, lectures and guided walks. There can hardly be an hour in the week with nothing happening in the town, from a weekend learning English ('It must be recognised, however, that a weekend is not a long period and that results will be considerably better in cases where clients can find time to attend further seminars'), to a Bingo-Abend in the Kurhaus, and from a botanical tour in the park to a reading by Martin Walser from his new novel.

But this solicitude, the care taken to ensure that visitors to Baden-Baden shall never feel bored, ill-at-ease or disgruntled, is a very serious matter; it is the philosophy of the town, and not only because obviously it is the visitors who keep the town prosperous; the concern to look after those who honour the place with their visits is genuine. And nowhere in Baden-Baden is the philosophy so meticulously and unwaveringly followed, and nowhere does it result in greater success, than in the mighty centre of luxury, comfort, pleasure, care, food, wine, relaxation, exercise and soft, deep sleep on soft, deep pillows that is called the Brenner's Park Hotel.

I have said that I believe Brenner's to be the best luxury hotel in Europe; certainly there can be few other contenders for the title.

Suvretta House at St Moritz, perhaps, the Kempinski in Berlin, Michel Guérard's gastronomic palace at Eugénie-les-Bains (but the rooms are too small), the Baumanière, Schloss Fuschl near Salzburg, the Cipriani in Venice (but it faces the wrong way); one or two in Paris might still qualify, and I think Britain has at least a *proxime accessit* in Chewton Glen; the list is inevitably short. But however much it is further shortened, Brenner's will remain on it.

I have always thought that the perfect symbol of a grand hotel which pays attention to the details was The Great Shoelace Trick at a strange hotel on Britain's south coast, called Bailiffscourt. (It still exists, but I have not been there for many years, and have no idea of what kind of place it now is.) It was strange because it looked like a medieval monastery, and most visitors must have assumed that it was indeed a medieval monastery adapted to a hotel, like the San Domenico Palace in Taormina, but the truth was that it had been purpose-built. Anyway, the Shoelace Trick worked like this: the guest would put his shoes outside his room for polishing (that in itself dates the period to at least thirty years ago, for there is hardly a hotel in Britain, and precious few elsewhere, which still has a 'Boots'). The staff assigned to the polishing would inspect the shoelaces (that also helps with the date, for very few men's shoes have laces now), and if either of them was in the least frayed or worn, or missing a tag, a new pair of laces would be inserted. The cost of that tiny service would have been almost too small to measure – a penny or two at most. But the goodwill the hotel gained in return was almost too large to measure; one proof of that claim, after all, is that I have remembered the trick for something like a third of a century.

At Brenner's Park they are not troubled by shoelaces, for, as I say, the shoelace has long been disappearing, and will soon be put on the list of endangered species; but they have a Great Shoe Trick of their own which rivals the shoelace system. At Brenner's the guest does not need to put his shoes outside the door; it is the chambermaid's duty to inspect them, and if she detects the smallest sign of a scuff or stain, *she* puts them in the corridor for the Boots.

Much of the goodwill generated by a fine hotel is, objectively examined, very easy to acquire; the flower on the breakfast trolley is nothing in itself, but it brightens up the trolley, the room and the guest himself, and presumably costs little more than the shoelaces of long ago. When a hotel guest rings the housekeeper and asks for someone to collect the laundry, he naturally wishes someone to appear quickly; but the difference between five minutes and ten is unlikely to worry him. At Brenner's, however, *they* worry; twice, I rang for the laundry service, and both times the knock on the door followed so hard upon my call that I could not believe it was connected with it. (But even Brenner's is beaten by the Mandarin. I once rang for the laundry service there; a youth appeared at my door exactly three minutes later, *and apologised for the delay*.)

It is easy to say that the mark of the best hotels is that they think of what their guests want and supply it before it is asked for. The really interesting question is: how is *that* trick worked? It seemed to me that the easiest way to find out was to ask the man responsible for it, so I went to talk to Richard Schmitz, Managing Director of the Brenner's Park.

It had occurred to me that such a man in such a position would have – must have – a system. What I had not foreseen was that he would have something that it is not absurd to call a philosophy. To start with, he spoke of his staff, without artificiality or obtrusiveness, as 'a family'; it was clear that not only does he regard his staff as his family, but his staff share the feeling. Again, easy to say, but what does it mean? Without drama, Herr Schmitz told me that not long ago a young unmarried girl among the Brenner's staff came to him in great distress, having found that she was pregnant; she could not bring herself to tell her parents or any of her relatives, or even her friends, but she could and did throw herself on the head of the Family Brenner, to seek the help she needed (and received).

It was not difficult for me to see why; Schmitz is clearly an outstanding man as well as hotelier – a great charm of manner and many layers of warmth, understanding and wisdom beneath it. His care for his family is plainly inseparable from his constant desire that the members of it shall work incessantly for the very highest standards of service. 'Perfection,' he said, 'is unattainable. But we must strive for it every day.'

Yet, in the hotel business as in any other, to stand still is to fall behind. I asked him how he kept up with competition; more and more hotels are installing more and more facilities (the first safari-park cannot be far away), and he, too, must be in this race, and always near the front. 'Yes,' he said; 'twenty years ago' (I was astonished that it was so recently) 'a hotel needed only three things: good rooms, a good restaurant and a good lobby.' No longer; now, more than one type of restaurant is essential. So is a swimming-pool; 'You couldn't run a luxury hotel today without a swimming-pool.' Is swimming really so popular? His answer was surprising; 'No,' he said, 'lots of the facilities we have to have are not used by three-quarters of our guests – but they won't come if such facilities are not offered.' So the fitness-room (some of them today are gleaming, fully equipped professional gymnasiums) is essential, as are conference-rooms, in-house entertainment, cocktail-parties and excursions. (But he still, surprisingly, resists credit cards.)

Another surprise: 'Hotel guests do not read notices put up in the public rooms.' So how does he communicate with guests? Every night, when the breakfast-order is collected from the doorknob, a hotel bulletin is hung in its place, describing all the events of the day, whether it is a trip by pleasure-steamer on the Rhine or a musical evening in the *salon*.

And his biggest problem? He breathed in, long and hard. 'You can never – never, in any circumstances or for any reason – be rude to a guest. Some guests are impossible; they set out to make life difficult for the staff; well, we decide that next time they telephone or write for a reservation, we will say we are very sorry, the hotel is full at those dates, but we cannot be rude or angry. In the most extreme circumstances I can ask a guest to leave, but even then I cannot shout or lose my temper: I say, Madam,* it is clear that my hotel cannot meet your wishes or serve you as you need to be served; therefore a taxi is at the door, your luggage will be brought down as soon as it is packed, and of course we will telephone to any hotel of your choice to make a reservation for you. But still we cannot be rude.' 'But that,' I said, 'must be very frustrating; you must sometimes want to break a chair over their heads. How do you get it out of your system?'

This time he breathed out. Every Thursday, he explained, with never an exception, he goes to the Friedrichsbad, has a full sauna and massage – it lasts about an hour and a half – and the cares of the hotel, the frustrations, big and little, the worry and concern, all slip away with the suds and the perspiration, and he leaves refreshed and restored in body, mind and soul. And to back up the baths, though it cannot be so regular, is his visit, gun in hand, to the forest. Richard Schmitz is a huntsman (he must have one of the 3000 licences that I learned about from my friends in the Black Forest); boar, deer, hares, anything suitable. But he talked about it, curiously, in the tones not of a hunter but

* Or 'Sir'? He *said* Madam.

of a fisherman; it was the same equanimity, the same patience, the same ultimate indifference to the prize. 'I take my hunting chair to the forest,' he said, 'and perhaps I will sit all day and not get anything. But it doesn't matter; it makes me calm and rested, and that is better than coming home with a deer.'

I suppose it is; but I suppose even more strongly that Richard Schmitz is another of the serene, contented men of the Rhine I had met on this journey, that although he did need the sauna and the forest murmurs, he needed them to restore his equilibrium, not to create it. He, too, had got hold of a corner of the secret; he, too, was a skilled craftsman, deeply happy in his work, knowing not only that man must earn his bread in the sweat of his brow, but that it is possible to derive from that knowledge a more important kind of knowledge altogether. If the Brenner's Park Hotel *is* the finest in Europe, it is no wonder, with Richard Schmitz in charge.

Next day, the doorknob bulletin announced an afternoon violin recital in the hotel *salon*, by Jenny Abel. Talking to her, I discovered that she was yet another pupil of Max Rostal, who must have worked with practically every leading fiddler in Britain (and elsewhere – he had a professorial post in Germany for many years) for two or three generations; all the pupils of his I have ever met, starting with the Amadeus Quartet, have all spoken of him in terms of gratitude, admiration and affection. He must have been one of the greatest of teachers, but I remembered him best for one little oddity; I reminded Jenny Abel of his habit of always playing a concerto from the score – in those days he was almost unique in doing so, but it is now, though still uncommon, not quite so rare. I never knew whether he had a bad memory, or whether it was some kind of psychological need for a security that could be obtained only if he had the music in front of him. She did not know, either, but she amazed and delighted me by telling me that Rostal was still alive – well into his eighties and in very good health.

Among the audience for the recital, I met the lady who runs the house (now a miniature museum) in Baden-Baden where Brahms spent part of the year for nine years in a row. I suppose it could be said that Brahms went where Clara Schumann went; it is one of the strangest and most touching of love stories, what with Schumann losing his sanity and Clara being older than Brahms (surely material for a film, or better still a musical, though I have never heard of either being done), but it is strange mainly because it is almost impossible to imagine Brahms as a passionate man, on fire for love. Perhaps it is the beard and the cigar; perhaps it is because we know about his settled bachelor existence, Clara or no Clara; but my theory is that generations of English-speaking music-lovers have had their image of Brahms created and sustained by the portrait of Brahms in the old *Oxford Companion to Music*, the work of Percy Scholes. 'Scholes', as it was always known, was one of the best single-volume musical compendiums ever published; it does what William Rose Benét did for literature with his *A Reader's Encyclopaedia*. But anyone who cut his musical teeth on Scholes (and they must be many, for it lasted for many years and went through many editions, until, only a year or two ago, it was finally laid to rest and replaced by a new and excellent two-volume version by Denis Arnold) will remember those lamentable drawings of composers by Batt that are strewn through the book.

Batt was a dreadful artist, but an extraordinarily powerful one; not just Brahms, but a dozen composers have had an image fixed for ever in the minds of many thousands – millions, perhaps – by the decisive images conjured up by Batt, together with the caption beneath the pictures, which impressed the image still more firmly, with its anecdote or summary. For Brahms, the picture was of the composer pouring himself a cup of coffee from a kind of primitive percolator; the caption told us that he would never trust his landlady to make the coffee, because none would make it as strong as he liked it.

Yet he did love Clara, I dare say no less passionately than Robert did, and history, whether it is Batt's fault or not, has been unkind to him. And he could be romantic in other ways, too; when a lady at a ball asked him to autograph her fan, he wrote the opening bars of the *Blue Danube*, and added, 'Unfortunately, not by Johannes Brahms.' Poor Brahms.

To Karlsruhe by train; another city which belies the claim that the tram is disappearing, or even has disappeared, from the cities of Europe. Karlsruhe ('Charles's peace') commemorates the Emperor Charles V, but I have long since abandoned any attempt to remember, or even understand, the complexities of the vanished dynasties of Germany. Throughout the eighteenth century, and much of the nineteenth, Emperors were five pfennigs a bushel; Dukes, Margraves, Princes, Electors were to be found on every street corner; Palatinates, Duchies, fiefdoms of every kind crowded the map; with what relief must the average citizen have greeted the unification of Germany!

A mousy little town, I thought; provincial, anyway. Not without heart, though; a citizen offered me shelter under his umbrella when it came on to rain and he discovered we were going in the same direction, and he even gave me a guided tour along the way until our routes diverged. They diverged hard by a department store, in which I bought an umbrella of my own, fearing that I might not get a lift under somebody else's next time. But here there was another demonstration of the modern world being too clever for its own good. Not wanting to buy a big and cumbersome brolly, I found one of the collapsible kind, which folds into a sheath only a foot or so long, but opens up into quite a sizable area of protection.

That, at any rate, is the theory; the practice is somewhat different. There was no problem about opening it; a touch of a button and it sprang ferociously apart, nearly taking my thumb off as it did so. And certainly it did its job of keeping the rain away. The difficulties began when I tried to get on a tram with it. There was, of course, no magic button that would snap it shut and folded; indeed, there was no way of closing it at all except by brute force exerted by grabbing the ferrule and squashing the ribs together, then pushing the telescopic action until the handle slid back into the closed position. The trouble with *that* was that it did not lock; the moment the unwary owner relaxed his hand's pressure on the bunched ribs it sprang open with an even angrier snarl, and all was to do again. Moreover, it was, remember, raining; that was the only reason I was dickering with umbrellas at all. That meant that the fabric was wet, and cold as well, making the operation even more difficult and unpleasant. Eventually, by holding the covering tube in my teeth, thus freeing both hands for the fight to get the thing closed, I managed to shove the ferrule and a bit more inside the tunnel before it exploded open again, and thereafter it was only a matter of forcing the rest of the damned thing into the sheath.

That raised another mystery. The man who designed that umbrella was, to put it with a moderation I did not feel at the time, unfit for his job; he had not thought about what he was doing, beyond the point at which the umbrella opened, at all. He should never have been allowed to meddle with things beyond his understanding; but his incompetence was nothing compared to that of the manufacturers who put it into production without discovering that it was useless, and the retailers who sold it without finding out that it was unfit for anything except hitting burglars on the head with.

Now the terrible truth about our world is that that sort of thing is happening every day; goods are manufactured and sold without anyone testing or examining them to find out whether they work, whether they can be made to work, whether they meet their specifications. The most extreme example of this tendency is provided by the manufacturers of computers and word processors, in the form of the books of instruction, almost all of which are incompetent, illiterate and impossible to follow; but anyone reading these words will be able to think of half a dozen examples at once. (If you are *very* seriously lacking in imagination, here are two starters; the hot-air hand-dryer and the cardboard milk-carton.) And yet we are told that we live in an age of consumerism!

Karlsruhe had a remarkable vista; the view was a full mile long, starting a little way from the railway station and running absolutely straight thereafter, until it was closed by the Castle. Just before the Schlossplatz a strange red sandstone pyramid reared up in the middle of the street; beneath it lay the founder of the city. But not far away I found the birthplace of a man who commanded no armies and ruled no subjects, but who had, and continues to have, an effect on the world that very few indeed of the princes of the earth have ever matched; Karlsruhe is the city that gave birth to Carl Benz, father of the motor-car. I looked at my useless umbrella, and thought dark thoughts.

The rain had stopped; I fought the monster to a standstill just in time for a bridal procession; bride and groom were in an open horse-drawn carriage, the wedding-guests followed in cars, sounding their horns as if they wanted to wake Carl Benz from his eternal nightmare of remorse. I raised my camera for a picture of the couple, and the boy indicated to the coachman that he was to stop. Then, proud of his beauty, he turned her towards me for my photograph; it was a lovely scene – coach, bowlered coachman, white lace foaming over the carriage, the girl smiling and sparkling with happiness and her cavalier content to take second place. I took my picture and gave them a salute with my umbrella; the groom raised his top-hat, so I thought that deserved another salute and called out 'Glück und Freude', whereupon the girl waved a slim hand in thanks, and the procession moved on, the sun now shining for them.

9

The Madman of Mannheim

HEIDELBERG WILL NEVER live down its reputation as the centre of student duelling. The reputation is undeserved; the weird practice was common to all German universities in the nineteenth century and much of the twentieth, and elderly bullet-headed Germans with a scar on their cheeks (who think themselves superior to the primitive Africans who cut their cheeks for tribal or initiatory reasons) are still to be found, and indeed will be found for some time to come, for student duels continued until the Second World War, and even had a spasmodic revival after it. I suppose the last vestiges disappeared in the Sixties, when students all over the world turned serious, and the German ones would have stamped out the custom as an unacceptably bourgeois and reactionary habit. Yet Heidelberg became, and remains, the place where the rest of the world believes that all day long the students, on the smallest pretext or none at all, would take sabre in hand and slice away at one another.

It does have one genuine claim to uniqueness; Heidelberg's is the oldest German university, older even than Göttingen. (If the students no longer duel, do they at least sing the old student songs? After all, if the unbending Brahms could bend sufficiently to work all the traditional ones, ending with 'Gaudeamus igitur', into his *Academic Festival Overture*, they can surely bawl them in the streets as they make their way home after an evening's carousing in the Zum Roten Ochsen. Or perhaps they no longer carouse in the Zum Roten Ochsen, or at all.) 1986 marked the 600th anniversary of the University's foundation, and the celebrations went on all year; the original founders, however, would hardly have known it, nor would even those who reorganised it at the beginning of the nineteenth century (the single building that then housed it still stands, and is still in use), for the student body is now 27,000 strong, which must make it the biggest anywhere in the Western world outside the United States; even London University has fewer students than that.

Though Heidelberg is the place where you go to have your face cut, it is also the place where – a rather more satisfactory remembrance – you can go on the Philosopher's Walk. I suppose this must be one of the most famous thoroughfares in Europe, famous not in the sense that the Champs-Elysées or the Getreidegasse or Piccadilly are famous, but because its name – Philosopher's Walk – has caught the imagination of millions who have never set eyes on Heidelberg. Nobody seems to know how it got the name – whether it was thus called because a particular philosopher would stroll along it meditating on his forthcoming *Treatise on the Sublime*, or whether its peaceful air of *rus in urbe* makes even the most pragmatic walker philosophical, or whether all the philosophers in Heidelberg lived there, rather as some London streets (Tottenham Court Road for electronic goods, Charing Cross Road for books) have become highly specialised. But whatever the origin of the name, I felt that I could hardly visit Heidelberg without doing the Philosopher's Walk.

It began with a crossing of the Neckar, one of the Rhine's most beautiful tributaries – it enters it near here – and a memorable sign announcing that I was entering *Handschuhheim*, which means 'Glovehome' (the linguistically economical Germans call gloves 'handshoes'). Whether that meant that it offered a refuge for retired or enfeebled gloves in an Old Gloves' Home, or whether, less romantically, it meant that it was the centre of the glove-making industry in Germany, was not clear. But from the Glovehome side of the river the view of the town, nestling into the hills as if for protection (and not so 'as if', for Heidelberg has had its share of invasion and pillage, culminating in its total destruction by the French in 1693), was enchanting.

The Philosopher's Walk lived up to its name. It wandered up the hill, keeping roughly parallel to the river, past handsome *bürgerlich* houses, and after a short time became a wholly pedestrian way. This was a Sunday, and I was not alone on the *Philosophenweg*; all Heidelberg, with its children and its dogs, was out for a philosophical stroll. About a third of the way along the path I paused for a rest on a bench in a pretty little flowered enclave, with a splendid view down to the river and the Old Bridge. (Strictly speaking, it is the Theodor Heuss Bridge, named after the first President of post-war Germany, but nobody in Heidelberg ever calls it that, any more than anybody in New York calls Sixth Avenue the Avenue of the Americas, or for that matter anybody in Leningrad calls the Street of the October Revolution anything but the Nevsky Prospekt. Governments and local authorities may decree, but the people take notice of what is decreed if they feel like it and not otherwise.) The bridge is a splendid sight, with its towers and its portcullised gate on the townward side, its sides bright and brave with banners; it was built in 1788, just in time to shut the town against the armies of the Revolution.

My eyrie commanded more of a view than the bridge; it showed me the castle, high on its hill, a splendid ruin looking haunted, as well it might, in view of the history it had seen in its six centuries. But it also showed me, across the river and almost on its edge, a building of such superbly harmonious proportions that it seemed as though the Golden Mean had been found. Beside me on the bench was an elderly man, clearly a Heidelberger, and I asked him what the building was. He said it was called the Marstall, and was the former arsenal of the town; it had been destroyed, with everything else, in 1693, but rebuilt as a replica of the original. Now it was the student refectory, an improbable transmogrification.

My companion turned out to be a most fitting interlocutor for a Philosopher's Walk, because it speedily became clear that he was something of a Philosopher himself. He had about as much English as I had German; between us we managed quite well. I said that the Marstall, which was a simple and undecorated building, was made memorable and beautiful by the air of peace and serenity (despite its warlike origins) given by the balance of its dimensions; but why did something as simple as a building's proportions achieve such an effect? He asked me if I was a musician; no, I said, but I am an amateur of music. Very well, he said, harmony is something that encompasses far more than music; it is at the basis of all man's understanding. I pricked up my ears at his Pythagorean exposition, for harmony in its broadest sense has for many years been for me the candle with which I have sought the truth, and my belief that the universe always inclines to harmony (which is why atonal music and action painting and similar absurdities will never be accepted by more than a few, and will anyway wither and die, lacking the nourishment of proportion) has led me to the conviction that it is and must be true of human beings too.

My new friend and I got up to continue the Philosopher's Walk. He told me that Heidelberg had been lucky in the Second World War, suffering little bomb damage; but soon we got back to our subject. Why has the instinct for harmony, which led the architects of the Marstall to its perfect proportions, become so dangerously attenuated today? After all, the Marstall's builders did not say, 'Look – if we slope the roof like *that*, and place the tower just *there*, we shall achieve such an air of harmony that a maudlin Englishman on the other side of the river five centuries from now will feel better for the sight.' I asked him if he had ever been in Britain: 'Leider, nein – und jetzt, glaub' ich, es ist zu spät.' I told him that in Bath – 'Ja, von Bath hab' ich viel gesehen' – there were houses that now changed hands for anything up to a hundred thousand pounds or even more, though they had been built, in the eighteenth century, as the cheapest form of housing for the working class; they were now prized because even *their* builders had had an instinctive grasp of form and proportion. And the houses built today, he asked; would they be worth a fortune in two hundred years? I didn't answer the question, or need to. But at that point, I came to the very winding old path down to the bridge, and explained that my timetable demanded that I broke off the Philosopher's – and now philosophical – Walk. He said he would continue to the end, that being his invariable practice, rain or shine; we shook hands and parted, harmoniously.

The path down was called the Schlangenweg, or Snake Path, because it wriggled and writhed as it descended, very uneven and at times slippery, but delightfully shady, winding through the wood that covered the hillside. Some hardier spirits passed me from time to time going up the Snake rather than down, and two, who were surely taking things rather far, actually came *jogging* up; I forbore to wish them good day lest they should feel inclined to spare much needed breath in reciprocal greeting. But near the bottom, a thought struck me.

For the first time in many years, I had spent time in the company of a German who was a stranger to me and of an age which means that he was fully adult during the Nazi regime, without asking myself, even once, the obvious question: what was he doing in those days? As I say, it was only when I had almost descended the Snake Walk that the thought obtruded, and I put it confidently from me, for my new friend had breathed the same spirit of harmony as the buildings and music and people we had been talking about; such a man, of wisdom and a benign understanding, may have done nothing heroic against Hitler, but it was inconceivable that he had done anything wrong. And here I was, on the bridge; and soon, across it.

I wandered through the streets of this perfectly preserved and restored town, picturesque but unspoilt, marvelling at the Ritterhaus, wonderfully and intricately carved, admiring the handsome Rathaus, rejoicing in a lovely pink-façaded Baroque church, delighted to learn, from a plaque on a fine, large, eighteenth-century house, that at the beginning of the nineteenth century the Brothers Boisserée, who lived there, had amassed an art collection which subsequently became the foundation of the Alte Pinakothek in Munich. Fountains, statues, well-proportioned squares, well-kept pedestrian precincts through which a tiny bus, drawn by four handsome ponies, clopped carefully with its load of sightseers; I rejoiced more and more in this splendid old place, which had defied time as bravely as it had defied the French. I wavered, in my admiration for Heidelberg, for a moment, when I came upon a hotel, right over the bottom station of the funicular that goes up to the castle, plainly brand-new and so ugly that I felt that one final excursion by French troops bent on pillage could be justified if they would burn it down; I wavered again in the Fischmarkt, a tiny, ancient alleyway winding down towards the river and full of sixteenth-century buildings, when I saw that one of them proudly announced itself as a Sex Shop; I wavered for a third time, and this time my faith in Heidelberg nearly fell, when I turned the corner of the fifteenth-century Church of the Holy Ghost, which is, after all, Heidelberg's cathedral, and came face to face with the Court Apothecary.

This is a perfect, and perfectly restored and tended, masterpiece of vivid Baroque pink sandstone, with the coat of arms of the Palatinate picked out above the doorway, flanked on either side with identical arched embrasures, now windows. Of all the ancient chemist's shops I had seen on my journey, with their wonderful names, this one was housed in the handsomest building of all. I raised my camera, and as I peered through the viewfinder the name over the top of that beautifully proportioned central doorway, actually *in* the fanlight, registered with me for the first time: McDonald's.

Let there be hamburgers: let there be places where they are sold; let them be found in the ancient quarters of beautiful towns as well as the hurrying modern centres of ugly ones; but could Heidelberg not itself have found the money and the energy to restore and preserve its Court

Apothecary's, without handing it over to the hamburger, however firm the hamburger's promise to do nothing to the structure and however meticulously the promise had been kept? It was time to visit the castle.

A ruin, to be sure, but not a comfortable ruin, like those warm and grown-over ones. In its time, which was the sixteenth century – it is one of Germany's most notable Renaissance monuments – it must have been a formidable sight, looming over the town when seen from below, and dominating it from above. Nor is it difficult to imagine its power, if only because even the French invaders in 1693 were unable to raze it, and much of it still stands almost intact, starting with the stupendous Renaissance façade in the inner courtyard, decorated with a richness and profusion that Renaissance Florence itself could hardly match. It houses the Great Tun, a barrel so large that a platform has been erected on the top, on which dances and concerts are given; the Great Tun holds 50,000 gallons (or, as the Germans, being Germans, insist, 49,000 gallons), and is guarded by a sixteenth-century statue of Perkeo, the Court Jester, said to be the most prodigious drinker in Germany at that time (a considerable claim); it also houses the Apothecary's Museum, which I very nearly omitted, as time was passing and an Apothecary's Museum was not something to make my heart race. I thought I would just take a glance inside; two minutes later I had abandoned my timetable and stayed, marvelling, for an hour.

There were some ten rooms, filled – and beautifully arranged and laid out – with the old pots and jars and bottles, measures and scales, drawers and cupboards and shelves. There were *thousands* of containers, each with a lovingly painted enamel label, scores of instruments for mixing the potions (I don't suppose most of them would have done anybody any good, but that applies almost to most of modern medicine, much of which does almost everybody a great deal of harm), and an air of craftsmanship not only in the work of the apothecary, but much more in the making of the objects, so utterly fitting for their purpose, yet by some mysterious alchemy of harmony and proportion in the souls of the craftsmen who made them, profoundly and enduringly beautiful. Magic.

There was one final call to be made before I left Heidelberg. I have never been very interested in the origins of *Homo sapiens*; I remember feeling mildly pleased at the fact that Piltdown Man was a hoax, and the rival claims of *Pithecanthropus australis* and Java Man to be the most ancient of our ancestors have never induced me to take sides. But how could I visit Heidelberg without paying my respects to *Homo erectus heidelbergensis*, who is said to be half a million years old, and no hoax?

Heidelberg Man was something of a disappointment; there was nothing to see of him but a lower jaw, and even that looked like something my dentist makes a cast of when he has a patient with severe problems. Nor did the fragment, in its glass case, make me feel the link with a past of an unimaginably distant time. There simply wasn't enough of a relic to conjure up the image of such a pre-man. But the visit to the Palatinate Museum was not wasted; an upper room houses Tilman Riemenschneider's Altar of the Twelve Apostles, which ranks with the ones at Colmar and Breisach for power and self-effacing magnificence.

A merry town, Heidelberg, duelling-scars or no duelling-scars. It wears its antiquity lightly and beautifully, and there is no feeling of a conscious insistence on its bygone charms so carefully preserved. Heidelberg, unlike so many ancient places, does not seem out to draw attention to itself; there it is, visitors are welcome, a tour of the Old Town is recommended, and the Information Office distributes a map with the best route marked; after that, it is up to us, whether or not we wish to pause for a meal at McDonald's, *ehemaliger* Court Apothecary.

Across the river, the Philosopher's Walk could be glimpsed through the trees; I thought of my friend the Heidelberg amateur philosopher, and the harmony of the Marstall that had set off our conversation. Besides, Weber wrote *Der Freischütz* in Heidelberg. I waved it goodbye with affection and regret.

Like Karlsruhe, Mannheim was a fairly mousy place. It has what is said to be the biggest Baroque castle in Germany, and so it may be, though to my eye it was also the dullest. I wandered about the courtyards; the fabric was dilapidated, empty bottles rolled about; is this the inevitable result of the fact that the Mannheim Schloss now houses a university? I went round to the front, where the castle looked more imposing; too unimaginatively symmetrical, but with a certain grandeur, a square tower rising behind the façade, and well-kept lawns. But if this was the better side of Mannheim Schloss, it was also the better side of the effects of a university; the area sported an impressive number of enormous bookshops.

Much of Mannheim is as regular as the Schloss; the centre is laid out on a rigid grid pattern, like Manhattan but without Manhattan's dominating Avenues to break the evenness. But in this square kilometre I discovered what Mannheim does for a living: it shops. It shops in a vast complex of giant department stores, themselves mostly part of a giant chain, such as Hertie and Kaufhof; and it shops with grim and ruthless determination. For six streets each way Mannheim is composed entirely of shopping thoroughfares, with the mighty all-purpose stores set like watch-towers along them, and the individual shops crammed between. And at nine o'clock in the morning, it seemed as though the entire population of Mannheim (307,000 when last counted) was in the area, buying, buying, buying.

There is no better index to the general prosperity of a country than its retail trade. For all Britain's economic problems, starting with unemployment, a walk along Oxford Street is enough to show that, as usual, the British people have never had it so good. When shops are cheek by jowl for a mile, when prices are mercilessly competitive, when in the middle of a Saturday morning the pavements are impassable, only the very poor could (or would be entitled to) deny that this is a prosperous country.

But what if there were six Oxford Streets running east-west, criss-crossing six more running north-south? What degree of prosperity would *that* betoken?

The economic rise of Japan after the Second World War could have been predicted, and by some far-sighted analysts was; it can be compared to the explosion of Jewish talent and enterprise when the walls of the ghetto were thrown down at the end of the eighteenth century, and the reservoir of ability, dammed for so long by repression and separation, flowed out in a massive torrent. But the German Miracle (the extra capital letter does not seem at all incongruous), though when it started it was rapidly recognised for what it was, could hardly have been foreseen by Nostradamus, let alone Phillips & Drew. When the Germans dug themselves out of the rubble in 1945, they knew that no one would help them, and that they must therefore help themselves. And they did. They scrabbled about in the rubble until they found a whole brick, then went back into the rubble to find a second, then they put one upon the other; and the rebuilding of Western Germany had begun. Of course, the rebuilding also took forms other than the physical; Germany's mind, and her soul, had to be made over entirely, after the psychosis of Nazism and the crimes without parallel committed in its name. For that matter, her politics had to be re-created from nothing. But first, another whole brick . . .

I did not discuss Nazism with the shopping crowds of Mannheim, though I did discuss the shopping with the counter staff when they could get their breath. No, there was nothing special about today; yes, there were usually these numbers in the shops; no, it was not a recent development. It is pointless to debate whether the Germans, or the British (or the Japanese or the Americans), 'deserve' their respective economic fates. All we can say for sure is that the Germans sowed the seeds of *their* rising prosperity before anyone offered them any help, and in Mannheim I saw the fruit being plucked.

I saw it being sold, too; the department stores have not, happily, driven out the less well-organised sellers. Mannheim's Market Square was a true market; household goods, undercutting even the margin-shavers in the shopping precincts, abounded, as did clothes. But it was the food that carried the day; carts piled high with apples, cucumbers or tomatoes were doing business as good as anything in Mannheim beneath a ceiling, and I stood and marvelled at the sight of Strawberry Corner; an island of barrows, each piled two feet wide and five feet long and a foot high, each with a large tin scoop for shovelling them into the scales, none of the sellers showing any anxiety about getting rid of their whole crop by nightfall.

The scale and exuberance of the Mannheim market reminded me of that astounding hall in Barcelona, where a visitor is seized with the feeling that every apple and fish and carrot and beefsteak in the world has been culled for sale there; Mannheim's square would have fitted ten times into the wonder of Barcelona, but it had something of the same air of a plenitude so great that it need never be replenished. I have just said that it is a waste of time to discuss whether the Germans deserve their prosperity; nevertheless, I came away from the shops and stalls of Mannheim convinced that they do.

The shopping, however, was to remind me also that however solid the edifice man builds with his hands, the earthquake within can bring it down at any moment: Except the Lord keep the city, the watchman waketh but in vain. In one of the biggest of the department stores, I heard a commotion coming from another part of the forest; I followed the noise to see what was causing it. The cause, it turned out, was undiscoverable, but the causer was as visible as he was audible. He looked as though he came from somewhere a good deal further to the east than Mannheim; I guessed that he was a Turkish, or possibly Yugoslav, *Gastarbeiter*. What ailed him, though, was beyond guessing. Amid a throng of lookers-on, he screamed an unintelligible message of hate, rage and pain, clearly directed at one of the shop-assistants, a slight, fair-haired young girl. Whether he was denouncing her in her professional capacity – accusing her of giving him the wrong item or the wrong change – or whether (which seemed more likely) in her personal life – was he her husband, or lover, or rejected suitor? – I could not tell, no one could, particularly since his contorted face and deafening yells suggested a pain far beyond anything as logical as either alternative. The girl, pink and distressed, heroically got on with her job, serving customers as though nothing out of the ordinary was happening (perhaps it wasn't – for all I knew this might be a regular Saturday morning performance). It was noticeable that although there were men at the front of the watching crowd who were very clearly from the store's security personnel, they made no effort to seize the man, or hustle him out of the building; for all the noise he was making, the intruder made no attempt to get at the girl or hit her, and the security men were content to hold watching briefs until and unless he turned more than verbally violent.

Gradually, the storm blew itself out. He turned away several times, only to turn back for another burst, but each burst now was less intense than the one before, and eventually, when his shouting had subsided to a mutter, he turned away for the last time, and I saw him making his way, no more than dejected now, to the exit. The girl just shook her head, and carried on.

An ugly, strange, even frightening experience, not just because someone might have been hurt, including the raging man himself, but because of the reminder, which we all need all the time, of how thin the ice is. There was no telling whether the man was mad or provoked beyond endurance: but then, there is no telling where one of those ends and the other begins. All I knew was that there was a human being six feet away from me who was beside himself, in whom all the restraints of civilisation had collapsed, leaving the dark stream of the tormented psyche to burst its banks. In olden times, it would have been said that he was possessed by evil spirits, and as I watched the scene, the image came into my mind; after all, it would be natural for me to say that he was 'possessed by rage', but what is that but a feeble excuse for not saying that he was possessed by devils? Perhaps he was; perhaps there *are* devils, who laugh at our sophisticated certainty that devils do not exist, as well as at our pathetic belief that the ice will hold for ever, and who now and again visit some perfectly ordinary place like Mannheim, there to demonstrate, carefully and thoroughly, that we are wrong on both counts.

After that, the rest of Mannheim was straightforward. Its most striking sight was a handsomely ornate concert-hall, obviously post-war but no less obviously rebuilt as a replica of the old one which had gone the way of the bombs. It had a Stamitzsaal, presumably named after Johann, the man who made Mannheim's orchestra famous; or am I thinking of the contemporary of Mozart's who was not a composer but a clarinet-player? If so, and if one must salute great endeavour wherever it is found, he must have some kind of niche in some kind of Panthéon, because he had a unique record of borrowing money from Mozart. To borrow money from Mozart must have been a considerable achievement, not because Mozart was mean, but because he practically never had any, and whenever he had, he made haste to give it away to anyone with a hard-luck story to tell.

Back at my hotel, I asked for some ironing to be done; I had to leave early in the morning for an appointment which demanded pressed clothes, if only out of *noblesse oblige*. Alas, there was no one left on the premises who could do it. No one? *Leider, nein*. Then in that case, pray lend me the ironing-board and an iron. The lady at the reception desk, where this exchange was taking place, looked at me narrowly; could a *man*, and an English one at that, use an iron without electrocuting himself or setting the hotel on fire, or both? I made a short speech, implying that I had many silver cups and gold medals, won at international concourses of ironing, and that I was willing to take on any challenger in the Market Square of Mannheim at dawn the following day. Impressed, she relented, and shortly afterwards the equipment was brought to my door by the porter.

I have written elsewhere at the surprise many of my male friends and contemporaries express at my ability to sew; I have always pointed out that it comes from my schooldays, for any man educated at an English public school would perforce know how to sew, since the only alternative was to go through his schooldays with a shirt flapping in the wind for lack of buttons, and with his trousers at half-mast for the same reason. But my prowess with the iron went back further. My grandfather was the traditional unsuccessful tailor, and I would watch all the processes as a garment took shape, ending, of course, with the pressing of the finished item.

I was not disposed to follow in the family footsteps (my father was a tailor, too), but the memory of my grandfather at work with the 'press-iron', as he called it, has remained vivid for me all my life, and on many previous occasions, in similar emergencies, I had turned to with the iron and displayed a skill which had had the bystanders applauding. Of course, my grandfather's iron was not an electric one; I don't believe they existed at that time, and if they did would have been far beyond his pocket. It wasn't even a steam-iron; it was nothing but the traditional thing in the traditional shape, and was heated on a gas-ring. When it was ready, the cloth would be laid on the ironing-board and sprinkled with water, the garment was stretched along it, covered with another sprinkled cloth, and the pressing began. For me, at the hotel, towels provided the protective layers, and in no time my suit was unwrinkled and ready for the morrow. And the morrow, as I left, offered a tiny reward for my diligence; I passed what may have been the very last hostelry in the Germanophone countries still advertising itself, on a conspicuous signboard, as 'Bad Hotel'. In my walking youth, I was constantly coming upon these, and at first I would take photographs to show the unbelieving at home; after a time, they became so familiar that I gave up even noticing them. But as tourism from the English-speaking countries increased, and more British and American visitors, doubled up with laughter, told the hotelier of such a place that a bad hotel at home meant something very different from what it meant in German, more and more of the hoteliers abandoned the designation, and now a long day's march, however rural, would be unlikely to pass a Bad Hotel, which offered, in all innocence, a sauna and some local mineral-water, and got nothing but puzzling laughter in return.

The next city I visited was the one that has provided seventeen generations of English schoolboys with something to giggle at: the Diet of Worms. But before I sat on a bench and contemplated the extraordinary phenomenon called Luther, I walked round the Romanesque cathedral, the middle one of that stupendous trio of cathedrals which stand like giant sentinels on the Rhine: to the south is Speyer, and to the north Mainz, a chain of buildings for which I know no parallel in the world. Of course they were not conceived as a triple unity; for that matter, none of the three was finished until long after the original architects were dead, and their designs modified, added to and extended in ways they could not have imagined. But anyone who has seen these three Colossi within a few days, anyone who has wandered about those three echoing, mighty naves, anyone who has heard even one of the three organs, let alone all of them, sounding amid the stone, must, if he has any imagination or wonder in him, have sat on a pew and thought about a thing that, beginning in an obscure corner of the Roman Empire, defied all attempts to ridicule it, crush it or absorb it, and within three centuries had achieved a position so dominant that instead of its being swallowed by or crushed by the Empire, the Empire had become its devoted follower.

What did the builders think, as the Cathedrals of Speyer, Worms and Mainz climbed towards the sky? Did they think they were lighting a candle that, with God's grace, would never be put out? Did they think about the origins of their religion, and wonder whether its founder would have burnt men and women for heresy? Did they guess what was about to happen, did they have a vision of the axe that was being forged to hew the Church asunder, a premonition that it was here, along this stretch of the Rhine, that the axe would come down?

I don't suppose they did. They built for their wages and for an instinctive feeling, rooted in their unquestioning faith (nobody ever suggested burning a cathedral mason), that what they were doing would find favour in Heaven, and that anyway to build was their duty to that Heaven.

Luther would have said no less. But Luther is so uncomfortable a figure that a brisk walk round Worms is recommended before settling down in front of his monumental monument. And in the course of my walk I chanced upon one of those tiny breaks in the world's cloud through which, if the eye is clear, a glimpse may be gained of something that makes a comment on the world that will not be forgotten.

There is a Jewish cemetery in Worms; it goes back to the eleventh century. Somehow, it escaped destruction under the Nazis, who were presumably too busy dealing with Jews in a manner that would make quite unnecessary anything so elaborate as a cemetery. They did find time, however, to destroy the synagogue, which was also eleventh-century; it has been rebuilt, and the street in which it stands, the Judengasse, has had honours heaped upon it by the new Germany. So far, so good; but now see how two standard guide-books, Michelin and Baedeker, respectively, treat the history of the Worms synagogue and the tragic and terrible implications of that history. Here is Baedeker:

> In the Judengasse (which is protected as a national monument) is the Synagogue (originally 11th C; ritual bath of 1186), rebuilt in 1961 after its destruction by the Nazis in 1938. Since 1970 the old Jewish

> quarter of Worms has been the subject of a comprehensive rehabilitation scheme. The old Jewish community house, the Raschi School (named after one of the most celebrated Jewish scholars of the Middle Ages), the area round the Synagogue and various dwelling-houses have already been completed.

And here is Michelin:

> This, the oldest synagogue in Germany, was founded in the 11C and rebuilt in 1961.

No word of why it needed to be rebuilt, no reference to the establishment of the area as a national monument, not even a capital letter for synagogue. How strange, touching and ironic that it should be the German book which honestly faces German shame (so, incidentally, does the local guidebook, published officially by the city), and the French one which dishonestly looks the other way.

Luther, as it happens, spent little time in Worms, but he spent it to considerable effect. The Diet of 1521 marked the turning-point of the Reformation; when Luther's wary patron the Emperor Charles V and the members of the Diet assembled to hear Luther defend his doctrines and explain his burning of the Papal Bull that had done everything but excommunicate him, he had either to retract or secede. He had no safe-conduct (not that that would have helped him if the example of Hus had been followed), and indeed the Emperor withdrew his protection from Luther in the course of the Diet; many of his friends and allies fully expected him to leave Worms as an urn-full of ashes collected at the peril of their own lives by his followers, and Luther himself must have thought it likely. But 'Here I stand; I can do no other.' The Reformation had begun.

Of course, it would have begun – *had* begun – anyway; not for nothing does the Luther Monument in Worms include statues of Hus, Wycliffe and even Savonarola, as well as Melanchthon and Reuchlin. But Luther is rightly regarded as the force behind it, or rather *in* it. His single-mindedness of purpose, his terrible conviction that mankind was in danger of eternal damnation because of the errors of the Church, his consuming zeal to get closer to God and lead others there too – this was the stuff that Martin Luther was made of, and although no sensible man would want to spend ten minutes in his company unless there were stout bars to keep the holy madman off, and although also Luther was brutal, intolerant, Jew-hating, foul-mouthed and vindictive, no one can deny him an enormous, profound grandeur of soul. Luther is as horrible as Erasmus is lovable; but it was Luther who changed the world, and as I looked at him on his central plinth, surrounded by his precursors and followers, his eyes directed upwards to Heaven, I could understand why.

And even if I could not, I would have only to remember his hymn, which I sang so often in my schooldays to that splendid tune, and the last verse, which surely sums up Luther, would remind me that such a man, with such a faith, would not and could not rest until he had indeed changed the world:

What though they take our life,
Goods, honour, children, wife?
Yet is their profit small,
These things shall vanish all,
The city of God remaineth.

After that, it was a positive relief to go and look at the Nibelungs' Bridge and the statue of Hagen throwing the Nibelungs' treasure into the river. Worms was the capital of those shadowy Kings – mostly legend but partly history – Gunther, Giselher and Gernot, and of the ladies for whom they fought and died – Brunhild and Kriemhild. Fourteen centuries after the events, Wagner took the *Nibelungenlied* and, with further borrowings from the Norse sagas, fashioned his *Ring of the Nibelung*, just as his – and legend's – Alberich fashioned the gold into mighty instruments of power. I would no more wish to spend time in Wagner's company than in Luther's, but no one could deny that he reshaped music and the theatre as profoundly and comprehensively as Luther did the Christian religion. Wagner should have written an opera about him; they were birds of a feather.

If Worms breathes Luther, Mainz breathes Gutenberg, though it goes back a lot further; the Romans fortified it, and Drusus, their chief military architect, built the strongpoint, as he built many more along the river. (Drusus died at Mainz, and Augustus came from Rome to give the address at his memorial service.) Having paid my respects to the final, most tremendous of the three consecutive Romanesque cathedrals (the guidebook said that the one in Mainz had six towers, and I dare say it did, but I walked round it several times, counting, and got a different answer each time), and explored the old town, full of winding alleyways, half-timbering, ancient inns, fountains and statues (the whole of Germany, I was by now beginning to think, was a set for Act Two of the *Mastersingers*), I made, inevitably, for the Gutenberg Museum.

Inevitably? Quite inevitably; I am Gutenberg Man personified, and have the authority of St John to say so: In the beginning was the Word. Many years ago, I was taking part in the BBC's radio programme *Any Questions*. One of the questioners was a blind girl – it transpired that she had not been born blind but blinded in an accident in her childhood – and she asked the panel, 'If you had the misfortune to go blind, what sight would you most miss?' The first of the four to answer was the Bishop of Llandaff, who said, 'The fields and trees that I see from my study window.' And I thought, instantly, 'How appropriately in character: a Christian priest, for whom all the beauties of nature are the work of God's hand – naturally that is what he instinctively thinks of.' The next to speak was Baroness Brooke, and her answer was, 'The look on a child's face when he is unwrapping a Christmas present.' And again I thought, how perfectly fitting: the speaker was a mother and grandmother, and would surely have felt that those roles provided the centre and purpose of her life, so of course the witness to that life would be what she would most regret not seeing. With mounting excitement, I listened to the third speaker, this time an MP, Christopher Mayhew. My theory held, watertight and unqualified: the public man, the legislator, the man whose metaphorical visibility must be translated into literalness, the man whose professional life is passed in the lime*light*, answered in character and on cue: Light.

It was my turn to speak, fourth and last. Enthralled by what had gone before, I opened my mouth to answer, and only then – for the moment the girl had asked the question I knew without doubt what my answer was to be – did I realise that my own reply said as much about me as the replies of my three colleagues had said about them. For my answer was, of course: the printed word.

The *printed* word, mind, not just the word itself. Like all journalists, I cannot feel the reality of a word until it is in print, and I carry the principle (here, too, I am by no means alone) somewhat further, in that even the printed word has no life in it until it is actually printed in the newspaper or book. (Many journalists, I among them, will tell you that they have frequently failed to see an obvious error, or even a dreadful and wholly accidental libel, in their typescript or even their proofs, yet have seen it instantly, with a scream of dismay, next morning in the paper, when it is too late to do anything about it.) Now words are taking forms undreamt of by Gutenberg (whether he 'invented' modern printing or not will be debated until the end of time, which will also be the end of words, but if we cautiously call him 'the father of printing' we shall be safe), and are turning into images on a screen, getting there by incomprehensible electronic means (I suppose John von Neumann stands in the same relationship to the computer that Gutenberg does to printing); Gutenberg Man finally faces a challenge that is not unlike the challenge faced by pre-men when *Homo sapiens* appeared. I think I shall become extinct, as they did. I can cope with the new machinery, but the words that come up on the screen, or roll out of the Fax machine, or go down a telephone line via a Modem (which to me sounds like one of the enemy creatures in *Lord of the Rings*), or even come up on the familiar doomed telex, are to me not words but only the raw material of words; I am willing to believe that there is a Fourth Dimension, but I cannot for the life of me see it.

At the Gutenberg Museum I could see where it all started: In the beginning . . . Downstairs, a little room had been fitted up with replicas of his own machinery and equipment, rather like the Froben workshop in the Erasmus exhibition at Basle. (Could that have been only a few weeks ago?) The rest of the downstairs area was in effect a history of printing, with printing presses of every era from that of Gutenberg's immediate successors to almost the present time. It is impossible to go among these presses, as they get more effective and elaborate, and then to return to Gutenberg's own, without wondering what the world would be like if it had never happened. Of course it is impossible to imagine such a world, but there is a reason for that impossibility. Gutenberg's invention was not like Arkwright's Spinning Jenny or Watt's steam engine, or 'Turnip' Townsend's solution of the problem of feeding cattle through the winter, or even gunpowder: all these symbols show how mankind has advanced from a state of immobility, poverty, insecurity and powerlessness. But printing changed the very nature of the world. Printing was not just a tool, not even the greatest tool ever devised; it was a creation that altered the fundamental consciousness of human beings, and for ever.

Would he, if he could have seen what uses his invention was to be put to, have smashed his machinery and burnt his blueprints? I suppose not; he would have said, and should have said, 'For good or ill, they must use it as they think fit.' And they did.

Johannes Gensfleisch Gutenberg (Gensfleisch means, if it means anything, 'Gooseflesh', which is an odd middle name for a man who changed the world) has dominated history as no figure other than the great religious avatars has done. Centuries were to pass before literacy prevailed in the Western world, and in much of the rest it still has a long way to go; but nobody, as far as I know, has felt since Gutenberg anything but that literacy was a goal to be striven for. My own grandmother never learned to read or write in any language, and my grandfather read only with great difficulty; I still feel the astonishment with which I discovered that fact, but no effort of the imagination will be great enough for me to feel what it must have been like to live in pre-Gutenberg times, when literacy, beyond a very small circle, was almost unknown, and little regarded.

Upstairs in the Gutenberg Museum I saw the fruits of his invention; very wisely, those in charge of it had realised that a static museum will quickly die, so that in addition to their examples of Gutenberg's first printings and other *incunabula*, there were examples of fine printing and book-making right up to the present day. All the same, it was Gutenberg's work that took pride of place, and I, as a man who has lived all his life – far too much, of course, and to the terrible neglect of things even more important – by books, found inexpressibly moving the sight of the Gutenberg Bible itself, sumptuously rebound.

In the beginning was the Word. If you transplant St John to the first chapter of Genesis, something starts to happen. The primordial Chaos is suddenly ordered and arranged by God, and the reader can, however dimly, grasp the formless form of Chaos (if the reader cannot, let him listen to the opening bars of Beethoven's Ninth Symphony). But as soon as St John appears, the grasp slackens; what was, what could have been, before words? Words themselves preceded their printed form by many millennia; even before the written form words had long existed. But the impenetrable mystery of the origins of language itself must be left to itself; the creation of the printed word took place in Gutenberg's little room: Let there be light, he said; and there was light. And from that day to this, the results and effects of that great Promethean blasphemy can be traced in the utmost detail. To have under my hands the very first pebbles that, rolling down the mountain, were to create that colossal avalanche, was an experience I shall not forget. Some minutes after I had left the Gutenberg Museum, I suddenly realised that I had done so, instinctively, on tiptoe. I did not feel at all surprised.

10

Fire, Water and Throstle Alley

AT MAINZ, THE river turns sharply to the west; a few miles further on, it swings as sharply again, and hardly deviates thereafter from its path due north until it is across the Dutch border. But at the second 'elbow' lies Bingen, and it was at Bingen, that, as dusk began to fall, I boarded the *Germania* for a view of what I had been told would be among the most spectacular sights of my life. Such claims are easily, and frequently, made; very rarely are they lived up to. This one was.

Every year this stretch of the river sees a ceremony called 'The Rhine on Fire'. (Cynics might say that the Rhine had been on fire too often for a peaceful custom to be so named, but the custom goes back a very long way, and it had been felt that the title might as well be kept, particularly as nobody could think of a new one that described the custom so well.) The ship I was on was one of a gigantic flotilla; I had been told that there would be forty-eight in the group, but in the event there must have been twice as many, and the river resembled nothing so much as the old photographs of Dunkirk. Clearly, many of the boats were freelance additions to the programme, but the people in charge did not seem to mind, nor would it have done any good if they had, for short of torpedoes there was no way in which the river could have been cleared. To the accompaniment of music, in our case provided by a middle-aged trio on accordion, saxophone and drums, the armada set off.

By nine, it was almost dark; the music had stopped, because there was no one left below to dance to it. Everyone was crowded on the decks, awaiting the moment when the Germans would defy the English proverb, and set the Rhine on fire. I had a perfect position, just forward of the bridge; the *Germania* was the flagship of the entire squadron. It was fairy-lit from stem to stern, as were all the other boats, which was just as well, as the gatecrashers, some of which were as small as fishing-boats, weaved in and out of the parade, and it only needed one of the big ones to swing in the current for them to be smashed to pieces. It was almost time for the show to begin, but first there was a curtain-raiser. An Army landing-craft, flying the flag of the Bundeswehr, made its way cautiously from the shore to a rendezvous, in the middle of the river, with the *Germania*. Something, it seemed, had been left behind in the rush to get under way; crates of beer were hoisted aboard (though from the glimpse I had had of the bars it would not have occurred to me that it might run out, so ample were the stacked supplies), followed by tables and chairs (presumably for the comfort of those who were to drink the beer), and, finally, some latecomers who had missed the boat and who, embarrassed, were swung up and on to the deck – baby, pram and all.

The armada was slowing down; a little manoeuvring and the ships were lined up with a view of both shores. As one mass, they began to move down-stream in convoy. Somebody struck a match, and the Rhine was on fire.

I have always loved fireworks, and so deep is the feeling they generate that I would think very little of someone who claimed indifference to them. A really good display, with a proper balance of individual displays and set pieces, is among the most thrilling sights imaginable, and if there is a real artist behind the design of the show – as nowadays there very often is, many resorts having discovered the attraction for tourists in a truly spectacular fireworks display – it can leave a memory that lasts for life.

The hillsides, where the vineyards and the castles scrabble for a precarious toehold, burst one by one into flame; the speed of the flotilla had clearly been worked out in conjunction with those on shore fanning the fire, and it seemed that every village and castle passed was determined to outdo the one before. Each began with a huge parachute flare, the marker for what was to follow; what followed was clearly limited only by the designer's imagination, for there was certainly no curb on extravagance. My favourite item in any firework display, apart from the set-pieces, is the ring of bursting rockets into the centre of which, before the star-burst circle fades, a tight cluster of a different colour is fired. There were scores of such demonstrations, together with hundreds of coloured lights streaking like tracer bullets through

48 Burg Rheinstein: Up to the eagle's nest 49 The highest vineyard? 50 A lot of loving cup 51 What song the sirens sang

MZ
J 5215
MZ
J 5215

49

0

1

52

53

the sky and criss-crossing in perfect symmetry, thousands of giant Roman Candles and monster Catherine Wheels, huge pictures painted on the sky in brilliant colours.

At first, each burst which lit up the night was greeted with gasps of admiration and delight from the crowd on deck; after a time, the gasps turned to shouts, the shouts to cheers, and as the display continued, all control was lost, and everyone, including me, was yelling with a huge, unquenchable joy at the glory of the spectacle. Earlier in the evening, the weather forecast had warned that there might be thunderstorms, and so there might have been, but if so they were unheard amid the roaring of the explosions, from the small-arms fire which marked the unleashing of a row of rockets, to the artillery which despatched a multiple warhead into the heavens, while all the spectators drew breath for the universal shout which greeted the giant bang a few moments *after* the shell had burst and showered its rainbow cargo over the sky.

The best, and most tremendous (where fireworks are concerned, the words are synonymous), was kept to the last. As the ship neared Rüdesheim, where the display ended, the pyromaniacs on shore paused for a moment, and the hillsides were black. Then, just as we had begun to think that the show was over, the curtain rose on an epilogue that eclipsed everything that had gone before. On both sides of the Rhine simultaneously there erupted a last blazing inferno; it was like a battle, poised on a knife-edge between victory and defeat, to which the opposing generals have committed their last reserves, their last ammunition, their last encouragement to their exhausted troops.

Victory or death! Blinding and deafening, battle was joined; fire crossed and re-crossed the river, the shells seemed to burst right over the mast, the thunder of the guns was continuous. It was not only the Rhine that was on fire; the sky, the shore, the hills, the whole world was one roaring, dancing, blazing conflagration that was echoed in the delirium of cheers from the sightseers. Then it flickered and died; and the night crept out of its air-raid shelter to take command.

It was over just before midnight, but I lingered on deck, though I was not expecting an encore. The bitter, not unpleasant, smell of cordite hovered thickly in the air; beneath me, lit now only by the ship's lights, the Rhine flowed on, the fire quenched in its limitless waters. Fire is embedded deeply in the human psyche; perhaps nothing more deeply. It marked the point at which man could start to develop; without fire, *Homo sapiens* could never have survived, or even existed. The most ancient of the world's myths concern fire; the deepest core of

52 *Where they crossed the Rhine* 53 *Adenauer's favourite study*

many of the world's religions contain fire; rituals of purification, rejoicing and death are built on fire. As I finally, reluctantly, left the boat for my bed on shore, I could understand the release into abandon that the Rhine, on fire, had engendered in me and all my fellow-spectators.

And now, at last, the Rhine as most people think of it. From Mainz to Cologne, along the river, is a distance of about 125 miles. In that distance the Rhine has twenty-one bridges, thirty-nine ferries, twenty-two islands, and rather more than sixty castles. (The number is disputed; how much must be left of a ruin for it to count?) This extraordinary parade of giant guardsmen would alone demonstrate the enormous importance of the Rhine throughout the centuries, for these castles were, almost without exception, erected to stand guard over the fief of some king or duke or princeling, who knew that if he was to be safe he must never lose his suzerainty over the stretch of the river his eyrie commanded. Today, every visitor's first thought is likely to be one of amazement at the fact that they got built at all, for many of them are perched on crags or ridges or slopes so precipitous that it is difficult to see how, with only the most primitive equipment and rudimentary techniques, the materials could have been hauled up to the site, and in some cases (where the base of the castle covers the entire available building area) how the workmen had any room to move. It is all very well to say that the lord of the castle would have wanted it that way because the more inaccessible his fastness the less likely it was to be successfully assaulted; however many pressed men worked on the building, the ingenuity of the architects and the foremen must have been very considerable indeed. (The inaccessibility of the castles reminded me of an even more intractable mystery. The castles *could* be built, provided those engaged in the work had enough ingenuity and muscle-power, and were prepared to take great risks. But how were the cables for ski-lifts – Seilbahns and Sesselbahns – got from the valley to the peak? The whole point of the lifts is that they do not go along the ground or even, except at the beginning and end of the journey, anywhere near it, and in some cases the car or seat is hundreds of feet up, crossing huge valleys on its way to the mountain. How was it done? Today, no doubt, it could be easily accomplished by helicopters, but some of Europe's ski-lifts long antedate aeroplanes, let alone the helicopter. They could not fire the cable across – it would be far too heavy – they could not engage a passing bird to take it in its beak and fly up with it, and I can hardly believe that they took the entire cable up to the top on foot, then patiently unrolled it down the mountainside, got it finally to the valley station, then hauled on it until it was stretched taut.)

The very names of the castles are a roll-call of granite rocks translated into granite syllables: Scharfenstein, Eberbach, Reinhartshausen, Vollrads, Johannisberg, Schwarzenstein, Boosenburg, Pixholz, Ehrenfels, Nollig, Sareck, Sterrenberg, Marksburg, Ehrenbreitstein, Seyn, Engers, Weissenthurm, Stolzenfels, Stahlberg, Fürstenberg, Sooneck, Kaiserpfalz, Klopp.

And Burg Rheinstein, where I spent the night; it is well over a thousand years old, its original name Vogtsburg. Near the end of the thirteenth century its lord was a Holy Roman Emperor, and a Habsburg one at that; he re-named it Königstein. The Archbishops of Mainz ruled it on and off, in their capacity of Electors of the Empire, but it was eventually abandoned, and by the beginning of the eighteenth century it had crumbled into ruin. It was restored at the beginning of the nineteenth century by Prince Friedrich of Prussia, who re-named it yet again, this time Rheinstein, the name it still bears. Friedrich lived in it, and even entertained Queen Victoria there; it passed to his son, thence to Prince Heinrich of Prussia, brother of Kaiser Wilhelm, from whom it descended ultimately to its last aristocratic owner, the Duchess of Mecklenburg. In 1975 a retired opera singer named Hermann Hecher bought it from her, and has ever since devoted himself to its restoration and upkeep; it seems unlikely that the modest charge levied on visitors, many though they are, makes it economic, but when I talked to Herr Hecher it quickly became clear to me that his interest was in maintaining this notable cultural monument, not in making money from it.

The first ceremony was my appointment as Burgherr, or Lord of the Castle, for my night under his roof. In token of my duties in the post, which were light, he presented me with an iron key eighteen inches long and weighing about five pounds; happily, I was not required to carry it about with me, and I explored the castle at my leisure. It looked more like a stage set than most stage sets do; it inevitably reminded me of poor mad Ludwig's Neuschwanstein (which actually *was* a stage set, for Ludwig designed it in collaboration with a theatrical designer, then handed it to his architect and told him to translate it into three dimensions).

Turrets, battlements, towers, spiral staircases, halls, gardens, embrasures, platforms, leaded windows, a drawbridge, a moat, a chapel, a crypt – on and on I wandered, and from almost every point on almost every level (my tour was constantly going up and down) there were spectacular views of the river, over which the castle beetles so ferociously that I felt that the very slightest tremor of the earth, or even a cannon-shot, would bring it crashing down from its 270-foot perch, to make the greatest splash the Rhine had known in all its history.

The views, as well as being spectacular, are instructive, reinforcing yet again the character of the Rhine as a transport artery along which flows a constant, placid, yet enormous volume of goods. And this time, the image had a further extension; from my perch in the eagle's nest, I could see the railway lines on both sides of the river, so close to it that they seemed to be running on the towpath, and the rail traffic might have been engaged (it probably was) in a ferocious campaign of competition for freight and passengers with the waterway, so many were the trains that passed. I mentioned it to Herr Hecher, who astonished me by saying that, counting both sides of the river, an average of five hundred trains passed in every twenty-four hours, most of them goods trains.

Across the river, where I stayed the following night at Assmanshausen, is Rüdesheim (Assmanshausen is really an extension of it, or *vice versa*), which I had been assured was as dreadful as Benidorm and for the same reason. (This news, which in any case I found improbable, disappointed me, because I recalled that Coleridge's howl of outrage and hate directed against Cologne had been modified by only two things he found there, and one of them was the wine of Rüdesheim.) From the Krone, my waterfront hotel, Burg Rheinstein looked magnificent, hung in the sky against a mountainous backdrop, but a walk of exploration led to a most forbidding omen; if Assmanshausen is the sophisticated partner of the naïve Rüdesheim, what was a sign doing in the window of a restaurant, promising, in English, sausages and chips, fried eggs and chips, hamburgers and chips? And if Rüdesheim was the naïve partner of the sophisticated Assmanshausen, what would the restaurants there be offering?

At the Krone, I found a large troupe of *Schuhplättler*, those extraordinary entertainers – I suppose you could call them the German and Austrian equivalent of Morris dancers – who yodel, dance and – above all, and the reason for their name – kick their heels and clash their shoes. The band at the hotel were meticulously dressed in the traditional *Schuhplättler* costume of (for the men) black velvet jackets heavily embroidered, knee-breeches, frilled shirts and floppy hats, and (for the women) dirndls, coloured stockings, lace blouses and bonnets. I thought that their presence so far up the Rhine was odd, for normally they are to be found only in Bavaria and Austria, but a moment later I discovered that their presence was a very great deal odder than I had thought, for they were all Americans, and another moment later it transpired that the whole business was odder still, because they did not do their shoe-plattling in America, except to practise; they come every year to give performances, in the traditional inns, in Germany. A more bizarre example of carrying coals to Newcastle I never expect to hear of, much less see.

I spent the evening on the river, to be precise on a pleasure-steamer cruising gently on the placid water. On both sides there was lovely, varied scenery, much of it thickly wooded and lushly green, but punctuated by vast caravan-parks (why flee from a terrace house to a house on wheels and then park it every night in another, and even more crowded, terrace?). Buzzards, hawks and owls swooped over the water as dusk came on and the riparian villages were tucked up for the night. The hills were alive with vineyards, most of them tiny patches, and some with their names painted right along the verticals of the terraces (I suppose it was no different from a neon sign at home). But the most striking sight along this stretch of the river is the Niederwald Denkmal, a monument to the German victory in the Franco-Prussian War. It dominates the sky itself, plonked down as it is on the very highest point of the very highest ridge, and even from a mile or two's distance it looked spectacularly hideous.

I determined to visit it next day, and as the evening wore on and it was still to be seen, I thought more about monuments of commemoration. A victory as complete, swift and humiliating as that of the Germans in the Franco-Prussian War would inevitably inspire any country to puff out its chest, and what more obvious form can chest-puffing take than the building of a memorial? But I think that in Britain we do not take this attitude. We have Nelson on his column, of course, but what else, apart from a railway station called Waterloo? Is there a monument anywhere in England to the destruction of the Spanish Armada? On the whole, our war memorials are to the dead; almost every little village has its obelisk, or fountain, or even a plaque on a wall, commemorating those who fell. Most of these were put up after the First World War, and most of *them* have an addendum to record the dead of the Second. But apart from Nelson, we do not, I think, go in much for the Siegesturm or Arc de Triomphe variety, and I rather think I am glad that we do not.

Next day, as I had promised myself, I toiled up to the monument. Close to, it proved to be far, far more hideous than it had been when seen from the river, softened by distance and the evening light. It was well over a hundred feet high, two-thirds of it being the base and the rest the figure of Germania; from the inscription on the base of the base, I learned that it commemorated also the unification of Germany that followed the war. The main part of the support consisted of a grotesque frieze, showing a throng of notable Germans of the time; the life-size figures ran right round the square plinth. Germania herself was cast in bronze that had not weathered well and had turned her mostly a kind of bird-dropping blue; the figure was more actively repellent than any I could recall in monumental masonry anywhere (the Victoria Memorial outside Buckingham Palace is a thing of grace and beauty by comparison). I thought of my friend the Lion of Belfort, who commemorates the vanquished in that same war, or more exactly the heroes who held Belfort to the end against everything Germania could hurl against them; he became even more friendly and comfortable beside this horror. If the Germans should ever feel the need to demonstrate again their rejection of the worst of their past, they could not do it better than by dynamiting this thing, base, figure and all.

The boat steamed majestically on; between decks, the pace quickened. Four enormous restaurants, all lavishly supplied with waiters who plainly hated not only their jobs, their lives, their relatives and their customers, but the whole of mankind, were doing good business, and so were the souvenir-shops. A trilingual commentary emerged inoffensively from the loudspeakers. It had started with the unkind version of the Mauseturm, the one with the wicked Bishop meeting a deserved fate; it ended, inevitably, with the Lorelei.

The Lorelei is always a disappointment; it is, after all, only a cliff, and there are plenty of those along this river, even though this one does beetle more than most. The bronze sculpture of the traditional image of the Lorelei as a mermaid combing her long hair, which sits on a spit of land running out from the cliff itself, is pretty enough, but if the rock and the maiden had been the most beautiful and awe-inspiring sights of the world, the tune, amplified throughout the ship, would have done for it. Played straight it is bad enough, but this version had been flossed up with a series of horrible descants, sung, as far as I could make out, by a four-part choir; on shore, I could make out a Lorelei café, a Lorelei mill and a Lorelei chemist. Happily, most of the rest of the river along this stretch is almost entirely unspoilt; St Goar, Bacharach, Lorch, Kaub, all these were bright with handsomely painted frontages, the shops and hotels looking like expensive toys, and the villages beyond determined not to suffer the fate of the Lorelei shore.

But if the fate of the Lorelei shore is to be bemoaned, what shall serve to describe the fate of Rüdesheim? Rüdesheim was, and largely still is, full of beautiful buildings, some of great antiquity and carefully preserved, those along the Rhine frontage no less attractive than the ones further down-river. But in what might be called High Street Rüdesheim it is not the buildings that a visitor would flee from, but the use made of them. From end to end, the river-front walk is composed of fast-food restaurants and souvenir shops, the souvenirs being not only of almost indescribable ugliness but restricted to a very narrow range, and every shop sells the same things; how they make a living I could not see, particularly when I heard an English voice saying, 'Come on – in that place round the corner they were fifty pfennigs cheaper.' (At the then prevailing rate of exchange, fifty pfennigs were worth fifteen English pence.) I finished my walk in a state of deep depression, but I had not, as it turned out, so much as touched the hem of Rüdesheim depression, for the full, dreadful reality awaited me in the evening, in the Drosselgasse.

'Drossel' is the same word as our 'throstle', and indeed, at the entrance to Throstle Alley, there was a large wrought-iron sign, in the shape of the bird. But the sounds which were issuing from the Drosselgasse as I arrived were by no means those of the throstle, and still less the nightingale.

I now believe that the Drosselgasse is the most extraordinary street I have ever walked down. 'Down' is the right word, for I found that it was very narrow and sloped gently from end to end; it was lined on both sides with restaurants and *Bierstuben*, nightclubs and take-aways. Almost every one of these establishments had a powerful, and amplified, band; it was a fine night, so everything was open to the street, and there were points at which I could stand and hear at least six bands going simultaneously, all (except for an occasional fugal coincidence) playing different tunes. The bands were there for dancing; the floor of every one of the places I looked into was crammed with merrymakers, and since the dancing was of the simplest kind, the tunes matched it with violently accented rhythms; as I reeled down the street I felt I was being beaten on the head not with one rubber truncheon but a dozen.

I wandered in and out; in a few I stopped long enough to take a coffee or a glass of wine and to observe (to talk was impossible above the din). I had wondered how the souvenir-shops could all keep going; there was no similar mystery about these places, for there seemed to be an infinite supply of patrons for all of them, and in every one the turnover was astounding, with a dozen waiters or more demonstrating a kind of *perpetuum mobile* (and, incidentally, not obviously despising the customers as those on the boat had).

The largest national group in the Drosselgasse was the British; I imagine more than half of the crowd throughout the street were my countrymen and women, and the next biggest contingent, reasonably enough, were the Germans, though the Americans were also represented in strength. It was Saturday night, and for a long time I believed that the Drosselgasse was not like this for the rest of the week, but when I finally found a quiet corner and shared a table with a local man, he assured me that there was the same throng every night.

I found the whole experience dreadful, but that did not surprise me; still, I was the only one in a vast crowd, and my opinion was of no consequence; what I wanted to understand was the reaction of the crowd in general. It was no use asking; no one could have heard the question, and I could not have heard the answer. But the eyes did what the ears could not; looking round, I asked myself whether a good time was being had. And I had to answer: very plainly, yes. The noise was close to brain-damage level, the food was of the most basic kind, the heat and jostling unbearable, but almost all the revellers were enjoying themselves immensely.

Now I have spent much of my writing life denouncing the superior people who disapprove of those whose tastes in entertainment they feel to be lower than their own; I was not inclined to despise the revellers in the Drosselgasse, still less to tell them they should not be enjoying themselves in such a fashion. But I could not help wondering what the scene said about the horizons of those (nobody, as far as I could see, was drunk) who were having, literally, the time of their lives. If this was the best they knew, what could their world be like?

I fought off cynicism and went to bed with a headache but without misanthropic feelings. That may, however, have been because after leaving the Drosselgasse I went further into the town, away from the front, and there found, in an alleyway not much wider than the Drosselgasse itself, a little traditional *Stube* called Zum Grünen Kranz, and there above the door was indeed the sign of a green wreath. Inside, there was music of a very different kind; a glee club of some twenty-five men. They came from Mönchengladbach, and every year took their holiday in a different German town, where their delight was to gather of an evening in a place as unlike the hostelries of the Drosselgasse as possible, and sing. They had no self-consciousness or artifice; they wore ordinary clothes, unlike the mad American *Schuhplättler*, and their leader, Matthias Schmitter, acted as a very mild conductor, merely steadying the beat (he had no baton, remained seated and sang with the others) and giving the note on a pitch-pipe, an instrument I had not seen for many years, to set them off in what was, I suppose, correctly called close harmony. The songs were mostly old German ballads, and the part-singing was quite complicated; this was no mere sing-along in a pub, but music taken seriously and rehearsed. The Green Wreath was a delightful place altogether, presided over by a woman of great charm, who went out of her way to please her customers; I insisted that she should allow herself to be photographed with me, and she played up beautifully; we stood, my arm around her waist, in the doorway, and she looked up at me with eyes full of life and mischief. I bought a round of drinks for the singers, and they sang a full-throated thank-you to the tune of 'God Save the Queen'; possibly they had a version to fit all the leading national anthems of the world, but they certainly sang ours in noble style. They then returned the compliment by ordering me, presumably on the principle of the sconce, a gigantic goblet filled to the brim with a beautiful golden white wine. Since it must have contained a full two bottles, I thought it wiser to decline the implicit challenge and treat it (as no doubt I was meant to) as a loving cup, so after I had drunk my fill I passed it round, and it was soon emptied.

The Drosselgasse and the Zum Grünen Kranz were perhaps two hundred yards apart; but they were two different civilisations. The question that had to be faced was: is the Grünen Kranz a stage of civilisation earlier than the Drosselgasse, so that in the course of evolution it will end up the same? I remain of the opinion that the Manichee is wrong; there is no entropy in the universe that makes the good tend towards the bad, and there are limits to Gresham's Law. *Edel sei der*

Mensch, hilfreich und gut. Even in the Drosselgasse? Even in the Drosselgasse.

I went by train to Remagen, and noticed again the extraordinary terror of *air* that lurks in the hearts of the Germans. Men and women, old and young, all seem to be possessed of a phobic horror of air, and in particular of the moving kind. On a day when the temperature must have been well over eighty degrees, I opened the window of the coach I was travelling in. It was one of the long, open carriages that are now replacing the old six-seaters that lay at right-angles to the track, and I opened the window not more than three inches, whereupon a woman sitting at least thirty feet away from me came down the carriage, quivering with fear and outrage, to ask me to close it, as there was a draught. Now, not only was there no draught, but even if there had been it could not possibly have reached her in her seat at the other end; what is more, if there *had* been a draught, it ought to have been as welcome to her as to me, especially with the sun beating through the closed windows and turning the train into an orchid-house. But she had seen me open the window, and worked out that if the window was open some air might get into the carriage, and might then, in some invisible and surreptitious way, creep down the carriage and *get at her*. I sometimes wonder why the Germans bother to have windows in their houses; with modern lighting they do not need daylight, and bricking up the apertures would certainly take care of the danger that air might get in through a crack in even a closed window. (Shaw was once accosted at a party by a woman who said to him, 'Oh, Mr Shaw, I cannot abide the night air.' 'Madam,' he replied, 'you will find that in certain hours of the twenty-four night air is the only kind we have.' I don't suppose the Germans would see the joke.)

Hutber's Law, discovered by the financial journalist whose name it bears, states simply 'Progress means deterioration', and I had rarely met a better illustration of it than the system of buying tickets at a German railway station. The system is massively computerised; the screen is linked to a huge cabinet which prints out the ticket. At first glance (though I should have guessed, from the length of the queue at every counter in the booking-hall, that my first glance was untrustworthy) it looked superbly efficient, and I even began to think it actually might *be* superbly efficient. So, no doubt, it was, as far as the machinery itself was concerned; so, for that matter, were the booking-clerks, for it was at once obvious that they had been properly trained in the use of the apparatus. So where did Hutber's Law come in? It came in via The System.

The System, I discovered when I got to the front of the queue, worked like this. The customer approaches the counter, and says he wants a ticket to Station X; he specifies the class of travel and whether he wants a return. So far, so good; that, after all, was how railway tickets had been sold in Germany and elsewhere since soon after the railway was invented. Now, however, the new technique diverged sharply from the old. I stated my requirements clearly and unambiguously. The clerk, with all the information necessary, proceeded to type first his autobiography (a four-volume work, apparently), together with a comprehensive history of Germany from the Iron Age to the setting-up of the EEC, equipped with a formidable battery of statistical tables, appendices and source-notes, and then a doctoral dissertation, accompanied by no less exhaustive *apparatus criticus*, on thirteenth-century Flemish altar-building.

He then turned to the machine from which the ticket was to emerge; at this point the gentleman in the queue immediately behind me suggested that I might like to go and have lunch, since I would have ample time to do so before anything else happened; he urged me to take my time with the wine-list. Fascinated by the system, however, I said that I would rather stay and see it through, whereupon he expressed surprise that I had apparently not brought a pair of pyjamas. Some days later – time had become a blur, so I was unable to say just how many days – the ticket emerged from the machine, and I went on my way. But the very next glass of wine I drank, I drank to the memory of Patrick Hutber.

On the other hand, all German trains run on time; few people under fifty will hear the echo in that phrase, but everyone over fifty-five will do so instantly. Before the Second World War, sympathisers with Italian Fascism would excuse Mussolini's brutal rule by saying, 'Well, at any rate, he made the trains run on time,' the implication being that whatever the cost in freedom, dictatorship was efficient. The parallel excuse for Hitler was the Autobahn; such motor-roads were unheard of in Europe when he began to build the network, and they were models for the rest of the world (though they have since become hopelessly inadequate for the modern volume of traffic, so that a vast programme of road-widening has been going on for years). But Mussolini's trains did *not* run on time, and I was delighted to have that fact conclusively established on this very journey.

Among the books I had packed was Denis Mack Smith's life of Mussolini; it is a classic among biographies, its sweep and historical understanding beyond praise, its exact tone just what is needed for such a study, its detail exhaustive yet never superfluous, its excitement unflagging throughout. But what must be particularly interesting to readers of my generation, for whom Mussolini is not a figure from history but a living presence who brooded darkly over the world we grew up in, is its treatment of Mussolini as buffoon. That was how, while he threatened us, he was portrayed – a windbag, a preposterous fraud, a man of no real substance at all – but in the years that have followed the war I had begun to recognise the portrait as propaganda; not surprisingly, the Allied picture of the two dictators showed a diabolically manipulative Hitler with a red-nosed clown as his stooge. What I had never suspected until I read Mack Smith's book was that not only was the original portrait authentic, it fell far short of the appalling reality. The adulation that he insisted on, and that his sycophants enforced, was even greater – this seems incredible, but the book leaves a reader in no doubt that it is true – than that demanded by Stalin or even by Mao Tse-tung. Mussolini was *worshipped*; he was praised as a writer far above Dante, as a thinker far beyond Socrates, as a general far superior to Napoleon. Augustus was the first Roman Emperor to insist that he was a god as well as a man; well, Mussolini was the last. When he spoke on the radio, it was a criminal offence for listeners at home not to stand up throughout his address. And yet he was nothing – nothing at all but a brute who gained power by criminal means and held it because for forty years no one could be found to prick the bubble. His Italy was a hopeless mess in every way – economically, politically, strategically; it was not only the trains. The book strengthened still further my lifelong conviction that it is the inefficiency of totalitarianism (which is inevitable, because totalitarianism must by its very nature inhibit initiative) which will in the end destroy it, however complete and murderous its rule.

There was an odd connection from Mack Smith's book to the next one out of my bag; A. N. Wilson's biography of Hilaire Belloc. Wilson's biography is not as substantial a work as Mack Smith's, of course, if only because Belloc's life did not involve events that shaped and changed history and the world. But the connection – Belloc's hero-worshipping of Mussolini, which continued until his death (Belloc's, not Mussolini's) – is not simply fortuitous.

Wilson's attitude to Belloc is curiously equivocal at the very point at which there is no room for equivocation: his subject's anti-semitism. He doesn't exactly minimise or condone it, but he makes clear that he doesn't think it mattered much, and he goes somewhat further; he clearly believes, the dear old-fashioned thing, that there is still something that used to be called The Jewish Problem (with the capital letters), a subject on which his hero wrote an entire book, in which, years after the question was settled for ever, he still could not bring himself to admit that Dreyfus was innocent. And Wilson has one entirely inexcusable lapse into cowardice; he quotes one of Belloc's viler anti-semitic utterances, and then says, 'Either you find this funny or you don't', *without any indication of which category he falls into himself.*

I must not make Wilson's book look like whitewash; it is far more honest and scholarly than, say, Maisie Ward's ridiculous hagiography of Chesterton, for instance, and although it excuses too much, there is no sign at all that it hides anything. But it won't do; Belloc comes out of it as perfectly vile in almost every aspect of his life, not just in the anti-semitism. He played the utterly devoted husband, but spent as much time away from his wife as he could, and in particular ran off every time she became pregnant, compounding this after her death with the oozing hypocrisy of keeping her room shut thereafter and kissing the door or making the sign of the Cross on it every time he passed. In his business dealings he was simply a crook; he sold the same article to different papers simultaneously, he demanded to be paid a full salary for work he had so completely neglected that another man had to be called in to do it, and he signed contracts, took the money, then didn't deliver. In controversy he was caught out simply lying, he wrote scores of books and would never check anything in them (he once dictated an entire book to a secretary and would not even look at the typescript, telling her to send it straight to the publisher, and capped that behaviour by refusing to look at the proofs either). I finished Wilson's book not in the least surprised that Mussolini was Belloc's hero; they were birds of a feather.

All of which I thought about – I had finished the Belloc book the previous night – as I sped, in a German train that ran on time, to Remagen. It is an undistinguished little place, and would never have been heard of had it not been for General Ludendorff, who had a massive bridge built across the river here during the First World War. In the Second, an American unit reached the western bank at Remagen to find that the bridge had not been demolished by the retreating Germans – the only Rhine bridge to have been found intact. The

Americans dashed across and established the first Allied bridgehead on the eastern side of the Rhine. Hitler, beside himself with rage, ordered all those in charge of the bridge defences to be shot, and they were, the executed including a number of officers who were in no way to blame. (One sergeant among those who were to be killed survived, because by the time the order reached those charged with carrying it out he was a prisoner-of-war in American hands.)

The bridgehead had been secured on March 7th, 1945; ten days later the bridge itself collapsed into the river, with considerable loss of life, presumably under the weight of the troops, supplies and, above all, armour now pouring across the only open road leading to the heart of Germany.

After the war the bridge was not rebuilt; its debris was cleared away, and nothing but the two massive towers on each bank, the size of castles, remained. Then the Mayor of Remagen, a man called Hans Peter Kurten, had an idea. He persuaded the town to buy the land, on the Remagen side, on which the towers stood; by some odd chance it belonged to the German Railways. The town agreed, and Kurten's purpose was unfolded; he turned one of the towers into a double museum, half of it devoted to telling the story, in words and pictures, of the bridge and its fate, the other half to a museum of peace. Outside, on the wall of the tower, a plaque tells, in simple but moving language, of the men who were shot, of Kurten's proposal, and of what it was meant for: 'Here, on the spot where a part of the world's history was made, Hans Peter Kurten showed also the madness of war and the need for peace. Let us all, every day, work for peace with hearts and minds, and let each person start with himself.' And the symbol that crowns Kurten's achievement can be seen on the twin towers: on one flies the flag of the German Federal Republic, on the other the Stars and Stripes.

11

The Nose of Cologne

WE MUST NOW face the Bonn Question, though we shall postpone it as long as possible by approaching it via Rhöndorf and Bad Godesberg. Rhöndorf is not of much interest, except that it was the home of Adenauer, whose house is now preserved as a museum in the memory of Federal Germany's first Chancellor. I toiled up the steep path (well, he toiled up it every day until his death in his eighties) and went first to the museum proper. This tells the story of his life in a vast panoramic montage of photographs, followed in the next two rooms by a display of memorabilia, chronologically arranged and ingeniously laid out, which provides the documentary evidence that fleshes out the bones of his life. And what a life!

After I left the museum proper the custodians allowed me into the beautiful little round summerhouse that he had had built for himself after retiring and where he wrote his memoirs. It was a most fitting eyrie; from it, he could look down on his beloved Rhineland, where he was born; in it, he had mounted a display of signed photographs of statesmen, crowned heads and other leaders of the world or bits of it whom he had encountered in the long years of his German governance. In this room, also, he had assembled his library; I have always maintained that if you will show me a man's books, I will deduce his character though I have never met him, and on visiting a house I have never before entered I have hardly shaken my host's hand before I am to be found sidling round the walls to examine his library. What kind of a man, then, was Adenauer, thus reconstructed *ex pede Herculem*? Well, he was a politician, a historian, an admirer of Bismarck, to whom an entire section had been devoted; no doubt he compared himself with the Iron Chancellor. (But why not? Certainly, there was no German statesman between the two who could be compared to either.) He was also, I discovered to my surprise, a knowledgeable art-lover; the art books filled a good deal of space, and they were by no means coffee-table works. There was a shelf of books about Israel, and just beyond it Martin Buber on the Jews; a massive documentary history of the Third Reich, a great deal of biography, some poetry. But in the end, the test failed; an Adenauer cannot be measured by his books. How fortunate it was for both their countries, for Europe and for the world, that de Gaulle and Adenauer were governing their respective nations in the immediate post-war world; Bevin or no Bevin, Churchill or no Churchill, Marshall Plan or no Marshall Plan, I remain convinced that without those two impossible and unlovable men Europe would not have survived.

Of the two, Adenauer had the harder task; he had to rebuild Germany in two senses, one physical and one moral. Germany's cities were rubble, her industry had been destroyed, her roads and railways hardly existed, people were still wandering through the ruins in the hope of finding something to live on; and it was in those circumstances that he began his postwar career, first taking up, in 1945, the post from which he had been dismissed by the Nazis in 1933: Mayor of Cologne. (He was dismissed from it again, shortly afterwards, by a British officer in the Army of Occupation, whose one claim on history's attention was that he had sacked Adenauer, presumably because the new mayor had proved as difficult for the new governors of Germany as he had for their Nazi predecessors.)

Adenauer presided over the reconstruction of Germany; but he had a harder task than that, which was to show the world that there was, or could be, another Germany, untainted by the foul and murderous frenzy of Nazism. The difficulty of the task lay principally not in the scepticism of the rest of the world, but, as he saw immediately, in rehabilitating the German people and at the same time giving them back an untainted pride. To go too far in purging the guilt would have risked damaging the all-important will to survive and rebuild; to go too far in instilling real self-confidence would have had the world crying out that the Germans had still not changed and never would. Adenauer walked that tightrope with courage and skill, and the upshot was that within an almost incredibly short span of time the Federal Republic had shown itself to be one of the most completely democratic countries in the world, and within a few years more was to show the same wondering world that the roots of her democracy had gone deep into the ancient soil of a Germany older, truer and far more enduring than what had grown from the poisonous grafts of the Nazis.

I sat at his desk, looking down at the green hillside below. Was it really a coincidence that Adenauer and de Gaulle were there, in position, when they were most needed? The call to glory is, of all summonses, the easiest to mistake, for there are so many trumpet-calls almost indistinguishable from the real thing, yet leading only to failure or worse. Adenauer and de Gaulle heard the call; two characters without self-doubt obeyed it instantly; Europe stands, free and prosperous, a monument to their genius; and no guns now point across the Rhine in either direction.

As I left the summerhouse to descend the path, I caught sight of Adenauer's walking-stick. It had been part of his image through his post-war life; he was rarely seen in public without it. It was very prettily decorated, and for a moment I felt a wild impulse to steal it.

Bad Godesberg is like those fashionable suburbs of Washington, which the politicians and commentators and agents of influence go home to at night. It is pretty enough, but so are the Washington suburbs, and both it and they know that they have no real purpose except to house those who move the levers of the world in the city by day. Bad Godesberg, unlike its American counterpart, has a castle, the Godesberg, and from the other side of the river it looks a noble pile, but as the visitor gets closer the truth is revealed; Bad Godesberg's fortress has been tamed, and is now, restored, a hotel. With which discovery I decided it was time to face the Bonn Question.

I faced it in the handsome Münsterplatz, over which the statue of Beethoven stands guard, ignored by the hoboes sleeping against the walls. These were interesting; I thought how easy it was to see the appeal of so free a life to those who care nothing for material considerations or comforts. It is much more difficult, for those who succumb to the appeal, to see the catch in it. Take the big red-bearded man, perhaps in his late thirties, stretched out asleep in the sun; he was warm and dry, and would worry about where his next meal was coming from only when he was hungry, and not before. But what does he do when the sun is gone for the year, and the wind howls icily across the square, and a bed on the pavement is a bed on the snow? Perhaps his kind have taken advice from the birds, and he flies south for the winter; if not, he would have to have an exceptionally hardy character not to regret his rejection of the workaday civilisation around him.

Now for the Bonn Question. Bonn suffers from the fact that it is an artificial capital. I have never been to Canberra, which is also an artificial capital, built as a compromise to silence the equally strident claims of Sydney and Melbourne; from what I hear and read from those who have been there, my failure to do so entails no great loss on my part. Brasilia, another such, I *have* visited, and a wonderful sight it is, too. Washington also is an artificial city; doubly so, in that the whole central area was laid out to a single plan, drawn up by L'Enfant as Paris was by Haussmann, and although it is now a huge and bustling city it has become artificial in a third sense, for it has only one topic of conversation, and those not interested in politics must have a thin and lonely time there, at any rate if they live in those fashionable suburbs.

Bonn, of course, existed before it became its country's capital; so did Washington, and even Canberra, though not Brasilia, which was simply carved out of the jungle. But Bonn was then a small, sleepy town; now it has 300,000 inhabitants, not counting Bad Godesberg. Well, 300,000 is not, by today's standards, a giant metropolis; still, it is a considerable city. Why, then, do even its inhabitants call it 'the Federal village'? Because it *is* a village. No doubt the choice of Bonn avoided the unfortunate associations of Munich or Nuremberg; no doubt if Cologne had been preferred Munich would have yelled blue murder, associations or no associations; no doubt if the only alternative that *was* seriously considered, Frankfurt, had been chosen, the perennial Socialist local government of the city would have caused friction whenever the Christian Democrats were in national office. So all in all, the choice of the Federal village was the right one, the inevitable one. But the truth about Bonn, which cannot be escaped, is that it is *boring*. It *looks* boring (its handsomest public building other than the Münster is the Post Office, which looks like a Baroque palace), it *feels* boring, and it *is* boring. The dead hand of government, particularly of *respectable* government, has lain upon the city too long, and it is not big enough to avoid being dominated by its role as a capital.

One place in Bonn is not boring: Number 20 Bonngasse. This pretty little house in a modest alley draws to it every visitor who comes to the city, no matter on what errand – every visitor, at any rate, who is capable of being stirred by genius, and wants to feel its presence. Genius? But what if the genius is one of the three or four greatest in all history, a figure who towers over the human race, dwarfing all but the greatest saints and the tiny handful of artists who can truly be compared to him? What, in short, if the genius is that of Beethoven, who was born in this house? Would not a visitor to Bonn who left it off his itinerary thus proclaim himself a man without imagination, even without a soul?

Beethoven was the most tremendous spirit Europe has produced. I sat in the house of his birth and thought of great, flawed geniuses like Luther, of great artists like Michelangelo, of my beloved friends Erasmus and Montaigne, of great readers in the book of nature like Galileo, of great writers like Tolstoy, Dante, Goethe, of great rulers like the Medici, even of the greatest geniuses of music itself, like Bach. (Mozart is *sui generis*; he cannot be classified here.) Still the sun of Beethoven gives light to them all; Socrates, Rembrandt, Shakespeare – has he any peers but these?

Beethoven's last piano was being played while I was there – the slow movement of the 'Pathétique'. I marvelled at the way he had been able to transcend the limitations of the available resources, for the instrument was horribly primitive and restricted. (But did not Shakespeare see centuries ahead, when he created his most womanly women knowing that they would be played by spotty boys, to a time when beautiful actresses would take the roles that had waited so long for them?) Then I wandered about the house. There were manuscript scores (for a few moments I had the original of the *Coriolan* overture in my hands), portraits galore, including the two most frequently reproduced on the covers of concert programmes, a few of his remaining possessions, his death-mask, and some of his hearing-aids, which look like medieval instruments of torture. But all those objects were forgotten when I looked into the little room upstairs (very little; a tall man would have had to take care of his head, but he would almost have been able, stretching out his arms, to have touched the walls on both sides). The room was entirely empty except for a marble column in the middle, on which there was a bust; the walls were whitewashed; this is where he was born. Just as, upstairs at Number 9 Getreidegasse in Salzburg, the corner of the room is roped off and empty except for a plaque which says simply 'Hier stand Mozarts Wiege' – here stood Mozart's cradle – so this bare room is roped off at the doorway and the visitor peers in.

This visitor peered in. I looked at the face, then narrowed my gaze to the mouth and chin, as I had done with the portraits. You could cut the mouth and chin out of a picture of Beethoven, leaving behind the nose, the eyes, even the familiar shock of hair, and no one who had ever seen the whole face would be in any doubt to whom they belonged. If you had never so much as heard of Beethoven, and were shown that mouth, you would know that it belonged to one of the most indomitable wills that ever inhabited a human body.

Leave Beethoven's life story out of account, and suppose that his music had been found, anonymous, in an attic, and could never be attributed. Would we not know, listening to it, everything his life exemplified? For the music tells the same story as the set of the mouth – how could it not? – and the story is that life is always and eternally a struggle, and must be a struggle, and would be useless if it were not a struggle. The purpose of any struggle is victory, but Beethoven's struggle was not for victory as the world counts victory (he made that clear when he tore out the dedication of the 'Eroica' to Napoleon after Napoleon had himself crowned Emperor); he cared nothing for the victories of conquerors; he sought, and taught, the inward victory, the victory over doubt and fear and loss, over pain, denial and resignation, over regret, flight, despair. All these are inevitable, inseparable from life itself; to be human is to suffer. But these inner demons are not invincible, and Beethoven taught us both that it is our duty to struggle against them, and that, if we arm ourselves to the fight in that invisible, intangible armour that is made jointly by man and God, we can triumph over them. There is an anecdote about Beethoven walking with Goethe, passing through a crowd; Goethe constantly stopped to acknowledge the greetings and admiring remarks, taking his hat off to return the salutes, while Beethoven shouldered his way through, bent on whatever business concerned him, the crowd being of no more concern to him than any of the other great obstacles he had overcome.

A rather solemnly pious young man, a pupil of Beethoven's, wrote at the end of an exercise, 'Finished, with God's help.' Beethoven, after correcting the set-piece, wrote beneath it, 'Man, help thyself.'

From Bonn to Cologne, the greatest city, at any rate measured by numbers (a million), of my journey. Was it also the greatest in other ways? I set out to discover the answer.

I set out from my hotel, the Excelsior; Cologne's two leading hotels (the other is the Dom) are both only a few feet from the cathedral; from my bedroom window it fills the view, the world, the sky; there is nothing else to be seen or thought about, even when the bells are not ringing to shake the building around me.

Cologne Cathedral is, without doubt, one of the most splendid and noble buildings in the world; the people of the city say, apparently without a smile, that if it should ever be finished the world would simultaneously come to an end. No doubt they say that in Barcelona, too, about the Sagrada Familia, but it is clear from a glance at that noble jigsaw-puzzle that it will never be complete, whereas Cologne looks, apart from the patches of scaffolding, as though it is as finished as a building can be. Then a visitor learns two things which correct the impression; the scaffolding, on one part or another of the cathedral, is permanent, and the twin towers, the crowning glory of the building, were built only in the nineteenth century, and are still unfinished.

It was begun in the eleventh century; most great churches have a long history of addition and alteration, but Cologne must hold the record for continuous building over nine hundred years, and an extra record for chagrin when, having at last got it nearly done, the bombs, though they did not destroy it, did very extensive damage to it, leaving Cologne to start, more or less, all over again.

It is made of yellow limestone, though none but an expert would recognise it as such; it has weathered to a grimy brown and a good deal of black, presumably because of pollution in the atmosphere, which in Cologne is said to be as bad as anywhere in Europe. Looking at the grime, I recalled the cleaning of St Paul's, completed in the 1960s, and the discoveries made in the course of it. First, the cleaning revealed carved figures on the columns that had been completely buried in the accumulated soot, which in places was nine inches deep; their very existence had been forgotten over the centuries. Second, they realised, from early drawings of the cathedral, that – since pollution in the years following its building had been at times even worse than in our own century – it had become entirely begrimed within some fifty years of its completion, so that we were the first people for 250 years to see it as it was when Wren finished it.

Like most such buildings, the size of Cologne Cathedral can only really be gauged from inside. It will hold 40,000 people, which was the entire population of the city when the building was begun. (What will the number of that population be when it is finished? I suppose if the legend is correct, and the world will come to an end when the cathedral is complete, it won't matter.) It is full of wonderful things, despite the destruction caused by the bombs and the much greater desecration (because most of Cologne's treasures were removed for safe keeping during the war) of a robbery that took place in 1975, when thieves broke into the treasury and stole many of the cathedral's choicest relics; the gang was eventually caught, and much of their haul recovered, but by then jewels had been prised out of the objects and disposed of, and some of the gold had been melted down. But Cologne's chief pride is the reliquary of the Three Kings, a huge golden triple sarcophagus in the form of a church, and that was too much for the thieves.

Then I stumbled upon two sculptures, as unlike as any two figures of Christ could be; the first was an immense St Christopher, nearly ten feet high, looking like a giant in a fable, ready to leap the river in a single stride with his precious burden on his right shoulder (who was looking quizzically down as if to counsel his benefactor *not* to try leaping the river). The second figure, just around the corner, is hardly three feet high; a *Pietà*, with the sorrowing mother cradling her dead son so gently in her arms that it seems as though she is concerned to avoid hurting him any more. But the energy and vigour of St Christopher fitted in a wonderful counterpoint with the gentleness and repose of the madonna.

The authorities in Cologne Cathedral have not only sought modern artists, goldsmiths, lapidaries and restorers to repair and renovate their damaged treasures; they have also embarked on a series of commissions for modern works. There was a pair of massive bronze doors, a set of stained-glass windows, and a miraculous stone pillar which acts as a tabernacle for the Eucharist; at first sight it seemed that it was carved identically all over with a regular pattern of leaves, and so it was, but as I looked more closely, I could see that every now and again, distributed at random, there was a tiny animal or human figure peering out of the otherwise regular foliage. There is even a modern organ.

I imagine the original architects and decorators of Cologne Cathedral would approve, indeed would not understand those who disapproved. It is only those who believe that such a thing as a cathedral can be 'finished' (even without the end of the world threatened if this one ever is) who *would* disapprove, and they would be people who fail to see that buildings like these are living organisms, for which to stop growing, changing, developing means decay and death.

But I lingered longest over the old, not the new; one of the most powerful sights in the whole building drew me back to it again and again, insisting each time that I had not seen enough of it. At the end of the chancel there stood an extended semicircle of figures, running down the choir on both sides; it showed the apostles, but at the end, where the two rows met, in the centre of the arc, were Christ and his

Mother. They were inclined towards each other, at an angle of perhaps forty degrees, and – there could be no mistake – they were both bowing very slightly to each other, and, as slightly, *smiling*. The smiles were grave, unfathomable in earthly terms, but they breathed a certainty, and a wonder at their certainty, which said, unmistakably: Death, where is thy sting?

At this point, I fell into conversation with an elderly, frail man, with a shock of white hair, spectacles, and hands that were thin and heavily veined; he looked like Bertrand Russell, and he also looked rather fussy and forbidding, even cross. It turned out that he was the Choirmaster of Cologne Cathedral; well, the Choirmaster of Cologne Cathedral would be a formidable figure by anybody's measure, and he was entitled to be testy if he wanted to. But before we had been talking for three minutes, it was apparent that my guess as to his character was wildly wrong; he was a gentle, wise and loving soul, steeped in his music and his beloved cathedral, of which he plainly knew every stone and echo. There was a miniature choir-concert taking place that evening; he showed me the programme and the music, asked my opinion of it, even wanted to know if it would do. I had met a benign, harmonious, true son and servant of St Cecilia.

As I turned away from the group of figures for the last time, a ray of the setting sun struck through the window and touched Christ's face. I looked again, half thinking it was an optical illusion, but it was not; from the chin to the hand there ran a cobweb. Somehow, it gave the whole figure an even more human look; to keep Cologne Cathedral clean, like any other building of its size and complexity (not that there are many to touch it for either), must be the – well, I can hardly say the devil's own job, so I had better describe the task as enough to try the patience of a saint. On my next visit, I vowed, I would check to see whether Christ had been dusted.

For anyone walking round a German city today, certainly one of any size, it takes time to realise how much of it is post-war. In the case of Hamburg or Essen, say (or Dresden, but that is in the other Germany), virtually all of it is, for there the devastation caused by the Allied bombing was almost as complete as that in Hiroshima or Nagasaki. But none escaped entirely, and very few with minor damage. The larger the city, of course, the more that survived; Cologne was not among the very worst hit, but photographs of its condition at the end of the war suggest a vast area that had been entirely obliterated, and after a time I began to greet with genuine surprise any building that was obviously old and not obviously restored. The oldest and least restored is a Roman tunnel-sewer that runs for a hundred yards beneath the city; there is a section of it on display above ground, and a formidable structure it is, with a huge vaulted arch six feet high.

Clearly, the Romans built to last, but there is one aspect of their building which I do not recall ever seeing discussed, and which the tunnel brought sharply to mind. The Roman sewerage systems were remarkably advanced and efficient; even more so were their aqueducts, many of which survive today to remind us of Roman architectural skills. But they should remind us of something else. The aqueducts were designed to bring not just water but *clean* water; the sewers were built not so that we may marvel at the solidity of their construction but to cleanse their cities. We are used to reading European history which depicts the noisome conditions in which people lived until late in the nineteenth century, with open cess-pits and sewers running down the middle of the streets, with water-supplies that brought round the cholera (and, earlier, the plague) every year like a fifth season, with no understanding of the importance of cleanliness and clean air. What we forget is that such conditions did not go back to prehistoric times, ended at last by the enlightenment that burst on the world at the end of the Victorian era; they were a *regression* from classical times. When and why did the world lose the habit of cleanliness for so many centuries, and regain it only with such difficulty and pain?

The new architecture of Cologne, like that of most German cities, suffers from its date and the circumstances of its building. With hundreds of thousands of acres levelled entirely, their planners and builders had, in theory, an opportunity like that which faced London after the Great Fire, or the City of London after the Blitz. London had met its seventeenth-century challenge bravely and magnificently; the City had failed the twentieth-century version completely and shamelessly, out of cowardice, lack of imagination and greed. The German cities had no choice; in their immediate post-war chaos and desolation the most urgent task was survival, and buildings were put up without thought for the morrow, or at least the day after the morrow. But the result was that for thirty years West German architecture, once the most innovative and defiant in all Europe, had languished, and the cities of Germany presented a picture of new but lifeless buildings and streets. Recently, the tide has begun to turn; the office blocks of the *Wirtschaftswunder* began to show some original features, the pedestrian precincts (West Germany's one serious contribution to post-war urban living, chanced upon when the rubble had been cleared but the rebuilding had not yet started) began to take on real character, and a new spirit of adventurous architecture began, very slowly, to emerge.

No one could call the Hohe Strasse the product of a new spirit of adventurous architecture; it is, however, a pedestrian thoroughfare of considerable charm. To walk from the cathedral to the top end of it (which is really the bottom, for the numbering runs the other way, towards the centre of the city) is to be struck by its extraordinary resemblance to Hong Kong, of all places. The shops and restaurants that line the Hohe Strasse from end to end are bright with vertical signboards and banners, and the street is very narrow; the Chinese shopping streets in Hong Kong are exactly the same except for their alphabet, and as I walked down the Hohe Strasse I might have been far away, in the East.

More closely examined, the Hohe Strasse in one important respect resembles New York more than anywhere in Europe, for there is no class distinction among the shops and other enterprises, as there is in London and Paris and indeed Munich. London, for instance, has an Oxford Street, a Bond Street and a Carnaby Street, and (at least until Oxford Street's precipitate decline began) they could be easily distinguished. Bond Street was for fine things, the upper crust of shopping. Carnaby Street sold throwaways for the young; jeans, hamburgers, short-life jewellery, shorter-life records. In the middle was Oxford Street, its wares unexciting but dependable, concentrating on necessities like furniture and household goods and sensible shoes. As in Fifth Avenue, in the Hohe Strasse of Cologne such divisions are unknown; in this Hong Kong of the Rhine the sellers of jeans and the latest cassettes, the McDonald's and instant photoprocessors, happily co-exist with giant department stores and little elegant boutiques. No doubt it makes shopping more complicated, but it surely also makes shopping a more agreeable experience.

Cologne has a most hospitable Town Hall; the modern building incorporates the remains of the old one (its Renaissance front miraculously escaped damage altogether), and a visitor can walk in and wander about the entire building without being asked his business, let alone told that he is not allowed in at all. I doubt if Birmingham, a city with almost exactly the same population as Cologne, and therefore presumably with the same municipal responsibilities, would be as accommodating. Nor, I imagine, would it have so fine a blend of ancient rooms carefully preserved and handsome new ones decorated with the paintings and sculptures of contemporary local artists; nor the tiny, innocent fountain tucked away in a corner, embedded in the only bit of the old wall at this point to survive, which has been carefully dovetailed into the new stone around it. Outside, in the square opposite, is a plaque to mark the spot where John Kennedy made his last speech to a foreign audience, in June 1963; that must have been the tour on which he had spoken the famous words: 'Ich bin ein Berliner.'

The Alter Markt, once Cologne's centre, had been almost entirely destroyed; only one or two of the half-timbered houses had survived. On one of the new ones, however, there was a striking sight; a modern reproduction in bronze of a legendary Cologne figure, a dwarf, was fixed to the façade just above the windows of the top storey. The dwarf faced away from the square, looking into the corner of it, but if his face was not on show to the people passing through the square, they were not entirely without greeting from him, for his breeches were round his ankles, and he was defiantly showing his buttocks to Cologne.

The back of the dwarf-bottom house, which belonged, I discovered, to Cologne's resident wit, prankster and cynic, was marked more decorously; two life-size bronze figures stand on the pavement. These were Tünnes and Schäl, to whom all the Cologne jokes are attributed, like Pat and Mike in the Irish stories and Graf Rudi and Graf Bobby in the Viennese ones. Tünnes is clearly the stooge; he has a clown's nose and wears clogs and a smock, while Schäl is bowler-hatted and bow-tied, and wears a smart suit. I soon learned that it was no use my asking for Tünnes and Schäl stories to take away, because they are all in the curious language that is Cologne's private *lingua franca*, a dialect unintelligible even to other Germans, let alone foreigners.

If Cologne has its way, though, the foreigners will be coming on errands more serious than a wish to learn dialect jokes. Cologne, whatever its other attractions, means business. Throughout the city, there are signs to the 'Kölnmesse', the Cologne Fair. The fair the signs mean is not a funfair, not even an industrial fair; it is a huge area of the city, covering a good many blocks, which is available for every kind of international gathering of sellers and buyers. In every hotel, in public buildings, at the railway station and the airport, the visitor is showered, confetti-like, with handsomely printed leaflets about the fairs currently going on and the availability of space for the staging of fairs on any subject to match the customer's sample. Cologne had clearly invested a very great deal in the industrial fair business; the ground area of the exhibition complex is getting on for 2·25 million square feet, on the eastern side of the river, and from the embankment on the western side it dominated the view.

Or rather, it would have dominated the view if the Rhine had not been there. The Rhine frontage in Cologne is a huge thoroughfare, matching indeed the huge thoroughfare that the river itself forms. As in so many cities, though few as big as this one, the town turns out of an evening to take the air with a stroll along its favourite walk; the most famous of these is the Ramblas in Barcelona, but Cologne, I realised, does pretty well with the series of embankments – Rheinufer, Adenauerufer, Nederlanderufer, Gustav Heinemann Ufer and, very much the odd man out among the names, the Agrippina Ufer. (Agrippina was Nero's mother, and he murdered her – kicked her to death, as I recall. What connection did that happy family have with Cologne?)

A few feet from the embankment walk, the river was crowded with ships, many of them vast pleasure-steamers; the embankment walk itself was crowded with ticket-offices and landing-stages for those who wanted to embark. But the Cologners were evidently content to sniff the evening air and let the world, and the river, go by.

It was time for dinner, during which I learned more about epoxy resin, at any rate in its commercial aspect, than I really wanted to know. At the next table to mine in Chez Alex there was a party of six men, discussing matters of mutual business concern; they were all in chemicals, and there seemed to be at least four firms represented. Was I about to hear a merger concluded, a price-fixing agreement arrived at, a proposal for shared overheads put forward? No, I was going to hear about epoxy resin, which all evening flowed more freely than the wine; I must have heard the words a hundred times.

I do not know what epoxy resin is, and did not discover in the course of the evening, but I do now know that the trade in it is going through hard times. Consignments and contracts were discussed in gloomy tones; prices now and only a few months earlier were compared, and the more recent ones found wanting; the psychology of allowing their regular customers a discount on a consignment ordered before the price fell was explored; and then the talk turned to Hermann.

Hermann was the villain. He was clearly in the same business as the six of them, but had not been invited to the feast, and it was soon clear why not.

Hermann had been undercutting them all, and they were very displeased with him; epoxy resin, it seemed, was in quite enough trouble without Hermann shaving the margins still thinner. The only consolation was that Hermann was going to come a cropper. It was clearly impossible for him to be getting or making his supplies more cheaply, so he could only be undercutting them in order to poach *their* customers for the future. This, obviously, was dangerous business practice for anyone at any time, and Hermann was gambling both on an upturn in the market and on his belief that the newly attracted customers would stay with him. Perversely, I began to take quite a shine to Hermann; he seemed to be the enterprising type that Germany's industry needs no less than Britain's, and their talk of his over-reaching himself and going smash sounded more and more like whistling in the dark. Surreptitiously, I raised my glass to Hermann.

When in Cologne, visit 4711; I did, first discovering where the number came from. It seems that when Cologne was occupied by the French in 1794 the French soldiers had difficulty in remembering where their billets were, so their commander proclaimed that every house in Cologne should bear a number. Herr Wilhelm Mühlens, who had already begun to make the famous elixir (the firm's history – or legends, the two being inextricably interwoven – says that he got the magic formula from a Carthusian monk), lived, and made the potion, in the house that was numbered 4711, and that was that. (The original house has long since gone, but on its site – still numbered 4711 – there stands the 4711 shop, an elegant treasure-house of beautiful smells, from perfume to soap, including, surprisingly, some famous brands from rival firms. It is still, in its sixth generation, a family concern.)

I suppose I thought that the 4711 firm made nothing but 4711. Not at all; just as Heinz kept its famous slogan '57 varieties' long after the 57 had become hundreds, so Mühlens & Co. now put their irritatingly unforgettable trademark on hundreds of scents, lotions and elixirs, magic creams and magic rubs, perfumed sprays and perfumed solids, every size, colour and variety of things designed to make people smell nicer than they would without such aids. Nor are they content to rest on their aromatic laurels; the hunt continues every day for a new combination of essences that will have noses all over the world sniffing in appreciation. Only four years ago, responding to the marketing analysts' revelation that girls of fourteen are now interested in fragrance, they devised 'My Melody Dreams' and 'My Melody Musk', bringing the total number of lines sold by 4711 to around 360; a little longer, and those who are exceptionally interested in smelling nice will be able to do so with a different smell every day of the year.

I felt that, by way of starting to investigate this extraordinary business, I could do no better than visit the alchemists' inner sanctum, where they presumably traffic with the devil in return for his advice on blending. The head of the laboratory was Dr Walter Hönig, and if he traffics with the devil, I suspect that he comes off best. The laboratory itself was an amazing place; there were uncountable numbers of jars and bottles and other containers, each offering its own ingredient. So many were there that there was simply no room for most of them on the shelves which lined the walls, and an ingenious system of racks had been devised; bulkheads some nine inches wide slid into the walls, and when they slid out they could be seen to be filled on both sides with yet more shelves containing yet more smells.

So my first question to Dr Hönig was: how many? How many liquids, spices, chemicals, essences, stuffs did he have around him? 'Five thousand,' he said, and added, calmly and with no sign that he expected me to be surprised, 'and I can recognise three thousand of them blindfolded.' Dr Hönig, then, is what tea-blenders call 'a nose', and a champion schnozzle he must be, for there can hardly be a tea-nose with such a repertoire, if only because there aren't that number of tea-fragrances for a nose to sniff, and the only other comparable field of such endeavour – wine-tasting – though it certainly could provide an almost infinite number of varieties for the tasters to try their blindfold luck on, could surely not produce an expert to match, in numbers recognised, the nose of Dr Hönig.

I had already thought of the analogy with the alchemist; now, as I wandered about this *omnium gatherum* of smells, I began to believe that Dr Hönig, having long since discovered how to transmute base metals into gold, and even longer ago how to make not one but a dozen love-potions, was now engaged in the hunt for the elixir that would abolish death, as well as – just in case that one failed – an ichor that would raise the dead to life.

Meanwhile, his job was to go on mixing ingredients in different combinations and different quantities until he hit upon a new scent or essence that could be stamped 4711 and sold. But after a few minutes it became apparent that he was not only a chemist and a nose, he was something of a philosopher of smell. Animals, he explained, recognise one another by smell, for each has its own; human beings still have a trace of this identification in their biological composition, and when hygiene was not as widespread as it is today (presumably the same is true in parts of the world where it has still not taken root) individuals had a specific body odour by which others unconsciously recognised them. Now we wash more often and thus kill our specific smell, but unconsciously we still need to give off a recognition signal to the noses of others, and that is why – well, it is why 4711 is so successful.

I watched him mix and stir and sniff; I asked him if anyone could learn to be a nose, and he said anyone could train the fifth sense. (On the other hand, anyone can learn to play the piano, but obviously there is an inborn quality which only a few have; no amount of practising will enable a player without it to be mistaken for Brendel.) He also said – I have heard the same from tea-blenders – that the nose gets tired after a couple of hours, and its ability to distinguish among odours declines rapidly, so that a rest is essential. ('What are you doing?' 'I'm resting my nose.')

Then I went exploring the whole building, and in particular the cellars, which reminded me of nothing so much as those of Jacques Mousset in his Château de Fines Roches at Châteauneuf-du-Pape.* There were huge metal vats and tubs and drums arranged in rows, all with their contents, and even the date they were laid down, carefully recorded on labels, but what clinched the resemblance was a vast area in which wooden casks – half-hogshead size – lay in avenues on wooden trestles, their vintages maturing until it was time for the bung to be removed and the spigot turned. I mentioned the comparison to Hönig, and he pointed out that it was hardly even a comparison, because eau-de-Cologne is 94 per cent alcohol, and, like anything based on alcohol, has to mature. And then – I knew it had to come, and had long ago braced myself for it – I heard the story of the Great 4711 Secret. We approached it via a discussion of the development of laboratory techniques; purity, weighing, analysis, temperature – all these and many more, I said, must surely have been primitive in 1792 and for a long time after. Hönig agreed, and added that distillation itself was unknown at the beginning of the Mühlens's family business; but through all the refinements the basic formula for 4711 had remained the same. We were off on the magical mystery tour.

The Carthusian monk appeared, beckoning his friend the first Mühlens into a corner and telling him that he had discovered an *aqua mirabilis*. Mühlens sniffed, agreed, and went into production at his still un-numbered house. And ever since then, children, The Formula had been handed down from father to son, and no one else in the firm – *no*

---

* See *Hannibal's Footsteps*, Ch. 3.

one other than the head of it – was allowed to know the details of the magic mix. It is not, apparently, a secret ingredient but the unique blend of familiar essences which constitutes the secret. I was taken to what was obviously a strong-room, a walk-in safe, in which the present head of the firm, like his forefathers before him, mutters spells and invocations, throws in the proper quantities of eye of newt and toe of frog, together with a due proportion of blind-worm's sting, wool of bat, tongue of dog, lizard's leg and even tiger's chaudron (whatever that might be) and – Peace! the charm's wound up!

The Sanctum Sanctorum remained firmly closed; I was told that it remained closed to everyone, at all times, except when Faust was at work, and even then only two men in the firm had the key of the strong-room, and both of them had to be present at the opening and shutting. Moreover, nobody other than Faust himself, not even the key-holders, was ever allowed *into* it at all. I pleaded for a glimpse inside – after all, the most I would see would be rows of jars and bottles, together with laboratory equipment, and such a glimpse would mean nothing to me, indeed would mean nothing even to an expert in this arcane science – but the door remained shut, and eyes were rolled up in horror at my blasphemy; another moment, and somebody would have said it was more than his job was worth.

And at that point I remembered Dr Johnson, and decided that credulity must take a stand. To put it another way, faint but unmistakable amid all the heady, fragrant, inviting scents with which the place was filled, my nose had caught a different odour: somewhere nearby there lurked, with a smile on its lips, a fine red herring.

Nobody could explain, at any rate to my understanding, what exactly Herr Mühlens and all the previous Mühlenses *did* in the sealed chamber. If he was mixing the ultimate essence, the flavour that distinguished 4711 from all its rivals, what did he do when he had finished? Did he go to the bottling plant and put three drops into each bottle as it came round on the conveyor-belt? If he did, he must have been an uncommonly brisk worker, because I visited the bottling plant, too, and watched many thousands of the bottles being filled (without a sign of Faust) at the rate of three a second. Or did he, once a week, make a tub of it, then wheel the tub out (remember that *no one* else was allowed into the heart of the mystery) and invite those excluded from the Promised Land to dip in and carry a measure of the elixir to their own mixing-vats? If so, it must have been an uncommonly hospitable tub, for 4711 is very big business indeed, and at even three drops of nectar to the bottle it would require a weekly Rhine to flavour them all.

And then again, if *nobody* but the head of the family has been allowed in since the early 1790s, surely the mysterious cave must be getting a little grimy by now? Does the boss sweep up, dust the equipment, wash the retorts, scour the pans? If the lighting or the heating or the wash-basin goes wrong, or if a table-leg collapses, does he hastily acquire the skills of an electrician, an engineer, a plumber and a carpenter? Or is he born with such abilities, merely by being a Mühlens? And further, at what age is the heir instructed in the mystery? Suppose the paterfamilias should be cut off in his prime by a heart attack or a car-crash, before little Wilhelm is old enough to understand the formula – would not the entire basis of 4711's fortune vanish overnight?

I decided that I didn't believe a word of it, though I conceived a considerably enhanced admiration for whoever had been doing the Public Relations for the firm of Mühlens since 1792. If all the head of the firm does when the great steel door swings shut behind him is to take out a volume of Goethe (an honoured client of the firm from 1802) or a solitaire-board, or even a frying-pan and a couple of eggs, I salute him for convincing the world for so long that he has been doing something much more mysterious.

Later that day, I went out for my last walk before leaving Cologne. Buoyed up by the entertaining absurdity of my day at 4711, I sought something by way of contrast. I found it in Kasinostrasse, which presumably means Casino Street, a most inappropriate address. For in that undistinguished thoroughfare, with its raffish name, there is the door to the last and greatest of Cologne's churches; dwarfed by the mighty cathedral, with its history and treasures, and by the quadruple-spired Great St Martin, its Romanesque magnificence lovingly restored after its extensive bomb-damage, stands St Maria in Kapitol, its simple exterior giving no hint of what lies within. I had learned that the original building on the site had been founded as a convent church by Plectrude, who sounded like a scientific instrument but turned out to be the step-mother of Charles Martel; more than that I did not know.

The door swung open; for an instant I thought I was standing in the great Basilica in Torcello, for the purity, innocence and sense of repose that swept over me as I entered was exactly the same as in that wonderful *cathédrale engloutie*. The interior walls looked as though they

54 *At Beethoven's piano*

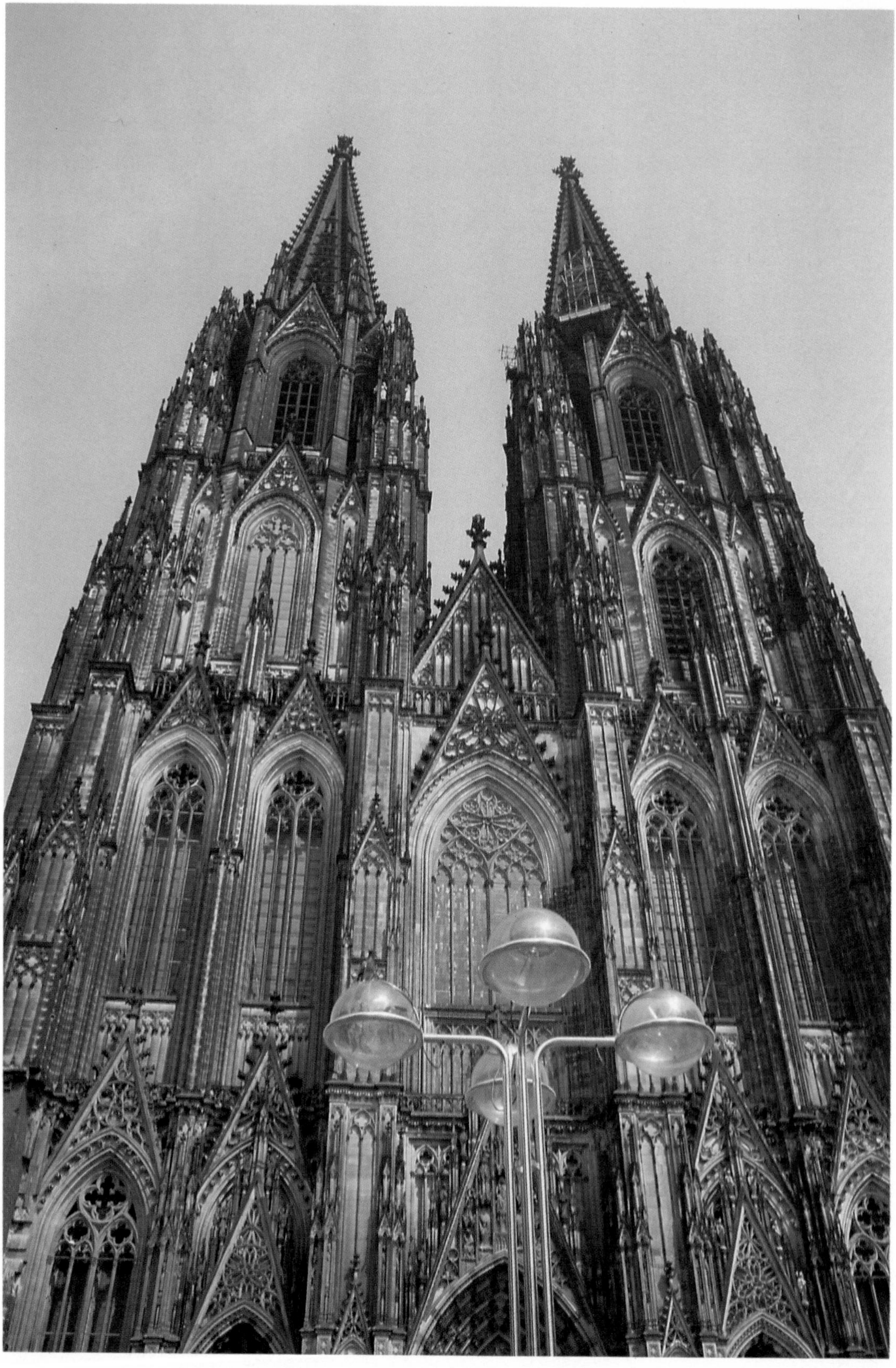

55

had been scrubbed, and great stretches of them were without decoration or anything else to break the flow; the spacious, triple-vaulted roof was like a divine hand stretched out in protection and blessing, the curve of the chancel had a Pythagorean harmony that vibrated like a plucked cello-string, and in conclusion I found a carved rood-screen, a Renaissance treasure recently acquired, with a series of panels depicting the life of Christ scene by scene.

Following the Rhine from source to sea had, from time to time on this journey (and I had now covered something like three-quarters of the route), struck me as rather an odd thing to be doing, and occasionally I had forgotten why I had ever embarked on it, having to go and look at the river to remind myself. But in the soaring peace of St Maria in Kapitol I needed no other excuse.

Cologne, I had felt, was a strange place. It had a long, varied and often glorious history; it was plainly a city of great wealth; it had a consciousness of its own identity (witness its dialect, clung to through all the vicissitudes of the German language around it). But no one could call it a lively place; there was no sign of the artistic ferment of Munich, the literary tradition of Frankfurt, the ostentation of Berlin, the cosmopolitanism of Hamburg. Cologne is not dead, like Vienna, or inhuman, like Birmingham, or neurotic, like New York, or smug, like Paris, or bewildered, like London. But it is torpid; it is a city that has had a very big lunch and is now too drowsy to attend to the afternoon's work. Not much of it is very beautiful or very ugly, not many of its citizens will ever write a symphony or murder their wives, no change in the political complexion of its government will cause any kind of upheaval, nor will its newspapers ever startle, let alone shock, their readers. Some ingredient is missing from Cologne's blood; its lack is not fatal, but it makes the circulation flow more sluggishly. And there is another thing, relevant here, which I must touch upon, though with the utmost circumspection.

I have contrasted Cologne with a number of other important German cities, and implied that Cologne lacks qualities that the others have, qualities which improve life in any city. I think that it is true, but it is also true that *all* German cities, certainly of any size and pretension, lack one particular element that has for centuries provided a certain extra quality in the life of any great urban centre which lays claim to an interest in the dramatic and pictorial arts, in music, in books, in trade and banking, in science and medicine, in

55 *The Unfinished Symphony*

opinion and argument, in scholarship and language, in journalism and humour.

In 1933 there were roughly a million Jews in Germany. Almost all of those who did not manage to get out of the country were murdered; very few indeed of those who did escape went back there after the war, and practically none of their descendants, born in free countries, did so. It is probable that there are no more than about 50,000 Jews in the Federal Republic today, and their numbers are very unlikely ever to increase. Now if we look at the contribution to the life of Europe made by Europe's Jews in the century and a half (roughly), from the throwing down of the ghetto walls begun by the French Revolution and Napoleon, to the advent of Hitler, the observer will see an explosion of talent and achievement with very few parallels in history. The reason for the explosion was not an inherent superiority in Jews but the removal of restrictions that, very widely accepted by the Jews themselves, had until then held them back from demonstrating the knowledge, talent and creativity that had been fermenting in them for centuries; when the dyke collapsed, the sea poured over the land.

From then until Hitler, Germany, like other European countries (and the United States, of course, but rather later), had experienced the quickening effect of the Jewish contribution to culture, commerce, discovery and thought. Indeed, anti-semitism (not only the Nazi kind) had long battened on this effect in its claim that Jews were too numerous and too successful.

The Jews of Occupied Europe were slaughtered in their millions, too; but many survived, and many of those who had got out in time (a larger proportion than the Jews of Germany) returned to their countries after the war. Only in Germany has the intellectual and commercial yeast of Jewry disappeared almost entirely, and with no expectation that it will ever return. The effect is difficult to define exactly, but there can be no doubt that it has been substantial in most areas and devastating in some. (For some twenty years after the end of the war Germany had no theatre to speak of – she has precious little *new* theatre even now – and few objective readers of German newspapers would deny that the loss of the curious salt that the pre-Nazi Jewish *feuilletonistes* supplied has diminished their quality.) As I have said, Germany, unlike Austria, has behaved almost impeccably, since the Federal Republic came into being, not only to her few Jews and to the State of Israel, but also in her unrelenting search for those guilty of participating in the Holocaust and still living within Germany's borders. But

Germany has not been able to repair the loss to German life which resulted from the destruction of German Jewry; and it shows. Perhaps it shows most clearly in Cologne, and perhaps that is what I had sensed when I felt that there was something missing in the greatest, richest and most powerful of all the cities of the Rhine.

12

The Black Hole of Duisburg

I CAN NO longer remember why I was in Mönchengladbach, staying at the Holiday Inn, but it must have a fair claim to the title of the least interesting town in the world, for all that the glee-singers of the Grünen Kranz lived there. The Michelin Guide is a good measure of the claim: in addition to their listings of hotels and restaurants, they are assiduous in leading the user to the interesting sights of the town under discussion, whether a noble cathedral, an art gallery or museum of interest, a handsome bridge, an old house still in use, a bas-relief on the Town Hall, even a spot where a fine view of the surrounding countryside may be had. Poor Mönchengladbach, though it has a population of 250,000, has no entry at all under the heading of 'Sehenswürdigkeiten', and although I walked round it for some time, trying to find something – anything – to take a picture of, I failed.

On the other hand, the Holiday Inn, though its architecture certainly did not rate as one of the leading sights even of Mönchengladbach, provided a different kind of interest. It is customary for the great chains of international hotels – the Hiltons, the Sheratons, the Holiday Inns – to be decried as fit only for the undiscriminating, a booking at them the indelible mark of the wimp (or wally). True, no one would choose such places for a month's holiday, if what is required is a friendly, attentive, wholly personal atmosphere, with an intimacy about the building itself which makes the visitor feel that it is the private home of a friend. Who ever knew the name of the hall porter at a Hilton, and who was ever served twice by the same waitress in the breakfast-room of a Sheraton? On all such tests, these monsters, some of them boasting a thousand rooms or more, fail. But there are other tests, on which these standardised chain hotels, now to be found in every country in the world where there is anything serious in the way of hotel business at all, score surprisingly well. They are without character, charm or soul, but the traveller, who is very likely to be staying only a few days and is therefore not in desperate need of such qualities (nor in expectation of them either), can rely without any danger of disappointment on an ironclad minimum standard, which is often not only surprisingly high, but absolutely uniform throughout the world. At any of these hotels, anywhere, the traveller will never find that there are no towels in the bathroom, he will never arrive and find that the Kleenex box is only half full, he will never feel the lack of a local telephone directory, writing-paper, a laundry service, a restaurant with reassuringly familiar food, some kind of room-service, lights that work and that are even ample. He will never come back in the afternoon to find that the room has not been visited by the chambermaids, nor will he discover that the furniture is dusty or the carpet stained or the sheets frayed; the bed on which the sheets are unfrayed, moreover, will be both comfortable and wide, and if he wants more pillows or blankets, they will be at his door within a few minutes of his asking for them. If you leave your room in such a hotel at mid-morning, you will invariably find the maids in the corridor with a trolley; if you look closely, you will see that the trolley is equipped with a check-list, which is identical, apart from the language it is couched in, in New York or Rome or Tokyo, or for that matter up-country Burundi. A tick will not be made against 'Laundry-bag' until the maid has inspected the wardrobe and either found or put a laundry-bag there, or against 'Room-service menu' unless it is standing on the dressing table.

The virtue of this system is, obviously, its reliability; such hotels are machines for living in briefly, but the only question anyone needs to ask about any machine is: does it work? The answer is that it does, almost invariably, and almost everywhere. The Holiday Inn at Mönchengladbach may not cherish its guests as individuals, but I have no complaint at all against a hotel which makes a carefully limited promise and fulfils it to the letter.

Düsseldorf, which I had not visited for many years, is the new Germany, with all its virtues and all its faults. To start with, it signals, for a traveller coming from the south, the beginning of the Ruhr, perhaps the biggest and most concentrated industrial area in the world.

Already it is impossible to say where Essen ends and Bochum begins; from Krefeld on the west to Dortmund on the east (a distance of nearly sixty miles) the map shows one continuous built-up area, and when the moving stain spreads down to Wuppertal, as it very soon will, there will be a similar monstrous conurbation from there to Recklinghausen, more than thirty miles to the north.

To this huge centre of steel, coal, labour, activity and grime Düsseldorf acts as the gateway, and indeed the office. The best way to see it is from above, and I saw it from a flat roof twenty-three storeys up. The roof itself was not without interest; it had a kind of railway running right round it, very near the parapet, with a bizarre kind of engine parked under a tarpaulin, clearly ready to be uncovered and to move round the track. But what was it for? I soon found out; it was the window-cleaning machine. From it was suspended the cradle that the cleaners used; the contraption is held fast to the tracks, then swings over the parapet and disgorges the cradle and its intrepid crew, lowering them, back and forth, steadily down one side of the building as they move across the face of each storey. When they get to the bottom, they are hauled right up again, the machine moves round to the next face, and the process is repeated. I had seen the future, and it worked.

The first image that comes to anyone a hundred yards or so above Düsseldorf is that of Christ's temptation in the wilderness, when Satan took him up into a high place and said, 'All the kingdoms of the earth I will give thee, if thou wilt bow down and worship me.' Christ resisted the temptation, but Düsseldorf clearly did not. From my eyrie I could see all the kingdoms of the earth, at any rate of the modern, international earth; as far as the horizon there stretched the gleaming office-blocks and shopping-precincts of the new Germany – to be precise, the second new Germany, for Düsseldorf is clearly far advanced in its second generation of post-war architecture, and some of it is surprisingly distinguished. Düsseldorf suffered almost total devastation in the war, and must now stand as a symbol of the heroic efforts the Germans made in rebuilding their country; it would be difficult for anyone today to claim that it is lovable, but no one would deny that it is prosperous.

Düsseldorf's prosperity comes partly from the economic success of Federal Germany, but more particularly from its character as the administrative and banking headquarters of the vast heavy industries of the Ruhr. The Ruhr, clearly, is told to wipe its boots before entering

Düsseldorf; it is a remarkably clean city, its own industries banished to the outer suburbs, and its huge network of commercial activities generating nothing dirtier than paper, which is anyway rapidly vanishing into the hungry maw of computerisation. It did not at all surprise me when I happened upon an Economic Museum – 'the Museum for People and Business' – where instead of paintings and sculpture there are graphs and tables, and in place of Roman coins and Egyptian pots the visitor can feast his business feelings on models of economic activity and accounts of progress made by the EEC.

Corelli Barnett's startling but persuasive book, *The Audit of War*, published in 1986, argued forcefully that Germany's prosperity and advance was made possible by the Germans' twin realisations, prompted by the urgent need to rebuild their country and equip it for the future before anything else, that their salvation would come from their own hard work and nothing else, and that the comforts of social policy must wait upon the achievement of the goal of reconstruction; his parallel argument was that Britain's continuing economic decline had been caused by our reversing those priorities, so that while we were building safety-nets for the economically unsuccessful and spending billions on sustaining the old, dying industries, we were falling further and further behind (and still are) in equipping ourselves for the real demands of the future. As Germany and Japan raced ahead in the post-war world, there was an uneasy joke in Britain about the advantages of losing a war rather than winning it, and it was suggested that we should provoke the United States to declare war on us. The joke died away in the end; from the twenty-third floor in Düsseldorf, I had a feeling that it might be time to revive it, now that nobody would find it funny.

In Düsseldorf the end of July marks twofold Carnival time. The first half was a parade of riflemen, a ceremony that had been going on for nearly 700 years; the riflemen are all dressed in eighteenth-century uniforms, and they are divided into rival companies from the different sections of the city – I was reminded of the *sestiere* of Siena's Palio. Like many, if not most, such ceremonies, the principal purpose behind it is the drinking of beer, and the Mayor of Düsseldorf, mindful that the beer tradition goes back at least at long as the riflemen's, knocks in the first bung of the first cask, with the traditional cry of 'It's tapped!' But it was the other half of Düsseldorf's summer celebrations that was to prove my undoing.

The other half is the Düsseldorf Fair, and this fair, unlike the severely commercial and industrial ones of Cologne and most other German cities, is a funfair. It is certainly the biggest in Europe, and must be the biggest non-permanent one in the world, for Disneyland and its like are fixed structures, whereas the Düsseldorf Fair is erected for only eight days and then dismantled (the eight days, incidentally, are estimated to take some 60 million marks). It is vast, crammed with 300 of the traditional funfair attractions, from roller-coasters to stalls selling toffee-apples, and the 300 represent all that can be packed into the space available, out of the 1000 applications that the Fair gets every year.

My undoing approached. I allowed myself to be coaxed on to the Ferris Wheel, a vast one some 180 feet high. Though it induced vertigo, and shivered uncomfortably in the wind, it was surprisingly unterrifying; the sixty or so cabins hung from cross-bars, and the wheel revolved fairly slowly, so that they were never tilted out of the vertical by more than a few degrees, and even when they began to revolve horizontally as well they went round at a reasonable speed. The view over the whole Fair was spectacular from the top, with the dreadful loops and inclines of the giant roller-coaster dominating it and the noise from the traditional fairground organs wafting up most pleasantly. I stepped off at last with a feeling that the terror instilled by these fairground frighteners had been much exaggerated. It was time for my undoing.

I had had enough sense to avoid the device which whirled its passengers round in little cars fixed to the ends of mighty metal arms and which, when the cars were revolving at maximum speed (which looked like ninety miles an hour, and may well have been), began to swing them at right-angles to the direction of flight, so that the victims were being acted on by what must have been an enormous centrifugal force in the horizontal plane, and at the same time a scarcely less powerful one in the vertical.

But now, reassured by my experience on the Big Wheel, and smug with my determination not to set foot on the double whirler, I came upon the Magic Carpet, and was undone. The Magic Carpet, may its operators suffer bankruptcy (alas, they were unlikely to, since there was a constant queue for the suffering it provided), was a flat car, gaily decorated, with room for about fifty people at a time, seated on benches in rows. It was suspended from one end of a horizontal arm, with a massive counterweight at the other end; the arm pivoted in the middle on a no less massive upright column. This meant that the car

56 A quick way through the traffic   57 The secrets of 4711   58 Hard hat area   59 The power house

56

57

THYSSEN

60

61

62

could describe a complete circle while remaining the same way up; that, I felt, was all the further reassurance I needed, and I stepped aboard. Once seated beyond hope of changing my mind, I was locked in by a huge metal rod which descended into my lap and held me fast; not only was it impossible for the passenger to fall out, anyone who had been seeking a novel way to commit suicide by *jumping* out would have found his ambition baulked. I have to add that although I had not gone aboard with the intention of committing suicide, I did, in the course of the ride, feel quite strongly that if the lock which pinned me to my seat could only be relaxed for a moment, it would be a most attractive idea.

Up, over and down swept the car; as it fell, I thought that the old cliché about leaving one's insides behind while falling had come, for me at least, literally true. Unable to open my eyes, lest they should fly out of my head, I clung to the locking bar and prayed for death, even a violent one. No such boon was granted me; instead, the Iron Maiden began to vary her repertoire. The arm swung us up to the top position, high over the pivot, *and there stopped*, clearly debating whether to fall forwards or backwards. When it had decided, it fell; then it climbed up again and fell the other way, or sometimes, when the alternating rhythm had been established, the *same* way, so that the body, braced in one direction, was hurled in the other. The worst trick of all was the moment at which the car paused not at the top of its climb but at the bottom of its fall, level with the boarding and alighting platform. Convinced, as I was meant to be, that the torture was over, I plucked at the restraining arm as it prepared to let me go, whereupon the car shot up again and went round completely three times at its maximum speed, and backwards.

I crawled off in a state of collapse. When I felt a little stronger, I wandered about the Fair, and found a number of devices, no less enthusiastically patronised than the Magic Carpet, which were actually worse. One, for instance, was similar to my enemy, except that the arm which held it did not pivot, so that the passenger was upside-down when the cage was at the top. Another was worse even than that; it, too, went right over with its passengers upside-down, but in addition, the cars in which they rode were also revolving on their own axis, so that the people in them were simultaneously being turned on a spit and whirled round and round on a string.

I bought a toffee-apple and sat on a bench, and thought about this extraordinary phenomenon. People, it seemed, would willingly travel

60 The heart of the mystery 61 Taking the air at Xanten 62 Halt! Who goes there?

long distances, and pay money, to be frightened and nauseated. 'Frightened' of course, needs qualifying; I knew that the Magic Carpet's machinery would have been inspected and tested, that the arm which held me in my seat was most unlikely to give way and let me be hurled out to my death. Naturally, I knew also that any kind of machinery can fail without warning, and that from time to time there are very serious fairground accidents from the collapse or malfunction of just such a device; but I do not think that I really felt myself to be in danger in the ordinary sense, as a man tiptoeing across untested ice is, and knows himself to be, in danger. So whence came the terror I experienced as the Magic Carpet whirled me round?

It was, I think, the appallingly lifelike *simulation* of real danger. To be flung about the sky, abruptly dropped like a man in a lift-shaft when the cable has snapped, threatened with flying off into space – all these things felt as though they were about to happen, or were actually happening. But if I am right, and the terror, though experienced, is at the same time known to be unjustified (like horror films, where the audience knows throughout that the madman with the axe is not going to come out of the screen and chop them up), the greater mystery remains: why do people *seek* such experiences? The Magic Carpet, as I say, had a constant queue for its delights; so did the machine that subjected its customers to being upside-down in two directions; so did the roller-coaster (some of these have mirrors fixed at strategic points along the course, so that the passengers in the hurtling car see another car apparently hurtling towards them on the same track); what is it that makes such things attractive rather than repellent? The popularity of horror films has never been greater, and the makers vie with each other to make them more horrible still, the only effect being that the queues grow longer all the time. And I remembered my exhilaration and laughter as I shot the rapids of the Black Hole.

My conclusion is hardly original, but it is the only one I find at all convincing. We in the comfortable West live in a world which, for all its threats, is largely devoid of direct and justified fear. We know that the nuclear holocaust may engulf us all, but we do not really believe that it will actually do so; as I have repeatedly said, not even the most passionate believer in unilateral nuclear disarmament, painting the most frightful pictures of the result of a nuclear war, ever finds himself unable to eat his dinner after a hard day's campaigning. More directly, we know the statistics of car accidents; most of us do not, though, go about the streets in terror of being knocked down. More dramatically, we read of thousands dying of famine or floods or volcanic eruptions or earthquakes, but we know that such things are very unlikely ever to touch us. (As it happens, surveys have shown that even those who live in earthquake zones do not worry about the very real danger they are in.) We do not even live in the fear of poverty, or at least the kind of poverty many of the poorer nations suffer, or the kind that was suffered even in Europe a few generations ago when state provision for hardship was unknown.

Our lives, then, lack the stimulating sensation of fear. Lacking it in reality, we seek its image and effect in imitations of it, frightening ourselves safely. Presumably, if real fear returned to countries like ours, we would not welcome it; presumably, also, when there was such fear, those who experienced it did not welcome it. We tweak the tiger's tail, knowing that the rest of it is safely behind bars; is this a healthy or an unhealthy attitude? We hear a great deal about the dangers of modern urban living, without exercise, without variety, without effort; do we unconsciously seek to disrupt our own placidity, feeling that it is in the long run dangerous, by frightening ourselves safely?

If so, it must be a healthy instinct. But even if it is so, I am quite unable to see why, in addition to frightening ourselves, we want to have our stomachs churned as well. Unless, of course, that desire is only an extension of the desire to experience fear, and is sought in order to simulate real exercise, as the mirror on the roller-coaster is sought to simulate real danger. Further than that I cannot go, and had better leave it there.

Duisburg, like Mönchengladbach, had nothing at all that a visitor is urged by the Guide Michelin to see; in this case, however, it was Michelin that was at fault, not the city. For Duisburg, which is on the edge of the Ruhr complex but fully part of it, contains one of the wonders of the modern world, and deserves, if not demands, a visit. But any visitor who seeks it out in search of something to rival the Taj Mahal for beauty, St Peter's for majesty, Niagara Falls for tremendousness, will be deeply disappointed. On the other hand, those who know in advance what they are to find, which is the greatest producer of steel in the world, will surely be struck by the same kind of awe, even if they conclude that it is a diabolic awe.

The Thyssen steelworks give the impression that they are not *in* Duisburg; they *are* Duisburg. That is not only a matter of the size of the works, which is twelve square kilometres and looks it; it *is* partly that, but partly also the ubiquity of the name throughout the city, and partly the massive installations at the city's docks, which seem to be an extension of the steelworks themselves, and perhaps mostly the film of dirt that seems to cover the entire city, though presumably covers only the area of the works and their surroundings. (It certainly does that; within half an hour of entering the place, and without touching anything, I was begrimed from head to foot, and when I washed my hair that night, the shampoo-suds falling to the bottom of the bath were black.)

The Thyssen steelworks looked like a combination of the nineteenth century and the twenty-fifth, half science-fiction and half dark satanic mills. Everywhere I went there were huge pipes and stacks, vast girders and columns, gargantuan cranes and railway wagons, monster cooling towers and heating vats, men walking about in moon-boots, looking like Wagner's *Rheingold* giants, the constant clang of iron, roar of fire, rumble of coal, rush of air. Many years ago, when I was just at the beginning of my career as a journalist, I applied for a job on a trade magazine called *Steel News*. I didn't get it, but some time later, when I had found another opening, I met the editor who had interviewed me; he told me that it was not his lack of faith in my journalistic ability that had led him to turn me down, but the fact that he couldn't, as he put it, quite see me wandering around a steelworks in a safety-helmet. Oh, if only he could have seen me at Thyssen's, hard hat and all, wandering about as if to the manner born!

The heart of this amazing place was the blast-furnace; in addition to the hard hat, I was issued with a coloured visor, to hold before my eyes while watching the fire. I thought for a moment that that was rather overdoing things, but the moment speedily passed as I peered into the inferno from behind my plastic protection and thought that I would not have refused the loan of a pair of the much darker and more comprehensively protective goggles that the men operating the furnace wore. It was impossible to go near it without all-enveloping protective clothing, but from some fifteen yards away it was still a sight never to be forgotten (and every now and again the fifteen yards shrank alarmingly as a huge spray of sparks and molten pellets was thrown out by the furnace); from a white-hot hole a yard across there rushed forth a torrent of white-hot molten metal, which poured off through a channel to be fed into the tubs that would take it away to be worked. The monster never paused; it went on vomiting the blazing metal as though it would go on for ever, until the whole world had been fed into its terrible, consuming fire and spat out white-hot. But then I was told that, for some necessary process the details of which I could not understand, the furnace had to be turned off from time to time, and that one of these switch-offs was imminent. At this, my bewilderment increased, because it seemed obvious to me that it would take days to run down the furnace. But there was no intention of running it down; what they did was to shut it. A hooter sounded a note of warning; men moved out of the way. Then, with a crash that shook the walls, a giant metal arm descended, and slammed into the roaring mouth of fire a colossal concrete plug, weighing God knows how many tons. I could see that the plug did not quite fill or close the hole; presumably if it had been literally sealed there would eventually have been the biggest explosion since Vesuvius, but I watched the frustrated furnace, with its white-hot glow now all round the plug, until it was time to move on to the next mysterious stage.

This was the transfer of the molten metal from the furnace to the area where it was to be turned into steel. A line of wheeled containers ran along a railway track; shaped like a submarine's torpedoes, they were black, indescribably grimy, encrusted with the droppings of hot metal. Each had a hole where the submarine's conning-tower would be, and as they moved beneath a gantry, the soup was poured from the saucepan into the Tupperware; the flaming liquid cascaded down, now orange tinged with a deeper red on the edges of the stream, a trace of white in the interior; the torpedo swallowed it, without any signs of indigestion, and moved on; another torpedo paused beneath the saucepan.

The heat was all-pervasive; from the moment I entered the heart of the plant I felt it, glowing from things that were not themselves glowing or even hot. It was like some kind of model of the universe, with dead stars still giving off energy reflected from some still-active body farther away. And the analogy from outer space went closer still; in the furnace-room I had seen two men dressed from head to foot in flowing, glittering robes. I assumed that they were not modelling Yves St Laurent's new season's collection of silver-lamé gowns, but only gradually realised that the ultra-fashionable garments were designed to reflect, and thus to diminish, the heat. The weirdness of their appearance was much increased when I went nearer; I had assumed that they were both black men, but they were not, they were white, with faces made absolutely black by their work – *absolutely* black, far more so than the familiar picture of the coal-miner emerging from his shift with his face begrimed by his trade.

Heavy industry is aptly named. Before I went to Thyssen's, I imagined that the whole place would be spotlessly clean, that technicians in white overalls would command gleaming, surgical-looking machines, while the processes of steel-making, cleansed of the ancient crudities, would proceed unseen in subterranean caverns using smokeless fuel; from ore to sheet-metal, I assumed that I would recognise nothing that had any connection with the Industrial Revolution. This illusion, I may say, had been considerably strengthened on my arrival at the plant: the administrative block was handsome and stylish, its entrance-hall decorated with modern pictures and sculptures as well as a fountain splashing into a beautiful stone pool with a line of stepping-stones running across it; an open-plan telephone-operator sat at a console of the latest communications technology, and paged the man I had come to see. A hundred yards away, time had rolled back a century and a half, and the monstrous iron jungle I was driving about in (some of the areas I visited were a couple of miles apart) would have been instantly recognisable to the ironmasters who, in the nineteenth century, laid the foundations of modern Western prosperity.

That, I decided, would not be wholly true. The original Thyssen works were set up in 1890; they were destroyed in the Second World War, so these could not be more than a few decades old. Possibly they had just missed a quantum leap in steel-making technology, so that, say, Japanese producers would regard Thyssen's as a museum. But its steel must be competitive, and plainly is; all over the world, Thyssen products and techniques are sought after and used. I concluded that the editor who had turned me down for a job among the makers of steel had been a wise and far-seeing man, and left. But as I did so, I looked about at the effects of the unspeakably polluted atmosphere on the buildings – it was mostly a residential area, and I imagine that the residents' net curtains would rot away in a month – and wondered what Thyssen's would do if Germany had a Clean Air Act like Britain's. (Perhaps it does, and industrial concerns like this are exempt from its provisions; for all I know, their equivalents in Britain are.)

On the other hand, when I went to lunch in the canteen, the workers certainly did not look emaciated, exhausted or harassed; many of them had bellies that cried out for a supermarket trolley to prop them in, there was a great deal of laughter, and all had cleaned themselves up before entering the administrative block. Nevertheless, I felt that the now ubiquitous and incessant warnings of the dangers of sedentary occupations, which sometimes seem to suggest that anyone sitting at a desk for more than an hour at a time will inevitably suffer a coronary, might be a little overdone, and I began to think of my own office, desk and comfortable chair with considerable affection.

I had been told that Duisburg was the biggest inland port in Europe, and no one visiting the harbour and its installations would have been inclined to doubt the claim. It also seemed to be entirely owned and directed by Thyssen; the name and emblem were everywhere, which was hardly surprising, as presumably a very large proportion of what arrived at these docks must be raw materials for the steelworks, and no less a proportion of what left from them must be the steelworks' finished products. But here the next century was on show rather than the last one, which dominates the works. A row of giant metal tubs, each the size of a gasometer, stretched for nearly a mile; whether they held oil or molten steel or grain or Thyssen's workforce I could not guess but, vast as they were, they were dwarfed by the cranes, which looked as though they could pick up not just these monster vats but a fully loaded aircraft-carrier. No doubt the cranes were made of Thyssen steel, like the storage-tanks; for that matter, no doubt the aircraft-carrier was, too.

Duisburg has to exist; the world cannot get along without steel, and that will remain true, despite the world-wide slump in steel-making, until a new Industrial Revolution sweeps away the last vestiges of the old one. We can argue that it can clean itself up (Pittsburgh was once synonymous with the grime of steel-making, but cleaned itself up many years ago), but that will not reduce the necessity for the moon-men in their moon-boots and Yves St Laurent robes. Gandhi dreamed of a world in which every man sat before his own door and spun the cloth for his own clothes; but India now produces steel in places that inevitably look like Duisburg-on-the-Jumna. I was reminded, as I left Duisburg and thought of India, of a recent visit to Bali. Driving along a country road, I came upon a vast complex of oil-installations, the very symbol of the modern world and of the inevitability of industrialisation. Two hundred yards further on, I saw a peasant wading through the mud in his paddy-field, preparing it for the rice-sowing with a wooden plough the design of which had not changed for at least 2000 years, pulled by an ox.

But there are no paddy-fields in Duisburg, and if there are any ploughs they are certainly made of Thyssen steel.

*

Xanten has few claims to fame today other than its unique position as the only place in Federal Germany which begins with an X. But I had to visit it, because it has a claim on legend, if not history: it is supposed to be the birthplace of Siegfried, hero of the *Nibelungenlied* from which, six centuries later, Wagner hewed much of the material for the *Ring*. (There is a Nibelungen Baths, with a Siegfried Pool where a friendly dragon pours water over the bathers from his nostrils.) Its most remarkable feature, though, is neither its X nor its position as the cradle of the Superman, but its Director of Tourism, Frau Angelika Hinder, a woman of whom it may be said that if Xanten is not world-famous, it is certainly not for want of action and energy on her part.

I shall come to her later, but my first discovery was that this undistinguished little town was in many ways very distinguished indeed. To start with, I doubt if any place in Germany has been so beautifully, harmoniously and ingeniously reconstructed; it had been almost entirely destroyed (it could hardly have had any strategic significance of its own, so I could only conclude that it had accidentally been in the way of the Allied advance and had been fortified by the retreating Germans), but it would be impossible to guess the fact from its present appearance, with its handsome Market Square, its discreetly restored St Viktor's Cathedral (a towering Gothic pile, the biggest between Cologne and the sea), its archaeological sites, now incorporated into a park set aside especially for the diggers and the relics of their digs and eventually intended for a reconstruction of the entire Roman city (the reconstruction of the amphitheatre is already complete), its Klevertor, also restored with a subtlety and care that Düsseldorf might with advantage have thought to emulate, and its air of purposeful but not urgent bustle. The tower was the original gate to the town, and the living quarters in the interior had been transformed into self-catering flats, roomy and pleasant and amazingly cheap to rent; Xanten claims that it has 700,000 visitors a year, but I think an extra nought must have been fitted on while Frau Hinder wasn't looking, or possibly when she was. But her enthusiasm for Xanten was not without independent support. 1975 was (I would never have known, and I daresay not many other people noticed either) 'European Monument Conservation Year', and Xanten was singled out for a commendation as a town which had restored itself with singularly handsome success. In 1978 another such honour came Xanten's way; the town won the gold metal in the nationwide German competition for the best example of municipal conservation and design in town planning.

Frau Hinder, passing through the open hall of the Information Office, heard an English voice and bore down on me, speaking my own language perfectly. What was I doing in Xanten? How could she help? What did I need? Had I found a room at a hotel? Did I know I could stay in the tower? What had I seen? What would I like to see? Did I need a guide? Would I like a guide? Had I ever been here before? How long had I been in the town? How long was I staying? When would I return? Would I tell people about Xanten when I got home?

That sounds like hard selling; it wasn't, though, because Frau Hinder's charm and sophistication robbed it of anything like commercial pressure. When she learned what my enterprise actually was, of my tour down the Rhine from source to sea, she was beside herself with eagerness to ensure that Xanten figure prominently; she managed to imply, without actually saying, that her town was far more important, interesting, beautiful, hospitable, artistic and historical than Basle, Strasbourg, Heidelberg and Cologne put together, and I am sure that only the fact that I had to leave prevented her from telling me that it was bigger as well. Her last exhortation was for me not on any account to fail to visit the harbour. I promised that I would do so, and – intrigued, because she had been most insistent, coupling her advice with a complaint about the cruise and pleasure steamers, which would not include Xanten on their scheduled stops – I kept my promise.

The harbour was half a mile or so outside Xanten, and that fact alone had a significance which no one could have guessed without instruction, because it was the result of the river shifting in its course in 1535, thereby ruining the town (I forbore to ask Frau Hinder why the town had not simply pulled up its Cathedral and Klevertor by the foundations and followed the river, though I was quite certain that if she had been around at the time that is what the town *would* have done). But down at the harbour I could see, despite my admiration for this most attractive woman with her devotion to her most attractive little town, why the big ships were reluctant to put Xanten on their maps. The 'harbour' consisted of a sloping plank-walk ending in a tiny stone jetty with a tiny pontoon moored to it; the whole thing could hardly have been more than eight feet wide, and a kayak would have had trouble in mooring first go. Siegfried's Journey to the Rhine could hardly have ended here, with not a sign of the Gibichung Hall to land at.

I sat on the jetty and thought about Wagner; I was due to go to Bayreuth for the *Ring* when my journey was over, and it nearly was. I had fallen under his spell in my youth, not long after I discovered music itself. For forty years I had been following his star, returning again and again to my addiction, like the drug-taker who falls back every time into the trap after being weaned from his poison, because, in the deepest reaches of his heart, he does not really want to be cured.

The analogy is neither so far-fetched nor so distasteful as might appear. Sometimes I do think that I would like to be cured of an addiction to the *Ring*, *Lohengrin*, *Parsifal* and *Tristan* (no one who has ever really been captured by *The Mastersingers* could ever want to be prised loose from its grip). What is this disease, which I cling to even while calling for skilled doctors to treat it?

It is not, for me, what it is for those who reject Wagner after one horrified hearing, or – more frequently – without even that. They are fleeing from something real; it is no myth that Wagner is rejected and condemned because he throws open, brutally and without warning, doors and windows that we struggle all our lives to keep shut. The currency he deals in – love and hate, betrayal and self-sacrifice, murder, incest and deception, faith, truth and compassion – is not legal tender for the Wagneroclasts, and as he goes probing into the deepest recesses of the human soul, where the greatest sins and greatest virtues jostle together in the darkness, they have good reason for their refusal to undergo such experiences as he provides.

I got past that in the first months of my addiction, which is how I know it was true addiction. The truth about Wagner-addicts is that we *want* those windows and doors to be smashed in, provided that the smashing takes place safely, in the very different darkness of an opera-house. We have only to clutch the arms of our seats to know that this is make-believe, that those terrible figures and feelings from within us are real to us only because of the artistry of the composer and the performers, and that we can put them away from us at the end of the performance just as easily as the performers their wigs and the conductor his baton. The collapse of every kind of emotional barrier at performances of Wagner, which is what so many Wagner-lovers seek because they cling to those barriers in their lives and fear beyond anything else their collapse in daylight, is safely experienced, and these Wagner-lovers are therefore not disturbed, indeed are comforted, by the fall of the ramparts.

But that is precisely why my reluctance now grows. Life is, in one aspect, a coming to terms with our limitations; at any rate, a terrible price in pain and frustration has to be paid by those who cannot do it.

Few achieve that nirvana completely; certainly I have not – there are barren areas in my life which I still dream might yet fructify. All the same, I have wrestled, with some success, against many of the dark angels of ambition and regret; I have achieved, with only a few important exceptions, a wide range of serenities. The result is that I do not *need* Wagner as I once did, and I can only conclude that the reluctance is a form of protest at the fact that I none the less cannot break free of the spell.

The spell, after all, for anyone who has ears to hear and a heart to feel, is some of the most glorious music ever written by any man; it is inexhaustible in the discoveries it continues to offer, the depth at which it touches us, the healing it offers for the hurt it has done, like the Spear with which Parsifal heals the wound it made. It is a curious fact that I no longer feel that I *need* Beethoven, at least the orchestral Beethoven, as I once did; I love him no less, but I have learned the great lesson that he teaches, and do not have to go back to school for a refresher course unless I want to. I cannot do without Mozart, though, and the intensity of my need for him grows all the time, as I sense, more and more urgently and directly, that I must understand what he is telling me before I die, lest my death should be meaningless to me. And foursquare in the middle of these feelings for the music I adore, there stands Richard Wagner, glaring at me in defiance of my belief that I can, or even should, do without him, as my phobia challenges me to face down the very thing which I cannot face at all.

Thus I reflected, as I sat on Xanten's mighty Rhine harbour and watched the truly mighty Rhine go by. The lapping of the water soothed my spirit, the sun warmed my back, and peace descended. Then, from deep inside me, there welled up, as it wells up in the *Rheingold* prelude, Wagner's Rhine; he had come to claim his due, to tell me I was still his sworn vassal and would be until I die. I let the music run its course through my head, and returned, not unhappily, to my hotel.

13

Erasmus of Rotterdam

AND SET OFF for Holland next day, having answered in my own mind one of Frau Hinder's questions at least: I shall return to Xanten.

When I do, I hope I have another glimpse of what I found at the station from which I embarked for the Netherlands: a wheel-tapper, a real, old-fashioned, long-hammered wheel-tapper, a character whom I had not seen for very many years. Nor was he a demonstration model, showing modern passengers how the safety of the trains used to be ensured in pre-scientific days, but a fully employed, and no doubt fully trained, wheel-tapper, and he went down the platform tapping wheels. I suspect that many of my younger readers will not so much as know what a wheel-tapper is (or, more likely, was – other than in tiny railway stations on the way from Germany to Holland); I had better explain. His long hammer was used to tap, with an exactly controlled force, the wheels of a stationary train; if there was a crack in the wheel, even the slightest hair-line, the note of metal gave off would be, at least to the expert ears of the tapper, significantly different from the clang of a perfect one, and investigation would at once be undertaken. I had presumed that train wheels are now differently made, so that they cannot crack, or that their testing is now done in a different and less visible manner, and so I was delighted to see at work what may well be the very last practitioner of an ancient and honourable trade, the very last wheel-tapper. I recalled two other such professions from my youth, one – the lamp-lighter – altogether gone; the other – the chimney-sweep – to be seen now (usually on a bicycle, with his brushes slung over his back) only very rarely. The muffin-man had gone before I was born; I dare say the window-cleaner, with his curious triangular ladder, will follow shortly.

The Dutch have long enjoyed a good press. Like Denmark, Holland is admired, in an affectionate but slightly patronising way, by the people of larger countries. This, however, is not a matter of size only; Switzerland ought to qualify by its population and area, but the Swiss are not much loved, and Luxembourg, though it should qualify even more easily on the same grounds, is almost entirely ignored. As for Belgium, it is regarded with some suspicion, regularly fed by its communal tensions between the Flemish-speaking and French-speaking areas. It also suffers, in the case of older observers, from memories of the days, not so very long ago, when Belgium was the last European country to have no driving test of any kind, so that anyone could get behind the wheel of a car and drive off, even if departure was delayed by the necessity of discovering the difference between the brake and the accelerator; in those days, the 'B' which denoted a car from Belgium struck terror into other drivers, and deepened the feeling that sympathy would be wasted on such a country.

The Dutch, however, have been almost universally smiled upon, with good reason. They managed the transition to a post-imperial role more successfully than most countries with overseas possessions (how strange does the word 'possessions' now sound in the era of self-determination!); and although they handled the Indonesian struggle for independence abominably (though the French, at any rate in North Africa, were far worse in their short-sighted cruelty), when it was over, friendly relations were established with remarkable speed, while the Dutch have probably the best record of all colonial powers in the way they have treated their immigrant population.

Not that such considerations count for much with the world's view of Holland, which is based on far less cerebral principles. The Dutch, for one thing, are seen as almost universally friendly; and so they are – at least, I have always found it so in all the forty-odd years I have been visiting the country. More; they have skilfully blended their rural, simple, traditional image – clogs, windmills and bonnets – with a well-founded reputation for efficiency and cleanliness, thus presenting a most inviting picture for foreign tourists, who commonly find to their delight that the picture corresponds very closely to the reality.

Also, they speak other nations' languages, particularly English (which is just as well, because the British are the second most relentlessly monoglot people on earth, the Americans being the very worst), which makes life easier for visitors. Also, their country is beautiful, even though, by a strange but touchingly understandable perversity, they are not content with its beauty; they must have contours, too. I was once driven seventy miles by Dutch friends to be shown some undistinguished dunes, in order that I might believe, by the incontrovertible evidence of my own eyes, that Holland is not entirely flat.

My own love for Holland is heavily influenced by my feeling for Rembrandt; other than Shakespeare, there is no artist, not even Mozart, whom I love so devotedly. I have often linked Rembrandt and Beethoven, not only because of the similarity of the set of their mouths, but because I find striking affinities in their conviction that suffering, which is inevitable in the lives of all mankind, and certainly in a great part of theirs, exists to be faced, challenged and overcome. But although I have said that the hold of Beethoven's blazing optimism is less strong upon me than it was in my youth, the hold of Rembrandt goes on getting stronger, and will plainly continue to do so until I die.

But Rembrandt must wait; these reflections occurred to me as I crossed the Dutch border, and there was much to see, and do, before I got to the Rijksmuseum.

Particularly do; for it was not far from a tiny scrap of a place called Weesp that I tried, for the second and last time in my life, to master the art of riding a bicycle, and failed, ignominiously and completely. My first attempt had been at school; all my contemporaries were skilled bicyclists, and insisted that nothing was easier than to learn, indeed that there was nothing *to* learn, and that all that was necessary was to get on and pedal away. I have explained elsewhere and in detail the farce that ensued when I did get on and pedal away; all I need say now is that I found that I could start without much difficulty, and keep going with even less, but I could not for the life of me make the thing go round corners, so that I was obliged, whenever I wanted to change direction, to stop, get off, haul the beast's head round by force, get on, and start again. This soon struck me as the most absurd means of getting about ever devised, and I abandoned it, I thought for ever. But I had reckoned without Iolande. Iolande was a cycling instructor (she was also very pretty, which was not at all a drawback); her firm (in Holland, the land of the bicycle, there are many such) specialised in cycling tours, and tuition in the art of bicycle-riding was also provided. I did not want to go on a cycling tour; for that matter, I did not want to learn to ride a bicycle, but Iolande's coaxing was irresistible, and before long I was mounted on the machine that had defeated me all those years before, and, under her guidance, was wobbling along the edge of a canal, a circumstance that did nothing to improve my confidence. I did not fall in, but neither did I master the art or science of bicycling, and after a time, though Iolande's patience was clearly inexhaustible, I surrendered. As a consolation prize, or at any rate a consolation, I was invited to mount a tricycle and see if I could do better. I could; I still found it difficult to turn, though not, as with its two-legged cousin, impossible, but at least I was no longer wobbling, and sped up and down the towpath, and indeed across bridges, as though I had been tricycling all my life. When the exercise was over, I bade my steed farewell, knowing that nothing would ever again tempt me into the saddle, not even Iolande.

Weesp amply repaid inspection, on foot. It looked a little like Xanten, though it had nothing in the way of St Viktor's Cathedral or the Klevertor; but tiny though it was, it had an extraordinary grace and charm, with handsome shopfronts, well-tended houses, perfect proportions, and a miniature canal flowing happily through the town. I decided that the people of Weesp must be uncommonly thoughtful, because the canal bore, every hundred yards or so as it went on its way, a square platform, with what looked like a large dog-kennel in the middle of it. I could not guess what purpose this served, until I looked more closely and realised that the platforms were duck-sanctuaries. The ducks sat and sunned themselves on the platform, and inside the duck-kennel I could see their eggs; presumably no one was going to row out in the middle of the night and steal them, let alone sell them to the local supermarket or dairy.

From Weesp I made a diversion, assured that Gouda, which I had never seen, would repay a visit. All I knew about it was that a cheese was named after it (I suppose it could have been the other way round), but Gouda turned out to have treasures far beyond those of the table, starting with a Cathedral, St John's, which must rank as one of the most glorious churches in the world. It had a strange basilica shape, the nave ending in a kind of arena for the audience; 'arena' was inevitable, so dramatic, even theatrical, was the feeling. The light fell on to the stage through what must be some of the finest stained glass in existence, the colours as bright and clear as though they had been made yesterday, and the gigantic windows ran down the whole length of the church on both sides. The combination of the soaring roof, the colours of the glass, the feeling of air and space, turned the building into thistledown; I felt it would float up into the sky at the first puff of wind. An aged sacristan greeted me; bursting with his pride in his miraculous place, a pride which had clearly lasted through generations of visitors and would last through as many more as he would welcome before his life ended, he showed me round. The windows told three series of biblical stories, and one of a more secular nature; the life of Christ and of John the Baptist; episodes from the Old Testament; and lastly, in a most extraordinary historical coup, a celebration of the Protestantism which in the sixteenth century had triumphed here. The Protestant windows were all on the western side of the church; it was as though the struggles of the Reformation had been fought out in the nave, with the battle swaying now to this side, now to that, and victory being marked by the window which announces itself as proclaiming the Liberty of Conscience. How easily we now take for granted that great principle, counting ourselves lucky only by comparison with those unhappy lands which, in our own world, still deny it; the church of St John in Gouda reminded me (though my guide, with true Christian forbearance, did not) that many men had to die before it was established.

That was by no means the end of the surprises Gouda offered a visitor. In the centre of the place there was the old Town Hall, still in use as Gouda's municipal offices; from the front, it looked like a church itself, and a pretty tremendous one, though far too exuberant to be consecrated as a place of worship, even if its interior had been that of Birnau or the Wieskirche. But the Stadthuis was seen at its best from the sides, for the two central storeys had symmetrical rows of windows running the length of the building, and each of these windows had its original shutters in red and white, all carefully set open at an identical angle to the walls, the effect being of an array of brilliant flags against the grey stone. Nearby a very friendly-looking lion sat, on his rear end, upon a column, staring fixedly at the Town Hall clock, presumably prepared to growl fiercely if it should begin to show the wrong time. And the square was completed by the old weigh-house, with a lovingly carved bas-relief of the weighing that went on inside; the weighing, inevitably, of the cheese.

But the sight of it led me back to my earliest days in journalism. Pye, the electronics firm, which I think had started with radios, was based in Cambridge. Somebody had dreamed up the idea of an exchange week with Leiden, also a university town, with its own well-established Dutch firm in the same business, Philips. A party of journalists, of whom I was one, was taken to Leiden for the week; it started in spectacular fashion, because not only did the plane taking us leave from the grass runways of Croydon, which was London's airport before the Second World War (pre-war memoirs were full of Bright Young Things buzzing over to the Continent from Croydon), but the aircraft we flew in was a biplane (I can even remember its name – it was a de Havilland Rapide). It didn't look at all safe, but I must say it flew very steadily, and since it also flew very slowly, and very low, we had a good view of everything on the way. When we got to Leiden, the sense of mild lunacy persisted, and indeed increased; the first thing I saw was a mock-up, in the town square, of a Cambridge court (only Oxford calls them quadrangles), and they had done it very thoroughly, because all round it they had built astonishingly lifelike façades which would have been the entrance to the Cambridge staircases, and dotted about the court were lifesize figures of students and dons, all in cap and gown.

The ceremonies of the week included a boat race between university crews, various musical and dramatic entertainments, and – which is where the gates of memory were opened for me in Gouda – the weighing of the Burgomaster of Leiden, who was a very fat man indeed, in Dutch cheese. The scales, specially built, were enormous; the Burgomaster, entering into the spirit of the thing, had donned his robes and chain of office, and an apparently infinite supply of cheese was stacked and ready. I forget now how many cheeses were needed before the Burgomaster rose from the ground, but His Worship, to look at him, would have tipped the scales at about eighteen stone, so the number must have been very considerable. I never did discover whether the high-jinks had improved either the corporate image (not that we used such jargon then) of Pye and Philips, or even their sales, but I can certainly attest to the fact that all those involved had enjoyed themselves.

From Gouda, with memories, to Monnickendam, via a tiny ferry – so tiny, indeed, that it had room for only three or four people at a time, and was hauled across, by hand, on a cable. The lady who operated it had a little mongrel terrier, who considered it his duty to shepherd the passengers across, so that every time the little boat set out, he would dash down the bank and leap aboard at the last moment, standing in the bow, ready to leap off as soon as the boat had grounded, only to re-board as soon as the boat set off on its return journey.

Monnickendam contained an etymological problem. In Dutch,

'dam' means dyke, so that all the Dutch place-names (and there must be thousands) from Amsterdam downwards, which end in the syllable, are referring to the dyke which originally protected them (and in many cases still does) from the ever-watching, hungry sea. That must have been true of Monnickendam, too, but I recalled that Monnickendam, in various spellings, was the surname of a very old and distinguished Jewish family. The Monnickendams of Britain, and presumably of elsewhere, too, were not of Sephardic origin, unlike the Sebags and Montefiores and the other higher-class Jews; they were plainly Ashkenazim, and in Britain at any rate their business was food – importing, exporting, preparing and serving. Later, they must have had some connection with the wine trade, for a Mr Monnickendam was for many years the British Railways adviser on wine, and he must have known what he was doing, because in those days not only was the wine at British Railways hotels well-chosen, interesting and good value, but so was the wine on the trains themselves, a fact which will be met with incredulity today among those too young to have known the good old days.

Did the Jewish Monnickendams come from Monnickendam and take the name of it with them, out of nostalgia? Or was there a meaning to the name, shared by the place and the people? Whatever the answer, Monnickendam had not only a handsome harbour, alive with a great forest of masts, but also a simple restaurant which at once restored the link between the family and the town, because it served a variety of smoked and fried fish, precisely the things that I remembered the Monnickendam firm for.

Amsterdam cannot have been the first foreign city I visited; that was Paris, as I suppose it was for most young people in Britain in those days, and probably still is. But it was the first that I got to know well, and my love for it, kindled thus early, had never waned, even though the city (over the years and like most Western cities everywhere) has deteriorated.

First love has a magic about it that lasts, in those who let themselves remain open to it, until death. That is as true of places as of human beings, and although no one would claim that the intensity is the same, there are real parallels. The glow that warms my heart still when I remember my own first human love remains a real presence in my life; I cannot imagine, nor wish to, how much more impoverished my life would be without that storm of youthful emotion recollected in tranquillity. But the same is true, in its more objective, less passionate form, of my first love among cities, and to this day I can remember even tiny details of my early explorations of Amsterdam. I stayed there first, for instance, in a private house where temporary lodgers were welcome for bed and breakfast. When I went sightseeing, I visited the famous House of Mr Trip's Coachman, built in the eighteenth century by Mr Trip, who overheard his coachman saying that he would be happy if he had a house no wider than his master's front door, and immediately decided to make his faithful servant's wish come true; well, I remember the house I stayed in because it could not have been very much wider than Mr Trip's front door itself, and although I could no longer find it, I am sure that if I were taken to it and the door thrown open, I would recognise it at once.

In those days (we shall come to these days in a moment), Amsterdam must have been one of the most relaxed and gracious cities in Europe. Nobody ever seemed to be in a hurry, and I believe that it was the grace and beauty of the city which had nurtured that attitude for both its citizens and its visitors. Those concentric rings of water, the old, simple houses along the quays, the spires of the churches poking up behind the roofs (some of them looking still as they were when Rembrandt drew or etched them), the big traditional hotels (certainly looking as they did when they were built in the nineteenth century), the herring-stands in season – where the seller, spotting a greenhorn, would cut up the raw fillet, put the pieces on a cardboard plate and offer a toothpick to spear them with (for the natives, and the more daring greenhorns, whom I rapidly insisted on joining, he just handed it over by the tail, the trick being to nibble it from bottom to top without getting the juice on your tie or even chin), the subtle but unmistakable Indonesian influence, the spotless shops and the quality of the goods therein, the ready helpfulness of the Amsterdammers, almost mid-American in their anxiety to ensure that a visitor would enjoy their town, the noble pile of the Rijksmuseum and the limitless array of treasures it housed – these were the things I loved about my new-found-land, and which made me a friend of Amsterdam for life.

But my friend changed, as some friends do, not for the better.

Amsterdam acquired a well-deserved reputation as the most tolerant city in Europe, in which young people whose style in clothes, hair, music and sleeping arrangements would have been frowned upon in London, icily reproved in Bonn and likely to lead to a bang on the head from a policeman's truncheon in Paris, were happily accommodated.

Soon Amsterdam, too glibly, became known as the hippy capital of Europe; the railway station was thousands deep in them, singing to their guitars and living, apparently, on air alone.

Amsterdam's hospitality, alas, was abused. The city began to deteriorate, visibly. It became dirty, with litter strewn everywhere and the walls sprayed with graffiti. The old, gentle shops disappeared, and were replaced by new, raucous ones, selling shoddy clothing and shoddier music and still shoddier food. The drug tide swept over the city, inevitably bearing crime with it; there were areas of Amsterdam – Amsterdam, which had always been as unfrightening as Venice! – that were off-limits for all but the hardy or the foolhardy. The red-light district became a tourist attraction; the waters became, with a grim symbolism, polluted; whole city blocks were given over to the pornography industry.

It was the pornography that was most noticeable, for it was not confined to the areas of the Amsterdam demi-monde; in many of the central shopping thoroughfares, there were shops, not at all furtive, crammed with rack upon rack of pornographic magazines, interspersed with sex-shops and pornographic cinemas.

The flower children came, saw and conquered; but the flowers withered, and when the city authorities finally woke up to what had happened, it was too late for them to do anything but make a half-hearted attempt, in any case soon abandoned, to clean off the graffiti. Saddest sight of all was the Kalverstraat, once one of the most elegant shopping streets in all Europe, and moreover without the chilly glitter of the rue Faubourg St Honoré or the huckstering spirit of the Kurfürstendamm; I remember a Christmas visit to Amsterdam, when the Kalverstraat was decorated from end to end, in beautiful, simple taste, with flowers and wreaths and candles, the shop-windows dressed similarly, and ancient Dutch carols hovering about the loudspeakers.

The Kalverstraat died; the fine shops took themselves elsewhere and were replaced with those selling instant and limited gratification, the litter piled up (I believe the street-cleaning service must have simply abandoned it – at any rate, for many years now I have not seen the Kalverstraat litter-free, at any hour of the day or night), and another victory for Gresham's Law was marked up.

So I was not surprised when, on this trip, I found that things had got even worse. I was staying at the Hotel Europe, one of the few places in Amsterdam which have not changed at all – its quiet, unobtrusive charm and discreetly efficient service the same as it was when I first stayed there decades before. I dropped my luggage and sauntered forth. Before I had sauntered five yards, I saw a litter-basket fixed to a lamp-post; it was crammed with rubbish to – literally – overflowing, and the base of the lamp-post was inches deep in more. Clearly, even those with the impulse to dispose of their litter, finding the basket full, had simply thrown it on the ground; how long it had been since the basket was emptied, and how long it would be before it was emptied again, there was no telling. Imagine such a sight practically on the doorstep of Claridge's, of the Meurice, of the Vier Jahreszeiten, of the Pierre! Where has Amsterdam's self-respect gone?

And yet, beneath the rubbish and the sadness, there remains the Amsterdam spirit that I fell in love with so long ago. Gradually, the city's timeless qualities asserted themselves; the walk-ways along the canals yielded their magic spell of serenity, I found that the churches had not been pulled down and rebuilt as McDonald's (they had not even been left up and rebuilt as McDonald's), the clock on the Muntplein chimed as it had done on my first visit, and indeed as it had chimed four centuries earlier, the Rijksmuseum beckoned (and so did the Van Gogh Museum, which had not even existed when I first visited the city), and in the end my eyes ceased to register the dirt and dilapidation, seeing only the grace, beauty, vigour and calm. And a stroll along the Singel, which is composed from end to end of flower-stalls, served to lift my spirits almost to the heights of the old days, and a visit to the cat-boat – which is a floating sanctuary for them – lifted them higher still.

And then there were the bicycles, inseparably linked with my oldest Amsterdam memories. Even if I had managed to learn to ride one, I would not have dared to do so in Amsterdam. With the exception of Peking, there is no city in the world with a greater number of bicycles; indeed, taking the Netherlands as a whole, the proportion of bicycles to population must be bigger even than China's. I discovered that there are 14 million Dutch citizens and 11 million bicycles; presumably that extraordinary figure is the fruit of having a country that is almost entirely flat.

But driving (not on a bicycle) near Amsterdam, another childhood memory was stirred, when I saw a signpost marked Hilversum. When I was young, radios (which were called wirelesses, or even wireless sets) had a dial covered not, as in the modern mode, with figures, or at most with colourless locations like 'Radio Three', but a vast range of places at home and abroad. I can hardly believe now that with such primitive instruments most of the overseas transmitters could be heard in Britain (though Radio Luxembourg certainly was), but among the places theoretically obtainable on even the simplest sets was, invariably, Hilversum. I seem to remember that I knew it was in Holland, but why was it supposed that large numbers of people in Britain should want to tune into broadcasts in Dutch?

I thought I should do what every tourist does, and indeed what I had done on my first visit, though not since: take the evening tour of Amsterdam by motor-boat. Within a few minutes I remembered why I had not done it for so many years; Amsterdam, though a city of canals and a river, cannot be seen properly from them. The reason is that, unlike Venice, very few of the interesting buildings or thoroughfares are on the water, and although Amsterdam had gone to great trouble and expense to illuminate the bridges – picking out the arches in lines of light-bulbs, for instance – it has to be said that, again unlike Venice, when you have seen one Amsterdam bridge you have seen most of them.

The tour started just as dusk was falling, which meant that the first building to which we had our attention drawn could be seen clearly in the evening light. That was a pity, because it was Amsterdam's new opera-house, just about to be opened, and an uglier building I have not seen go up, anywhere, for many years. It wasn't even positively and obtrusively ugly, like the Hayward Gallery and Queen Elizabeth Hall in London, or fashionably ugly, like the Beaubourg in Paris, or ridiculously ugly, like the Trump Tower in New York; it was just depressingly ugly, in its lifelessness and banality. The interior may be exciting, though I cannot see why it should be if it is designed by the architect, but that would be no excuse anyway. Somebody had plainly missed the point; if the opera-goer cannot approach his evening with a sense of excitement he might as well stay at home, and an opera-house which not only fails to instil that excitement but positively reproves it can hardly be called an opera-house at all.

The last thing I saw before night closed in was an amazing sign; neatly painted on the wooden arch above a landing stage, it read, in English, 'Love thy dentist'.

I got out when we arrived at the red-light district, and explored. There was a great deal of it; off the main thoroughfare there were a dozen or more streets apparently devoted to the same trade, if we are to include the shops selling venereal devices, the blue cinemas, the pornographic bookshops and ('Group Sex') the live stage exhibitions.

The first surprise was that it *was* a red-light district, literally. Many of the houses of prostitution had a red lantern in the doorway, and virtually all of them had a red strip-light over the top of the window; in the windows sat the ladies of the establishment (or, much more often than not, lady, for prostitution in Amsterdam seems to be largely a freelance occupation). When a client knocked on the door and was admitted, the curtain was drawn across the window; I assumed that this was not for excessive delicacy but as a sign that the lady of the house was for the moment engaged. Most of the women could be described by the traditional word, raddled; but a surprisingly substantial minority were genuinely attractive. I am not so foolish as to waste my time wondering how an attractive and, as far as I could see, sophisticated woman had chosen that trade; for centuries men have tried to answer that question, and failed. It was another puzzle, surely not so difficult to solve, yet for me insoluble, that occupied me.

Try as I will, I am, and always have been, unable to stretch my imagination far enough to encompass the man who, for his sexual gratification, frequents prostitutes, whether street-walkers, call-girls or the staff of brothels. I can just guess what animates a man who goes to a live sex-show, though I have never seen even a blue film; I can understand, I *think*, what the readers of pornographic magazines get out of their habit; but I can no more imagine myself resorting to prostitution than I can imagine myself attempting rape. In both cases I am certain I would be impotent, but that is not the foundation of my inability to comprehend either. What baffles me is the thought that some men can divorce the sexual act so completely from any other feeling – not just love but even lust – that they can find gratification in a solely commercial form, and – even more astonishing to me – some can get the gratification *only* in that form.

There is no logic in my attitude; I am not driven to it by the fear of disease or scandal, though those fears are real ones, nor by a belief that resorting to prostitution is itself an immoral act, which I do not hold, nor by a thrifty unwillingness to pay for that which can be obtained free by mutual consent. It is, clearly, a failure of imagination on my part, which prevents me from understanding what a man in that situation can possibly get out of it. But the failure is complete.

Next day, things were different, and not only because my nocturnal walk around the red-light district was accompanied by a persistent drizzle, whereas the day dawned, and stayed, fine. As big modern cities have increasingly suffered from congestion, pollution and excess population, more and more of them have resorted to a variety of inducements to persuade business, at least, to move out; the whole of the 'New Town' movement is based on the need to decentralise. And among the focal points of this problem are the great markets, which sprang up years – even centuries – ago, in very different circumstances, and in very different traffic conditions. The Covent Garden market, which had occupied the same area since Nell Gwyn was an orange-seller, moved across the Thames, Les Halles fled Paris for Orly (where, I learned, the rats had faithfully followed them), and the Amsterdam flower-market and flower-auction have moved out of the city to where the flowers are grown.

On my way to them I passed vast complexes of greenhouses, some of them many acres in extent, though they were nothing compared to the market building itself. This looked like a series of monstrous aircraft hangars, but for no aircraft outside science-fiction. These buildings are hundreds of yards long; standing at one end, with an unobstructed view, I had great difficulty in making out the other. There were six of these gigantic halls, each with its auction-room at one side; with the aid of what must be a vast computerised plan, an interminable series of open trucks, looking rather like much larger versions of the display racks in clothes shops, trundled on narrow tram-lines about the hall, crammed with flowers. Some of these 'trains' were composed of thirty or forty trucks, and the lines constantly criss-crossed each other, whence my conviction that the whole thing must be controlled from a central point by computer. But although the trundling and criss-crossing looked haphazard, I realised after a time that it was all directed to a purpose, because from whatever part of the hall the trains appeared, sooner or later they all chugged into the auction-room itself, and passed slowly across the front of it. This looked like the dress circle of a theatre, with semi-circular rows rising steeply. In this forum sat the bidders, the flower-merchants of Amsterdam; each was equipped with a microphone and a loudspeaker, the one to make his bids, the other to learn what his rivals were bidding. Like all such auctions, the effect is very different from the stately calm that reigns at Christie's or Sotheby's; even at those places it is difficult for an outsider to see where the bid lies for the moment, but at the Dutch flower-auction it was quite impossible, with scores of bids being shouted at once as the flower-trains paused briefly before trundling on out of the room.

63 Popcorn at 180ft 64 Man, woman, dog and bicycle 65 No, these *are the handlebars*

Talking to one of the market officials, I discovered – I had to ask him to repeat it, thinking that I must have misunderstood – that *millions* of blooms are traded in this place every day. When I had got over my surprise, the obvious thought occurred to me; with such a gargantuan market (in both senses of the word), and with so many buyers (I had seen only one of the six auction-rooms in action), the prices must be desperately competitive, making it difficult to see how anyone could offer even a fraction of a cent more or less than anyone else – so why all the fuss and screaming? The official agreed that if the market were confined to Amsterdam or even the whole of the Netherlands there would indeed be no great eagerness to win the bid, but these flowers go all over the world; pointing to a bank of flowers, he said simply, 'Those will be in America tonight.'

On the way back to Amsterdam, I stopped at one of the greenhouses supplying the market. It was bigger – a good deal bigger – than a full-size professional football pitch,* and everything except the picking was controlled, I learned, by yet another computer-system: temperature, humidity, light. The picking was done by hand, but so nonchalantly expert were the pickers that they might have been robots. Up and down the rows they went, using a slight twist for each flower before the knife cut it, and tucking the cut flower, in a gesture that flowed so seamlessly out of the cutting itself that it made the whole action one, into the crook of the arm. At the end of the row (they harvested lengthways, not across) they emptied the crook; their bundle was taken away to be readied for market, and before it had moved three yards on its way the harvesters were already moving down the next file. (Unfortunately, it was not tulip-time, but there seemed to be every other flower I had ever seen and a good many I had not.)

At this point, or thereabouts, I recollected that I was not supposed to be in Amsterdam at all, or even near it. It is not on the Rhine, and although my river, when it crosses the Dutch border from Germany, not only breaks up into what becomes the huge delta that stretches almost to the Belgian border, with countless little Rhines (and a few good-sized ones), but even changes its name to such unrhinelike things as Waal, Lek and Merwede (to say nothing of Haringvliet, which must surely be the name of the main fishery-vessel line), the truth is that although one baby Rhine (the Kromme Rijn, which pre-

* Which is 130 yards by 100.

sumably means the Crooked Rhine) goes as far as Utrecht, where Dr Strabismus (Whom God Preserve) came from, there is no denying that the only water flowing from there to Amsterdam is the Rijnkanaal; even the northernmost bit of the river itself, under the name of Oude Rijn, goes only as far as Leiden.

A fig for geography; despite all the foreboding with which I now visit Amsterdam, how could I be in Holland and not go there, even briefly? Would we cease to visit a lifelong friend on the grounds that he has aged, and become rather doddery? And if Amsterdam is not a lifelong friend, then friendship must be a very odd quality. Besides, I don't just visit Amsterdam out of friendship in general; there are three things that I must do there, without which no visit, however limited, is complete. I must visit the Rijksmuseum; I must have a long, aimless walk along and across the canals; and I must eat a *rijstafel*.

The Rijksmuseum is inexhaustible, as inexhaustible as the Rembrandts that constitute its greatest glory. There is an essay by Hermann Hesse, written when he was twenty-eight, but full of the ripe wisdom that might have been thought to have come to him only in his maturity, in which he sounds an alarm that is growing ever more urgent today, for all that it was published more than eighty years ago. It is worth quoting here.

> Let not the man who subscribes to a weekly theatre series feel that he is losing something if he makes use of it only every other week. I guarantee: he will gain.
>
> Let anyone who is accustomed to looking at a great many pictures in an exhibition try just once, if he is still capable of it, spending an hour or more in front of a single masterpiece and content himself with that for the day. He will be the gainer by it.
>
> Let the omnivorous reader try the same sort of thing . . . And let any man who cannot bring himself to use any other kind of restraint try to make a habit of going to bed at ten o'clock at least once a week.

How keenly I feel the rebuke! For I am the very man to whom Hesse was addressing his exhortation. Again and again I have tried to take his advice, and failed. Whether it is greed, or the sound of time's chariot, or a fear of missing whatever is round the next corner, I cannot content myself with the part while the whole is spread out before me, even though I know that Hesse is right, and that I would be the gainer from his recommended moderation. And in the Rijksmuseum, of all places, the temptation to gorge is irresistible; I have written at length elsewhere* about its treasures, and I shall not repeat myself here. For that matter, I have written about the walk and the *rijstafel*. So let me practise Hesse's moderation in something at least; one of these days I shall try to go to bed at ten o'clock – but not yet.

Stepping over the young people napping in the sun outside the railway station, picking my way between the heaps of bicycles, and declining the various kinds of happydust promised me, at astonishingly modest rates, by the gentleman who materialised from behind a pillar and plucked me by the sleeve, I took train for Rotterdam. My thousand-mile Rhine journey was almost over.

Rotterdam is not a gracious city, but no one who knew anything of modern history would be so tactless as to draw attention to the fact. For it fell to the lot of the second city of the Netherlands to be the test-bed of the aerial *Blitzkrieg* perfected by the German armies which in May 1940 brought the 'phony war' to an abrupt end and swept across Western and Northern Europe in one of the swiftest and most complete military victories in history. Partly to instil panic in the Netherlands, and partly to test theories of bombing which had had only a very limited rehearsal during the Spanish Civil War, the Luftwaffe launched a series of raids on Rotterdam which destroyed virtually the whole of the centre of the city; not even Coventry, when the Blitz began, was so devastated. Indeed, not until, with the turn of the tide of war, the saturation bombing of German cities by the Allies began was there greater destruction. So the reason.for Rotterdam's lack of ancient grace is that practically every building that had any was destroyed in those few days in May.

Rotterdam has had its revenge, but the revenge has taken a form that no one could have guessed at while the bombs rained down. The place was rebuilt long ago, mostly, of course, in a strictly utilitarian architecture, with only Zadkine's monumental sculpture of 'The Destroyed City' to remind the world of what happened. But gradually, like some huge sea-creature, Rotterdam has engorged most of the maritime traffic of Europe. Its port is now the largest in the world, and the harbour tour by road is *ninety* miles long; I wandered for hours through this astounding landscape-waterscape, with its thousands of

---

* In *Enthusiasms*, Ch. 3.

acres of docks and basins, storage-tanks and container-terminals, derricks and locks, bridges and dams, factories and canals.

Rotterdam harbour is Rotterdam's reply, which is what I meant by saying that the city had had its revenge. Here you may see the modern world at work, incessantly taking in and sending out unimaginably stupendous quantities of goods, from mountains of cement and pig-iron, armies of locomotives and machine-tools, thousands of tons of grain and coal, to light-bulbs and nail-scissors, toys and flowers, hand-mirrors and coffee-grinders, frozen peas and saucepans to thaw them in, tins of paint and boxes of chocolates; and somewhere, in huge cardboard containers marked 'This way up' in half a dozen languages, there were millions upon millions of microchips, coming and going all over the world, to feed the voracious and ever-increasing appetites of the computers and computerised industrial and business systems on which, in some mad kind of self-perpetuating circular argument, everything depends.

Gazing out on this undiscovered new planet, I saw the huge metal containers, the monstrous cranes, looking like giant herons waiting for their fishy prey, the fleets of barges, the wharves covered with hundreds of identical freight containers, the railways that fetch and carry; thus gazing, I contemplated, uneasily, the inter-dependence that it all demanded, as well as – even more uneasily – the fragility of the entire structure. In Karel Čapek's *The Absolute at Large* (a singularly prophetic book about the power unleashed from the atom) one scene is set in a factory where tintacks are made. The new energy is pouring them out in an unstoppable flood; the sorcerer's apprentice is in charge, the entire system of the factory is overwhelmed, and soon the area around the building is covered with mountains of tintacks, the size of slag-heaps, with no one able to utter the secret password that will staunch the haemorrhage. As I looked over the port of Rotterdam, stretching to the horizon, it occurred to me that it would not take much to bring this mighty edifice of iron and steel and concrete and aluminium and wood to a halt, and with it the flow of Europe's life-blood. Certainly another Blitz would do it, but it is not necessary to imagine so brutal (and unlikely) a cause; a lack of fuel, a series of key strikes, a malfunctioning of a central computer system, and the machine stops. Industrialisation, and in particular specialisation, has made much of the world prosperous beyond all the dreams of less than a century ago, and in time it will make the rest of the world prosperous too. But the price paid has been frightful, and in nothing more frightful than the fact that no one can any longer make a *thing*; people can only make *components*. What happens if – when – the supply of a vital component gives out, or the techniques of assembly fail? A carpenter, if there are any left by then, will still be able to make a table or a chair; but who can make, single-handed, a telephone system, a printing-press, an electric generator, a combine harvester, an aeroplane, an oil-refinery?

Half sad, half scared, I went back into the city to greet the friend whom I had not seen since Basle. Erasmus styled himself 'of Rotterdam'; despite the fact that he got out of his native city as soon as he could, and never set foot in it again, the Rotterdammers are proud of him, as the Bonners are of Beethoven, who did the same, and have given him a handsome statue, not quite so eloquent as the one in Basle, but enough to make the passers-by stop and stare, and to guess, even if they had never heard of him, that they were in the presence of a very great man. For me, he is a lifelong hero, but on this journey he was a symbol, too, for he straddles the river from the point at which it becomes navigable to the point at which it empties itself into the sea, and no man in all the turbulent history of the Rhine would have been more pleased to see the post-war progress – faltering, painful, constantly checked by selfishness, greed, fear and treachery, yet slowly moving forward – towards a Europe that will truly be one united band of nations. His *Complaint of Peace* is still, after nearly five centuries, the noblest and most passionate call to mankind to sheathe the sword and learn to love one another. Very little notice indeed has been taken of his plea for most of these five centuries, yet he has had the last laugh, for although the world is still full of war and the threat of war, at least the Rhine is free of it.

The day was wearing on; I had not many more hours before I would be saying goodbye to the Rhine. My last exploration was a tiny, unspoilt little complex of canals and eighteenth-century houses, the remains of Rotterdam's Old Quarter, most of which was destroyed in those May days; handsome old drawbridges, a charming little antique-shop, a converted windmill, a few boats fussing self-importantly about as if they were on the other side of the town in the mighty harbour area.

Attempts to preserve a vanished past by turning part of a city into a museum, or a museum into part of a city, rarely succeed; the artificiality shows through, and if the inhabitants have been persuaded to dress up as their ancestors, it becomes less convincing still. The Old Quarter of Rotterdam, however, had a real life of its own, and managed to combine its bustling present with a glimpse of the long-gone past. I wandered up and down, drinking in the scene, watching the pigeons strutting pompously about; I felt soothed by the gentle bobbing of the boats at anchor. I am nothing of a sailor, but occasionally I think I can understand what the sea-struck feel. Looking out across the water, I was reminded of the Marseilles trilogy of Marcel Pagnol, where the boy Marius hungers for the sea with such an intensity of longing that it is clear he will die if he remains ashore; I was very conscious that Holland and England, on opposite sides of the North Sea, were among the greatest of maritime nations. It is easy to see how the latter trusted to her wooden walls; there was no other way off the island, and throughout England's history her sailormen have steadily gone a little further, and a little further, and a little further, until lands thousands of miles away were part of her dominion. But why the Dutch? They, surely, could have remained on their fertile land, particularly since for them the sea must have been an eternal enemy, always threatening to swallow their entire country alive, and often almost succeeding.

The mystery was not solved in the Old Quarter of Rotterdam, but the tranquil air of this world in miniature did much to dispel the great sadness that mysteriously accompanies the end of a journey. I sat on the edge of a canal and dangled my feet over the water, wondering about that sadness. Is it a presage of the last journey we must all take? Is it the realisation that however far we go, we cannot leave behind our fears and doubts and failures, since here we are, back where we started, and nothing has really changed? Is it the parting from our comrades on the voyage? Whatever the cause, I was running out of time for thinking about it. I had a few minutes, enough for only one more stroll beneath the blue sky, among the cafés, the tethered craft and the idlers, and then I must be gone.

One of the idlers spoke English; he was old enough to have remembered the war, but when I approached the subject – and, after all, I was talking to him in one of the worst-bombed cities in Europe – he showed a noticeable reluctance to talk about it. Well, I had long ago learned not to press Europeans on what they had done during the war, ever since, many years ago in Paris, I had made a naïve enquiry and unleashed a flood of bitterness, accusation and self-reproach. My idler explained that very near where we were there was an area of modern architecture built into just such an ancient quarter as this, but by then the clock was hard behind me, and anyway I did not want to end my journey in the modern world. I made my way back to my last rendezvous, at the ferry that was to take me home.

The ferry was enormous; it held 700 cars and more than 2000 people. I dropped my bag in my doll's-house cabin and went exploring; I had had an invitation to take a drink with the captain a little later, and thought it courteous to have a look at his ship first. I had not been on any kind of ship for almost twenty years, when, as I have related, I had gone on the last transatlantic voyage of the *Queen Mary*; the North Sea ferry-boat jerked another memory of that journey out of me. My steward had put the studs and cuff-links into my dress shirt, attached the braces to the trousers, then laid them diagonally across the bed, so that they hung down, the ends almost touching the floor. Immediately beneath the ends of the trousers he had put my shoes; the only possible conclusion was that I was expected to put on my trousers by climbing on to the bed and wriggling my legs into them until my feet protruded from the bottoms, when I would have nothing more to do than to put my feet into the shoes, which had been waiting there all the time.

But on the Hook to Harwich ferry the passengers, even the ones with cabins, did not dress for dinner, and the ubiquitous fruit-machines made clear at once that the year was not 1938. I went in search of the captain and his hospitality.

I am not a very tactful man, but I had enough sense not to ask him about the ambitions he had as a young man just staring out as a seafarer. Surely every such youth must have dreams of commanding a great ocean liner or a mighty battleship? And surely there must be a pang of unfulfilled dreams in a man who pilots only a car-ferry across the North Sea? But my captain displayed no disappointment; he was as cheerful a sailorman as you could hope to find, taking his job seriously but with an exact understanding of its scale. Silently, I marked him as the last of the contented men of my journey, as the first had been Christian Patt. I turned in after our drink, and soon after I was in bed I felt the ship leave the quay. It was a fine, still night, and the treacherous North Sea was on its best behaviour. But I stayed long awake, nevertheless.

It seemed years (though it was only ten weeks) since, far up the Swiss mountains, I had seen the Rhine take its first faltering steps. A little further down, I had shot the rapids, drenched and laughing; lower still, I had seen Switzerland's amazing citizen army on its annual manoeuvres, and explored a hospital below ground, equipped, empty and waiting. Then I had passed through Liechtenstein – well, passing through it is easy, but I had *stopped* there, and learned what I would have to do if I ever became a millionaire and wanted to stay one. On to

Lake Constance, with Kurt Waldheim at one end and the Schaffhausen Falls at the other, marking the end of the cold and rain, for from here to the end of my journey the weather was kind.

From Basle I recalled the ingenious ferry with its trolleybus-wire to get across by, and the mighty Erasmus exhibition; I had been allowed into the little room reproduced as his study, where he stood at his writing-desk, and I peered over his shoulder as he wrote.

At Mulhouse, I had almost learned to love motor-cars; a little further on I greeted again the Isenheim Altar of Grünewald, and slipped off to dine at Belfort. Then the Babel of Strasbourg, then the unspoiled grace of Baden-Baden, followed by the very thoroughly spoiled grace of Karlsruhe and the heady air of antiquity at Heidelberg, with its Philosopher's Walk on one side and its mighty ruined castle on the other.

At Worms I shivered at the thought of Luther; in Mainz I wondered whether the world would be so much worse off if printing had not been invented there or anywhere else; beyond Mainz the giant march of Rhine castles had begun, and continued as far as Koblenz.

In Bonn, Beethoven and the administration of a modern state seemed ill-matched partners; Cologne was a little more provincial than its reputation had promised; Düsseldorf, for good or ill, was the way the world is going; Duisburg is the way it had already gone.

At Xanten there was the mighty harbour, second only to Rotterdam's; beyond, I had resisted the deviation that would have taken me between the Scylla of Arnhem and the Charybdis of Nijmegen; further into Holland, Gouda, Weesp and Monnickendam had made a brave show in the sunshine, and Amsterdam had lowered my spirits before finally raising them.

And now I was on the sea; beneath me, as I lay in my narow bunk, were the waters of the Rhine, now inextricably mixed with those of other rivers, strangers to me. But the Rhine, my Rhine, which had started as a hero and finished as a friend, was finished. The history, the wars, the legends, the music, the castles, the frontiers, the languages, the people I had passed the time of day with and the ones I had got to know, the terraced vineyards and the wine they made, the vast traffic by barge on the river and the hardly less vast traffic beside it, the bridges I had crossed, the eagles wheeling over Burg Rheinstein as I looked out of my eyrie in its tallest tower, the old choir-master in Cologne Cathedral, with his fierce expression and gentle nature, the naked ladies in the Friedrichsbad and the geniality of Herr Schmitz of the impeccable Brenner's Park, the fresh running water in the streets of Freiburg, the astounding dome of St Blasien and the little dog who had appointed himself captain of the ferry so small that it could be hauled across by hand, the other-worldly roaring of the blastfurnace at Thyssen's, the green baize of the Baden-Baden Casino, the view of the Alps from Divisionnaire Gadient's helicopter, the little painted town of Stein am Rhein, my little friend Sophie on the Bouret barge, dawn over Assmannshausen and sunset over the Lorelei, the innocence of the Grüne Kranz in Rüdesheim and the desperate gaiety of the Drosselgasse a hundred yards away, the sight of Ashkenazy, about to embark on the 'Waldstein', shooing away with infinite tact an importunate photographer, the smell of the baking at six o'clock in the morning at Strasbourg, the hunters of the Black Forest and their toast with the glass in the left hand – all these made only a few pages in the vast catalogue of memories of my journey, as they came crowding in between me and sleep. But one more memory came, to dominate them all.

It was from Remagen, which encapsulated the lesson the Rhine taught. The story was set in war; it had courage – the courage of the forward American units of the Allied armies, racing for the bridge, and across it, knowing that it was probably mined and would be blown up with them on it; it had triumph, when they got across safely; it had injustice – the very injustice against which the Allies were fighting, when the German officers were shot on Hitler's orders for their failure to destroy the bridge; it had a terrible irony, when the bridge, ten days after its capture intact, collapsed into the river; and above all, it had its epilogue, in the purchase of the remaining towers of the bridge on the Remagen side of the river, and their transformation into a museum which tells the story of the bridge and concludes with a plea that no such conflict shall ever take place again.

Nor will it. And to testify to that resolution, the German and American flags fly side by side on the twin towers, illuminating the sky with their promise, like the sign God gave Noah. The last vision from my Rhine journey that I saw before I sank gently into sleep was of those two flags; my last thought was of what they meant.

I awoke as the ship bumped gently at Harwich Quay. It was a beautiful day in England.

Index

Note: Hotels, restaurants, institutions will be found under place.
n = note
Aus = Austria; Fr = France; Ger = Germany; Holl = Holland; Sw = Switzerland

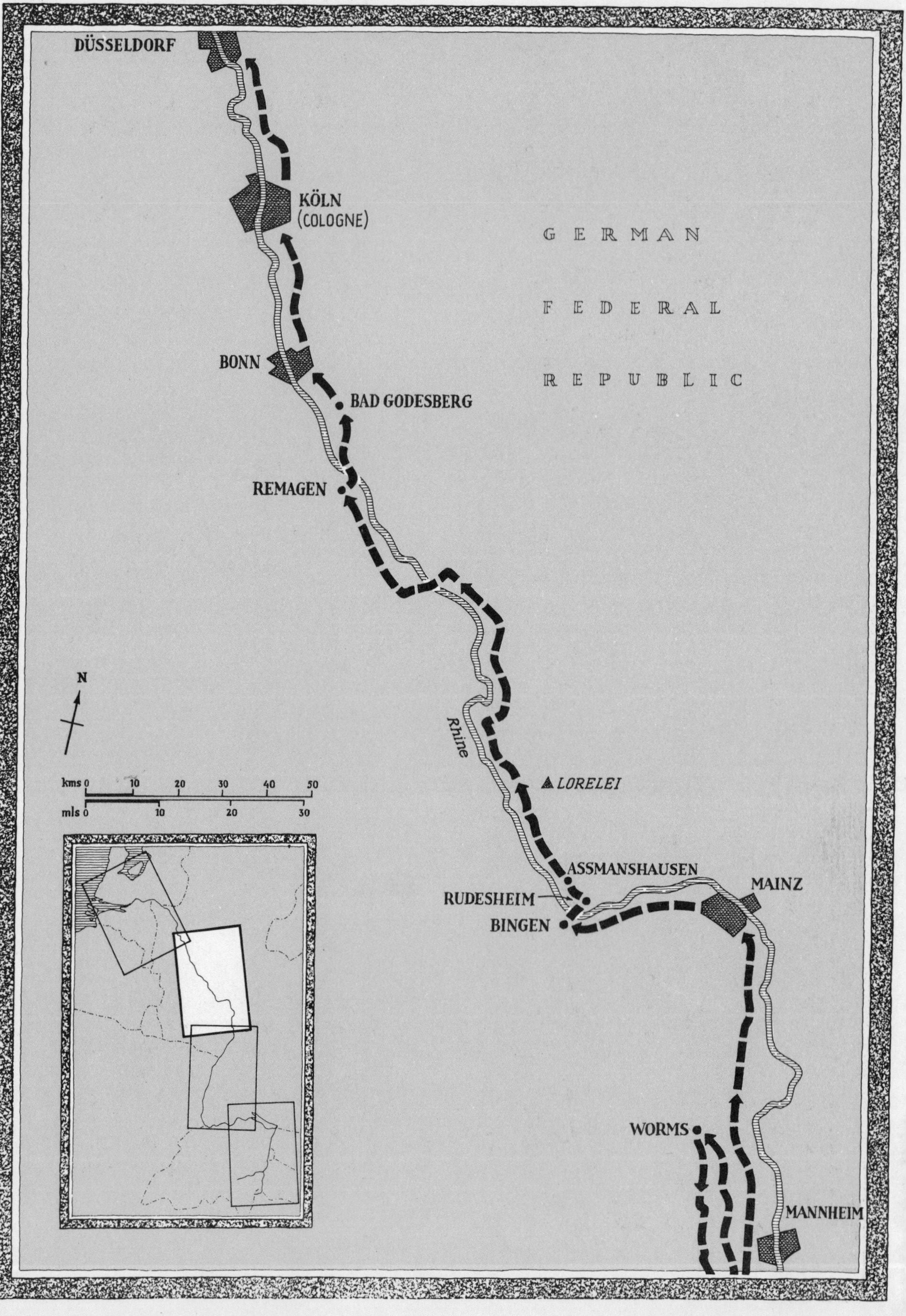
DÜSSELDORF
KÖLN
(COLOGNE)
GERMAN
FEDERAL
REPUBLIC
BONN
BAD GODESBERG
REMAGEN
N
Rhine
LORELEI
kms 0 10 20 30 40 50
mls 0 10 20 30
ASSMANSHAUSEN
RUDESHEIM
BINGEN
MAINZ
WORMS
MANNHEIM